CERTAIN APPLICATIONS OF FIXED POINT RESULTS IN VARIOUS METRIC SPACES

USHABHAVANI CHALUVAGALI

UPENDER REDDY GUJJULA

NARESH PARKALA

ABSTRACT

This book is an attempt to give a systematic presentation of results and methods which concern the fixed point theory of multivalued mappings and some of its applications. In selecting the material we have restricted ourselves to studying topological methods in the fixed point theory of multivalued mappings and applications, mainly to integral equations and Homotopy theory

we studied about fixed points, coupled fixed points and triple fixed points using various contractions in S_b-metric spaces, Bipolar metric spaces, C^*-algebra valued fuzzy soft metric spaces and partial b-metric spaces. This includes a few presentations of applications to integral equations and homotopy theory. Additionally, it includes some pertinent examples, which supports to main theorems in each Chapter.

In Chapter 1, we mentioned basic Definitions, Examples, Lemmas, Previous results and notions which are going to explain brief survey of literature as well as basics of our remaining Chapters.

In Chapter 2, we establishes some unique fixed point theorems for the self mappings in complete S_b-metric spaces. We provided applications to integral equations as well as homotopy. We also furnished some corollaries and example to support our main results.

In Chapter 3, we obtain some unique common coupled fixed point theorems via C-class function involving altering and ultra-altering distance functions in complete Bi-polar metric spaces. We gave applications to integral equations as well as homotopy and also mentioned some corollaries and exmaple to support our results.

In Chapter 4, we obtain some unique common coupled fixed point theorems via C_*-class functions in complete C^*-algebra valued fuzzy soft metric spaces along with applications to integral equations as well as homotopy. We also discussed some corollaries and example to support our results.

In Chapter 5, we obtain some unique common tripled fixed point theorems by $(\alpha, \varphi) - K$-type contraction in complete partial b-metric space and mentioned corollaries, example to support our main result. Also, we gave applicaions to integral equations and homotopy.

Contents

Contents

CHAPTER 1

INTRODUCTION AND PRELIMINARIES

Introduction and Preliminaries

1.1 General Survey

Fixed point theory is an essential branch of the rapidly expanding sciences of nonlinear analysis. It is a relatively new and well-developed research topic. The study of fixed points comes into numerous fields such as classical analysis, functional analysis, operator theory, topology, algebraic topology, and so on. Fixed point theorems are primarily useful in the existence theory of differential equations, partial differential equations, integral equations and also used in homotopy theories. Fixed point theory has several applications, including eigen value problems, boundary value problems, approximation theory, and nonlinear analysis etc. For details one can see Martin [71], Smart [108], Collatz [27], Moore [75], Kreyszig [65], Cronin [28], Cesari [25], Leggett and Williams [66] etc.

Brouwer [22] was the first to prove a fixed point theorem which states that a continuous mapping of a closed unit ball in n-dimensional Euclidean space has at least one fixed point. Several proofs of this basic result can be found in the existing literature. Alexendroff and Hopf [5] proved Brouwer's theorem by using the tools from algebraic topology while Birkhoff, Kellogg [19], Dunford and Schwartz [32] used classical methods of analysis and determinant to prove the same theorem. Theorems confined to the subspaces of $\mathbb{R}^n$ are not of much immediate use in functional analysis, where one is usually concerned with the case that E is infinite dimensional subset of some function space. Over a four decades ago Birkhoff and Kellogg [19] were the first to obtain the first infinite dimensional fixed point theorem.

In fact, Brouwer's fixed point theorem was used by Birkhoff and Kellogg in 1922 in proving the existence theorems in the theory of differential equations. Afterwards Schaiider ([101],[102]) extended Brouwer's fixed point theorem to the case in which E is a compact convex subset of a normed space.

Later on, Tychonoff [121] extended Schaiider's results from normed spaces to an arbitrary locally convex space. In 1922, when Stefan Banach [16] obtained the fixed point theorem for contraction mappings which is very famous because its proof is simple and does not require much topological background.

Sessa [106] began research on common fixed point theorems for weakly commuting pair of mappings in 1982. Later, in 1986, Jungck [45] expanded the idea of weakly commuting mappings to compatible mappings in metric spaces and proved compatible pair mappings commute on the sets of coincidence point of the involved mappings. When they commute at their coincidence points, Jungck and Rhoades [46] introduced the idea of weak compatibility in 1998 and demonstrated that compatible mappings are weakly compatible but the converse is not true.

The idea of coupled fixed point(CFP) was first developed by Guo and Lakshmikantham [38] in 1987 . Later, employing a weak contractivity type assumption, Bhaskar and Lakshmikantham [37] developed a novel fixed point theorem for a mixed monotone mapping in a metric space driven with partial ordering. See study results in ([1], [2], [4], [51], [52], [67]) and related references for additional results on coupled fixed point outcomes.

Berinde and Borcut, [18] were generalized Banach contractions and established few tripled fixed point findings with mixed monotone qualities in partially ordered metric spaces. Borcut et al. [20] have created the concept of a tripled coincidence point for a pair of nonlinear contractive mappings.

Aydi et al. [14] have studied the common tripled fixed point theorem for ω-compatible mappings in abstract metric spaces.

In recent years Kannan ([49], [50]), Husain, Sehgal [42] and Caristi [24] etc. have considered several generalizations of contraction mappings and proved a multitude of results.

In this chaper it is discussed about the fundamental definitions and results which are crucial to the subsequent chapters. For a detailed study of fixed point theory one is referred to the books of Istratescu [43], Rus [96] and Smart [108]. Three survey papers by Rhoades ([92], [93], [94]) are also of special significance for the comparative study of various metrical fixed point theorems that exist in the literature.

The concept of metric space was introduced by Frechet [35] which furnishes the common idealization of a large number of mathematical , physical and other scientific constructs, in which the notion of distance appears. The objects under consideration can be most varied, they may be points, functions, sets etc.

Now we mention some basic definitions of metric fixed point theory.
Throughout this section $\mathcal{B}$ is a non empty set.

Definition 1.1.1. ([35]): A metric space (MS) is an ordered pair $(\mathcal{B}, d)$, where d is a metric on $\mathcal{B}$, i.e., a function $d : \mathcal{B} \times \mathcal{B} \to [0, \infty)$ satisfying the following axioms for all points $x, y, z \in \mathcal{B}$

(i) $d(x, x) = 0$ i.e., The distance from a point to itself is zero;

(ii) if $x \neq y$ then $d(x, y) > 0$ i.e., Positivity;

(iii) $d(x, y) = d(y, x)$ i.e; Symmetry;

(iv) $d(x, z) \leq d(x, y) + d(y, z)$ i.e; Triangle inequality.

Using the above definition we can introduce the concept of open sets, closed sets, convergence of a sequence, Cauchy sequence in the space, completeness in the space. The pioneering result of fixed point theory in metric space is due to Banach [16]. It has applicability in various disciplines.

Theorem 1.1.1. ([16])(Banach Contraction Principle): Let $(\mathcal{B}, d)$ is a metric space and $\mathcal{T} : \mathcal{B} \to \mathcal{B}$ is a self mapping such that $d(\mathcal{T}a, \mathcal{T}b) \leq \kappa d(a, b) \ \forall \ a, b \in \mathcal{B}$ and $\kappa \in [0, 1)$, then $\mathcal{T}$ has a unique fixed point, say α in $\mathcal{B}$ (i.e., $\mathcal{T}\alpha = \alpha$). Further for any $p \in \mathcal{B}$, the sequence $\{\mathcal{T}^n p\}$ converges to α.

This is the backbone for the development of fixed point theory in metric space. It is the simplest of all the fixed point theorems so far established and its proof does not require much topological background. This contraction mapping is used to establish the existence-uniqueness theorem for ordinary non-linear differential equations. For various other applications of the contraction mapping theorem one is referred to Kolmogrove and Fomin [64], where one finds excellent illustrations of the use of fixed point theorems in analysis.

Since then many generalizations of the Banach Contraction theorem have appeared. Wardowski [123] was introduced the idea of F-contractions in 2012 and has become a key component of the current fixed point theory research trend. Following that, F-weak contractions and generalised F-contractions were added to the idea of F-contractions by Wardowski, Dung [122], Dung and Hang [33], respectively. Gopal et al. [36] introduced the concept of α-type F-contractions and α-type F-weak contractions by combining the idea of α-admissible mappings with F-contractions [123] and F-weak contractions [122]. Hafida Massit et al. [40] introduced the (ϕ, F)-contraction to be inspired by the work done in ([84], [116]) and proved some fixed point results. Later, many researchers extended or generalised this sort of contraction (See.([31], [83], [103], [112]).

Recently, Samet et al. [98] demonstrated fixed point theorems for such sort of mappings in the complete metric spaces and developed the notion of α-contractive and α-admissible mappings. As may be seen in ([3], [8], [15],[21], [54], [87], [89], [90]), numerous researchers have established tripled fixed point results for various spaces.

Definition 1.1.2. ([53]): A self mapping $T : \mathcal{B} \to \mathcal{B}$ and $\alpha : \mathcal{B} \times \mathcal{B} \to \mathbf{R}^+$ be a function defined on nonempty set $\mathcal{B}$

$$\text{if } \alpha(\ell, \varsigma) \geq 1 \text{ implies } \alpha(T\ell, T\varsigma) \geq 1 \text{ for all } \ell, \varsigma \in \mathcal{B},$$

then we claim that T is an α- admissible mapping.

Karapinar et al. [55] defined the concept of triangular α-admissible mappings and proved some fixed point results.

Definition 1.1.3. ([98]): Let $\alpha : \mathcal{B} \times \mathcal{B} \to \mathbf{R}^+$ and $T : \mathcal{B} \to \mathcal{B}$ are two mappings defined on a non-empty set $\mathcal{B}$. A triangular α-admissible mapping is described as T if and only if

(a) T is an α- admissible mapping;

(b) $\alpha(\ell, \varsigma) \geq 1, \alpha(\varsigma, \aleph) \geq 1 \Rightarrow \alpha(\ell, \aleph) \geq 1 \ \forall \ \ell, \varsigma, \aleph \in \mathcal{B}$.

Note:[53] A triangular α-admissible mapping T shall be assumed. If $\{\varsigma_p\}$ is a sequence with $\varsigma_{p+1} = T\varsigma_p$ and $\alpha(\varsigma_p, \varsigma_{p+1}) \geq 1$, then we obtain $\alpha(\varsigma_p, \varsigma_q) \geq 1$ for all $p, q \in N$.

Definition 1.1.4. ([124]): Let (B, d) is a metric space. A mapping $T : B \to B$ is called $\mathcal{F}$-contraction if there exists

$\mathcal{F} \in \mathcal{X}$ and $\tau > 0$ such that $\tau + \mathcal{F}(d(Tx, Ty)) \leq \mathcal{F}(d(x, y))$

where $x, y \in B$ with $Tx \neq Ty$ and $\mathcal{X} = \{\mathcal{F}/\mathcal{F} : R^+ \to R\}$.

Definition 1.1.5. ([124]): Let $\mathcal{X} = \{\mathcal{F}/\mathcal{F} : R^+ \to R\}$, and $\mathcal{L} = \{\varphi/\varphi : (0, \infty) \to (0, \infty)\}$ be the family of mappings satisfying;

(a) for $l'_1, l'_2 \in R^+$ such that $l'_1 < l'_2$, $\mathcal{F}(l'_1) < \mathcal{F}(l'_2)$ (i.e $\mathcal{F}$ is strictly increasing);

(b) $\lim\limits_{p \to \infty} \chi_p = 0$ iff $\lim\limits_{p \to \infty} \mathcal{F}(\chi_p) = -\infty$ whenever, $\{\chi_p\}_{p \in N}$ be a sequence of $+ve$ numbers;

(c) $\displaystyle\lim_{\ell \to l_1'^+} \inf \varphi(\ell) > 0$ for all $\ell > 0$;

(d) there exist $\lambda \in (0,1)$ such that $\displaystyle\lim_{\beta \to 0^+} \beta^\lambda \mathcal{F}(\beta) = 0$

(e) $\mathcal{F}$ is continuous on $(0, \infty)$.

Definition 1.1.6. ([123]): Assume that $\Gamma : \mathcal{B} \to \mathcal{B}$ is a mapping and $(\mathcal{B}, d)$ is a CMS, then Γ is called a $(\varphi, \mathcal{F})$-contraction if there exists $\varphi \in \mathcal{L}$, $\mathcal{F} \in \mathcal{X}$ with

$$d(\Gamma\ell, \Gamma\zeta) > 0 \Rightarrow \varphi\left(d(\ell, \zeta)\right) + \mathcal{F}\left(d\left(\Gamma\ell, \Gamma\zeta\right)\right) \leq \mathcal{F}\left(d\left(\ell, \zeta\right)\right) \forall\, \ell, \zeta \in \mathcal{B}$$

Definition 1.1.7. ([36]): Assuming that $(\mathcal{B}, d)$ is a metric space, $\Gamma : \mathcal{B} \to \mathcal{B}$ and $\alpha : \mathcal{B} \times \mathcal{B} \to R^+$ be the functions. If there is $\theta > 0$ such that for any $\ell, \zeta \in \mathcal{B}$ and $\mathcal{F} \in \mathcal{X}$

$$d(\Gamma\ell, \Gamma\zeta) > 0 \Rightarrow \theta + \alpha(\ell, \zeta)\mathcal{F}\left(d\left(\Gamma\ell, \Gamma\zeta\right)\right) \leq \mathcal{F}\left(d\left(\ell, \zeta\right)\right),$$

then it is claimed that the function Γ is an α-type $\mathcal{F}$-contraction.

Definition 1.1.8. ([16]): Let $\mathcal{F} : \mathcal{B} \to \mathcal{B}$ be a self map on $\mathcal{B}$. If $\mathcal{F}(\alpha) = \alpha$ where $\alpha \in \mathcal{B}$ then α is known as a fixed point of $\mathcal{F}$.

Let $\{\mathcal{F}_\delta : \delta \in I\}$ be a non empty family of self maps on $\mathcal{B}$.

If $\mathcal{F}_\delta(\alpha) = \alpha$, $\forall\ \delta$ in I then $\alpha \in \mathcal{B}$ is known as a common fixed point of this family.

Definition 1.1.9. ([37]): Let $\mathcal{F} : \mathcal{B} \times \mathcal{B} \to \mathcal{B}$ be a mapping, if $\alpha = \mathcal{F}(\alpha, \beta)$ and $\beta = \mathcal{F}(\beta, \alpha)$ then the pair $(\alpha, \beta) \in \mathcal{B} \times \mathcal{B}$ is known as a coupled fixed point (CFP) of the mapping $\mathcal{F}$.

Definition 1.1.10. ([1]): Let $\mathcal{F} : \mathcal{B} \times \mathcal{B} \to \mathcal{B}$ and $\mathcal{S} : \mathcal{B} \to \mathcal{B}$ be two mappings and an element (α, β) in $\mathcal{B} \times \mathcal{B}$ is called

(i) a coupled coincident point (CCIP) of $\mathcal{F}$ and $\mathcal{S}$ if $\mathcal{S}\alpha = \mathcal{F}(\alpha, \beta)$ and

$\mathcal{S}\beta = \mathcal{F}(\beta, \alpha)$.

(ii) a common coupled fixed point (CCFP) of the mappings $\mathcal{F}$ and $\mathcal{S}$ if $\alpha = \mathcal{S}\alpha = \mathcal{F}(\alpha, \beta)$ and $\beta = \mathcal{S}\beta = \mathcal{F}(\beta, \alpha)$.

(iii) $(\mathcal{F}, \mathcal{S})$ is called ω-compatible if
$$\mathcal{S}(\mathcal{F}(\alpha, \beta)) = \mathcal{F}(\mathcal{S}\alpha, \mathcal{S}\beta) \text{ and } \mathcal{S}(\mathcal{F}(\beta, \alpha)) = \mathcal{F}(\mathcal{S}\beta, \mathcal{S}\alpha)$$
whenever for all $\alpha, \beta \in \mathcal{B}$ such that $\mathcal{F}(\alpha, \beta) = \mathcal{S}\alpha$ and $\mathcal{F}(\beta, \alpha) = \mathcal{S}\beta$.

Definition 1.1.11. ([18]): Let $\mathcal{A} : \mathcal{B}^3 \to \mathcal{B}$ be a mapping, then an element $(\chi_1, \chi_2, \chi_3) \in \mathcal{B}$ is called a tripled fixed point if $\mathcal{A}(\chi_1, \chi_2, \chi_3) = \chi_1$, $\mathcal{A}(\chi_2, \chi_3, \chi_1) = \chi_2$ and $\mathcal{A}(\chi_3, \chi_1, \chi_2) = \chi_3$

Definition 1.1.12. ([20]): Let $\mathcal{A} : \mathcal{B}^3 \to \mathcal{B}$ and $\mathcal{V} : \mathcal{B} \to \mathcal{B}$ are two mappings, then an element (χ_1, χ_2, χ_3) is said to be a tripled coincident point of $\mathcal{A}$ and $\mathcal{V}$ if $\mathcal{A}(\chi_1, \chi_2, \chi_3) = \mathcal{V}\chi_1$, $\mathcal{A}(\chi_2, \chi_3, \chi_1) = \mathcal{V}\chi_2$ and $\mathcal{A}(\chi_3, \chi_1, \chi_2) = \mathcal{V}\chi_3$.

Definition 1.1.13. ([20]): Let $\mathcal{A} : \mathcal{B}^3 \to \mathcal{B}$ and $\mathcal{V} : \mathcal{B} \to \mathcal{B}$ are two mappings,then an element (χ_1, χ_2, χ_3) is said to be a tripled common point of $\mathcal{A}$ and $\mathcal{V}$ if
$$\mathcal{A}(\chi_1, \chi_2, \chi_3) = \mathcal{V}\chi_1 = \chi_1, \ \mathcal{A}(\chi_2, \chi_3, \chi_1) = \mathcal{V}\chi_2 = \chi_2, \ \mathcal{A}(\chi_3, \chi_1, \chi_2) = \mathcal{V}\chi_3 = \chi_3.$$

In [105], S.Sedghi, N.Shobe and A.Aliouche have introduced the notion of an S-metric spaces as follows:

Definition 1.1.14. ([105]) An S-metric on $\mathcal{B}$ is a function $S : \mathcal{B}^3 \to [0, \infty)$ satisfies the following conditions, for each $\alpha, \beta, \gamma, a \in \mathcal{B}$

(i) $S(\alpha, \beta, \gamma) \geq 0$;

(ii) $S(\alpha, \beta, \gamma) = 0$ if and only if $\alpha = \beta = \gamma$;

(iii) $S(\alpha, \beta, \gamma) \leq S(\alpha, \alpha, a) + S(\beta, \beta, a) + S(\gamma, \gamma, a)$

Then the pair $(\mathcal{B}, S)$ is called a S-metric space.

Czerwik [29] needs an extension of metric space. Using this idea, he presented a generalization of the renowned Banach fixed point theorem in the b-metric spaces (see also ([30], [57], [78]).

Definition 1.1.15. ([29]) A function $d : \mathcal{B} \times \mathcal{B} \to [0, \infty)$ is said to be b-metric if for all $\alpha, \beta, \gamma \in \mathcal{B}$ and for all $\kappa \geq 1$ the following conditions are satisfied:

(i) $d(\alpha, \beta) = 0 \Leftrightarrow \alpha = \beta$;

(ii) $d(\alpha, \beta) = d(\beta, \alpha)$;

(iii) $d(\alpha, \gamma) \leq \kappa \left(d(\alpha, \beta) + d(\beta, \gamma) \right)$

Then the pair $(\mathcal{B}, d)$ is called a b-metric space.

In 2014, Z. Ma et. al [77] initiated a concept of C^*- algebra valued metric spaces and investigated some fixed point results for mapping under different contractive conditions in these spaces established (see, eg. [9], [17], [23], [26], [34], [48]).

Definition 1.1.16. ([77]): Consider B is a non-empty set and Let the mapping $d : \mathcal{B} \times \mathcal{B} \to \mathcal{A}$ satisfies the following axioms, where $\mathcal{A}$ is C^*-algebra

(C_1) for all $l, m \in \mathcal{B}$, $\theta \preceq d(l, m)$ and $d(l, m) = \theta \Leftrightarrow l = m$;

(C_2) for all $l, m \in \mathcal{B}$, $d(l, m) = d(m, l)$;

(C_3) for all $l, m, n \in \mathcal{B}$, $d(l, n) \preceq d(l, m) + d(m, n)$.

Then d is described as a C^*-algebra-valued metric on $\mathcal{B}$ and $(\mathcal{B}, \mathcal{A}, d)$ is termed as a C^*-algebra valued metric space.

It is obvious that C^*-algebra-valued metric spaces generalize the concept of metric spaces, replacing the set of real numbers by $\mathcal{A}_+$.

In 2014, Thangaraj Beaula et.al [118] initiated the notion of fuzzy soft metric space in terms of fuzzy soft points and proved some results. On the other hand Thangaraj Beaula, R. Raja and other authors proved few results on complete fuzzy soft metric spaces (see, eg. [68], [76], [95], [119], [120], [125]).

Definition 1.1.17. ([118]): Let U be an initial universe set and Θ is the set of all parameters and $C \subseteq \Theta$, then the pair (F, C) is called soft set over U if and only if $F : C \to P(U)$ is a mapping from C into $P(U)$ the set of all subsets of U.

Definition 1.1.18. ([118]): Let $C \subseteq \Theta$, then the mapping $F_\Theta : C \to P(\tilde{U})$ defined by $F_\Theta(e) = \mu^e F_\Theta$(a fuzzy subset of U) is called fuzzy soft set over (U, Θ). Where $\mu^e F_\Theta = \bar{0}$ if $e \notin C$ and $\mu^e F_\Theta \neq \bar{0}$ if $e \in C$. Here $P(\tilde{U})$ is the collection of all fuzzy sets of U.

Definition 1.1.19. ([118]): A mapping $\tilde{d} : \tilde{\Theta} \times \tilde{\Theta} \to \mathcal{R}(\mathcal{C})^*$ is said to be a fuzzy soft metric on the fuzzy soft set $\tilde{\Theta}$ if $\tilde{d}$ satisfies the following conditions:

(S_1) $\forall$ $G_{x_1}, G_{x_2} \tilde{\in} \tilde{\Theta}$, $\tilde{d}(G_{x_1}, G_{x_2}) \geq \bar{0}$;

(S_2) $\tilde{d}(G_{x_1}, G_{x_2}) = \bar{0}$ iff $G_{x_1} = G_{x_2}$;

(S_3) $\forall$ $G_{x_1}, G_{x_2} \tilde{\in} \tilde{\Theta}$, $\tilde{d}(G_{x_1}, G_{x_2}) = \tilde{d}(G_{x_2}, G_{x_1})$;

(S_4) $\forall$ $G_{x_1}, G_{x_2}, G_{x_3} \in \tilde{\Theta}$, $\tilde{d}(G_{x_1}, G_{x_3}) \leq \tilde{d}(G_{x_1}, G_{x_2}) + \tilde{d}(G_{x_2}, G_{x_3})$.

The fuzzy soft set $\tilde{\Theta}$ with a fuzzy soft metric $\tilde{d}$ on $\tilde{\Theta}$ is called a fuzzy soft metric space (F.S.M.S) and denoted by $(\tilde{\Theta}, \tilde{d})$, which is based on fuzzy soft points.

The notion of partial metric space was introduced by Matthews [72]. Later Matthews ([72], [73]), Oltra Valero [81] and Altun et al. [10] have proved some fixed point theorems in partial metric spaces.

Definition 1.1.20. (See [72], [73]) A partial metric on a nonempty set $\mathcal{B}$ is a function $P : \mathcal{B} \times \mathcal{B} \to [0, \infty)$ such that for all $\alpha, \beta, \gamma \in \mathcal{B}$:

(p_1) $\alpha = \beta \Leftrightarrow p(\alpha, \alpha) = p(\alpha, \beta) = p(\beta, \beta),$

(p_2) $p(\alpha, \alpha) \leq p(\alpha, \beta), p(\beta, \beta) \leq p(\alpha, \beta),$

(p_3) $p(\alpha, \beta) = p(\beta, \alpha),$

(p_4) $p(\alpha, \beta) \leq p(\alpha, \gamma) + p(\gamma, \beta) - p(\gamma, \gamma).$

Then the pair $(\mathcal{B}, p)$ is called a partial metric space (PMS).

Remark 1.1. It is clear that the partial metric space need not be a b-metric space, since in a b-metric space if $\alpha = \beta$, then $d(\alpha, \alpha) = d(\alpha, \beta) = d(\beta, \beta) = 0$. But in a partial metric space if $\alpha = \beta$ then $P(\alpha, \alpha) = P(\alpha, \beta) = P(\beta, \beta)$ may not be equal zero. Therefore the partial metric space may not be a b- metric space.

1.2 Preliminaries of S_b-Metric Spaces

In 2012, S. Sedghi et.al [104] described S_b-metric spaces (S_b-MS) by applying the concept of S-metric spaces (S-MS) [105] , b-metric spaces [29] and established common fixed point results in S_b-metric spaces (S_b-MS). Subsequently to improve many authors established numerous results on S_b-metric spaces (S_b-MS) (see, eg. [47], [60], [88], [109], [110], [114]).

Now we mention some basic definitions and results of S_b-metric spaces (S_b-MS).

Definition 1.2.1. ([104]): Let $\mathcal{G}$ be a non empty set and assume that $\kappa \geq 1$ is a real number. Consider a function $S_b : \mathcal{G}^3 \to [0, \infty)$ that satisfies the following conditions:

(S_{b_1}) $0 < S_b(\Delta_1, \Delta_2, \Delta_3)$ for all $\Delta_1, \Delta_2, \Delta_3 \in \mathcal{B}$ with $\Delta_1 \neq \Delta_2 \neq \Delta_3,$

(S_{b_2}) $S_b(\Delta_1, \Delta_2, \Delta_3) = 0 \Leftrightarrow \Delta_1 = \Delta_2 = \Delta_3,$

(S_{b_3}) $S_b(\Delta_1, \Delta_2, \Delta_3) \leq \kappa(S_b(\Delta_1\Delta_1, \Delta_4) + S_b(\Delta_2, \Delta_2, \Delta_4) + S_b(\Delta_3, \Delta_3, \Delta_4))$ for all $\Delta_1, \Delta_2, \Delta_3, \Delta_4 \in$ $\mathcal{G}.$

Then the pair $(\mathcal{G}, S_b)$ is called as S_b-metric space and the function S_b is referred to as a S_b-metric on $\mathcal{G}$.

Remark 1.2. ([104]):It should be noted that, the class of S_b-metric spaces is effectively larger than that of S-metric spaces. Indeed each S-metric space is a S_b-metric space with $b = 1$.

Example 1.1. ([104]) Let G is a non empty set, define $S_* : \mathcal{G}^3 \to [0, \infty)$ by $S_*(\nabla_1, \nabla_2, \nabla_3) = S(\nabla_1, \nabla_2, \nabla_3)^\kappa$, when $\kappa = 2^{2(\tau-1)}$, where $\tau > 1$, then $(\mathcal{G}, S_b)$ is a S_b-metric space

Definition 1.2.2. ([104]): Let $(\mathcal{G}, S_b)$ be a S_b-metric space, then, for $\alpha \in \mathcal{G}$, $r > 0$ we define the open ball $G_{S_b}(\alpha, r)$ and closed ball $G_{S_b}[\alpha, r]$ with center α and radius r as follows respectively:

$$G_{S_b}(\alpha, r) = \{\beta \in \mathcal{G} : S_b(\beta, \beta, \alpha) < r\} \text{ and } G_{S_b}[\alpha, r] = \{\beta \in \mathcal{G} : S_b(\beta, \beta, \alpha) \leq r\}.$$

Definition 1.2.3. ([104]): Let $(\mathcal{G}, S_b)$ is a S_b-metric space. $\{\zeta_p\}$ is a sequence in $\mathcal{G}$

(1) If p_0 in N exists such that $S_b(\zeta_p, \zeta_p, \zeta_q) < \epsilon$ for each $q, p \geq p_0$, then the sequence is known as the S_b-Cauchy sequence.

(2) S_b-convergent up to a certain point $\zeta \in \mathcal{G}$ if, for each $\epsilon > 0$, $\exists p_0 \in N$ such that $S_b(\zeta_p, \zeta_p, \zeta) < \epsilon$ or $S_b(\zeta, \zeta, \zeta_p) < \epsilon$ $\forall p \geq p_0$ and write it as $\lim_{p \to \infty} \zeta_p = \zeta$.

(3) An S_b-metric space $(\mathcal{G}, S_b)$ is said to be complete, if every S_b-Cauchy sequence must be S_b-convergent in $\mathcal{G}$.

Lemma 1.2.1. ([104]): In a S_b-metric space, we have

$$S_b(\zeta, \zeta, \aleph) \leq \kappa S_b(\aleph, \aleph, \zeta) \text{ and } S_b(\aleph, \aleph, \zeta) \leq \kappa S_b(\zeta, \zeta, \aleph).$$

Lemma 1.2.2. ([104]): In a S_b-metric space, we have

$$S_b(\zeta, \zeta, \aleph) \leq 2\kappa S_b(\zeta, \zeta, \eth) + \kappa^2 S_b(\eth, \eth, \aleph).$$

Lemma 1.2.3. ([104]): Given that $\{\alpha_p\}$ is a S_b-convergent to α and that $(\mathcal{G}, S_b)$ is a S_b-metric space with $\kappa \geq 1$, we obtain

$(i) \quad \dfrac{1}{2\kappa} S_b(\beta, \beta, \alpha) \leq \lim_{p \to \infty} \inf S_b(\beta, \beta, \alpha_p) \leq \lim_{p \to \infty} \sup S_b(\beta, \beta, \alpha_p) \leq 2\kappa S_b(\beta, \beta, \alpha)$ and

$(ii) \quad \dfrac{1}{\kappa^2} S_b(\alpha, \alpha, \beta) \leq \lim_{p \to \infty} \inf S_b(\alpha_p, \alpha_p, \beta) \leq \lim_{p \to \infty} \sup S_b(\alpha_p, \alpha_p, \beta) \leq \kappa^2 S_b(\alpha, \alpha, \beta) \forall \beta \in \mathcal{B}.$

In particular, if $\alpha = \beta$, then $\lim_{p \to \infty} S_b(\alpha_p, \alpha_p, \beta) = 0$.

Definition 1.2.4. ([69]): Let $\Gamma : \mathcal{G} \to \mathcal{G}$ be a self mapping and $\alpha : \mathcal{G} \times \mathcal{G} \times \mathcal{G} \to \mathbf{R}^+$ be a function, then Γ is called an α-admissible mapping, if

$$\alpha(\ell, \ell, \zeta) \geq 1 \Rightarrow \alpha(\Gamma\ell, \Gamma\ell, \Gamma\zeta) \geq 1 \ \forall \ \ell, \zeta \in \mathcal{G}$$

Definition 1.2.5. ([69]): Let $\Gamma : \mathcal{G} \to \mathcal{G}$ and $\alpha : \mathcal{G} \times \mathcal{G} \times \mathcal{G} \to \mathbf{R}^+$ are two mappings defined on a non-empty set $\mathcal{G}$, then Γ is called a triangular α- admissible mapping, if

(i) Γ is an α- admissible mapping;

(ii) $\alpha(\ell, \ell, \zeta) \geq 1, \alpha(\zeta, \zeta, \aleph) \geq 1 \Rightarrow \alpha(\ell, \ell, \aleph) \geq 1 \ \forall \ \ell, \zeta, \aleph \in \mathcal{G}$.

1.3   Preliminaries of Bipolar Metric Spaces

In 2016, Mütlu and Gürdal [7] have introduced the concept of bipolar metric space and they investigated certain basic fixed point and coupled fixed point theorems for covariant and contravariant mappings with contractive conditions (see, e.g [6], [7],). For more works on fixed and coupled fixed point theorems in bipolar metric spaces, we refer ([59], [62], [63], [113],).

Definition 1.3.1. ([7]): The mapping $d : \mathcal{S} \times \mathcal{T} \to [0, \infty)$ is said to be a Bipolar-metric on pair of non empty sets $(\mathcal{S}, \mathcal{T})$, if

(B_1) $d(u, v) = 0$ if and only if $u = v$;

(B_2) if $(u, v) \in \mathcal{S} \cap \mathcal{T}$, then $d(u, v) = d(v, u)$;

(B_3) $d(u_1, v_2) \leq d(u_1, v_1) + d(u_2, v_1) + d(u_2, v_2)$,

for all $u, u_1, u_2 \in \mathcal{S}$ and $v, v_1, v_2 \in \mathcal{T}$, and the triple $(\mathcal{S}, \mathcal{T}, d)$ is called a Bipolar-metric space.

Example 1.2. ([7]): Let $\mathcal{S} = (1, \infty)$, $\mathcal{T} = [-1, 1]$ and $d : \mathcal{S} \times \mathcal{T} \to [0, +\infty)$ as $d(l, m) = |l^2 - m^2|$, for all $l \in \mathcal{S}$ and $m \in \mathcal{T}$. Then the triple $(\mathcal{S}, \mathcal{T}, d)$ is a Bipolar-metric space (BMS).

C-class function:

In 2014, A.H. Ansari [11] introduced the notion of C-class function,which is pivotal result in fixed point theory. Subsequently, many scholars were interested in fixed point theorems for C-class function (See, eg. [12], [13], [41], [82], [97], [111], [117]).

Definition 1.3.2. ([11]): Let $C = \{\Delta/\Delta : [0, +\infty) \times [0, +\infty) \to R\}$ be a family of continuous functions is called a C-class function if for all $s^*, t^* \in [0, \infty)$,

(a) $\Delta(s^*, t^*) \leq s^*$;

(b) $\Delta(s^*, t^*) = s^* \Rightarrow s^* = 0$ or $t^* = 0$.

Example 1.3. ([11]): Each of the functions $\Delta : [0, +\infty) \times [0, +\infty) \to R$ defined below are elements of C.

(a) $\Delta(s^*, t^*) = s^* - t^*$;

(b) $\Delta(s^*, t^*) = ms^*$ where $m \in (0, 1)$.

(c) $\Delta(s^*, t^*) = \frac{s^*}{(1+t^*)^r}$ where $r \in (0, \infty)$.

(d) $\Delta(s^*, t^*) = s^* \eta(s^*)$ where $\eta : [0, \infty) \to [0, \infty)$ is continuous function.

(e) $\Delta(s^*, t^*) = s^* - \varphi(s^*)$ for all $s^*, t^* \in [0, +\infty)$ where, the continuous function $\varphi : [0, \infty) \to [0, \infty)$ such that $\varphi(s^*) = 0 \Leftrightarrow s^* = 0$.

(f) $\Delta(s^*, t^*) = s^* \Omega(s^*, t^*)$ for all $s^*, t^* \in [0, +\infty)$ where, the continuous function $\Omega : [0, \infty)^2 \to [0, \infty)$ such that $\Omega(s^*, t^*) < 1$.

On the other hand, Khan et al. [56] and A. H. Ansari et al.[12] introduced the concept of altering distance function and ultra altering distance function, which are control functions that alters distance between two points in a metric space. Afterwards, many mathematicians obtained fixed point theorems associated with altering distance functions (see, eg. [39], [70], [74], [80], [85], [99]).

Definition 1.3.3. ([56]): Let $\mathfrak{F} = \{\psi_* / \psi_\star : [0, \infty) \to [0, \infty)\}$ be the class of all altering distance functions and $\mathfrak{G} = \{\phi_* / \phi_\star : [0, \infty) \to [0, \infty)\}$ be the class of all ultra altering distance functions satisfying the following condition:

(ψ_0) $\psi_\star$ is nondecreasing and continuous;

(ψ_1) $\psi_\star(t) = 0$ if and only if $t = 0$.

(ϕ_0) $\phi_\star$ is continuous;

(ϕ_1) $\phi_\star(t) > 0$, $t > 0$ and $\phi_\star(0) \geq 0$.

Definition 1.3.4. ([7]): Let $\Omega : \mathcal{S}_1 \cup \mathcal{T}_1 \to \mathcal{S}_2 \cup \mathcal{T}_2$ be a function defined on two pairs of sets $(\mathcal{S}_1, \mathcal{T}_1)$ and $(\mathcal{S}_2, \mathcal{T}_2)$ is said to be

    (i) covariant if $\Omega(\mathcal{S}_1) \subseteq \mathcal{S}_2$ and $\Omega(\mathcal{T}_1) \subseteq \mathcal{T}_2$. This is denoted as

        $\Omega : (\mathcal{S}_1, \mathcal{T}_1) \rightrightarrows (\mathcal{S}_2, \mathcal{T}_2)$;

    (ii) contravariant if $\Omega(\mathcal{S}_1) \subseteq \mathcal{T}_2$ and $\Omega(\mathcal{T}_1) \subseteq \mathcal{S}_2$. It is denoted as

        $\Omega : (\mathcal{S}_1, \mathcal{T}_1) \leftrightharpoons (\mathcal{S}_2, \mathcal{T}_2)$.

Particularly, if d_1 is bipolar metric on $(\mathcal{S}_1, \mathcal{T}_1)$ and d_2 is bipolar metric on $(\mathcal{S}_2, \mathcal{T}_2)$, we often write $\Omega : (\mathcal{S}_1, \mathcal{T}_1, d_1) \rightrightarrows (\mathcal{S}_2, \mathcal{T}_2, d_2)$ and $\Omega : (\mathcal{S}_1, \mathcal{T}_1, d_1) \leftrightharpoons (\mathcal{S}_2, \mathcal{T}_2, d_2)$ respectively.

Definition 1.3.5. ([7]): In a bipolar metric space $(\mathcal{S}, \mathcal{T}, d)$ for any $\xi \in \mathcal{S} \cup \mathcal{T}$ is left point if $\xi \in \mathcal{S}$, is right point if $\xi \in \mathcal{T}$ and is central point if $\xi \in \mathcal{S} \cap \mathcal{T}$. Also, $\{\alpha_i\}$ in $\mathcal{S}$ and $\{\beta_i\}$ in $\mathcal{T}$ are left and right sequence respectively. In a bipolar metric space, we call a sequence, a left or a right one. A sequence $\{\xi_i\}$ is said to be convergent to ξ iff either $\{\xi_i\}$ is a left sequence, ξ is a right point and $\lim_{i \to \infty} d(\xi_i, \xi) = 0$, or $\{\xi_i\}$ is a right sequence, ξ is a left point and $\lim_{i \to \infty} d(\xi, \xi_i) = 0$. The bisequence $(\{\alpha_i\}, \{\beta_i\})$ on $(\mathcal{S}, \mathcal{T}, d)$ is a sequence on $\mathcal{S} \times \mathcal{T}$, in the case where $\{\alpha_i\}$ and $\{\beta_i\}$ are both convergent, then $(\{\alpha_i\}, \{\beta_i\})$ is said to be biconvergent.
The bi-sequence $(\{\alpha_i\}, \{\beta_i\})$ is a cauchy bisequence if $\lim_{i,j \to \infty} d(\alpha_i, \beta_j) = 0$.

    Note that every convergent cauchy bisequence is biconvergent. The bipolar metric space is complete, if each cauchy bisequence is convergent (and so it is biconvergent).

Definition 1.3.6. ([7]): Let $(\mathcal{S}_1, \mathcal{T}_1, d_1)$ and $(\mathcal{S}_2, \mathcal{T}_2, d_2)$ be two bipolar metric spaces (BMS).

    (i) The mapping $G : (\mathcal{S}_1, \mathcal{T}_1, d_1) \rightrightarrows (\mathcal{S}_2, \mathcal{T}_2, d_2)$ is said to be left-continuous at a point $l_0 \in \mathcal{S}_1$ if for every $\epsilon > 0$, there is a $\delta > 0$ such that $d_1(l_0, m) < \delta$ implies that $d_2(G(l_0), G(m)) < \epsilon$ for all $m \in \mathcal{T}_1$.

(ii) The mapping $G : (\mathcal{S}_1, \mathcal{T}_1, d_1) \rightrightarrows (\mathcal{S}_2, \mathcal{T}_2, d_2)$ is said to be right-continuous at a point $m_0 \in \mathcal{T}_1$ if for every $\epsilon > 0$, there is a $\delta > 0$ such that $d_1(l, m_0) < \delta$ implies that $d_2(G(l), G(m_0)) < \epsilon$ for all $l \in \mathcal{S}_1$.

(iii) The mapping G is called continuous if it is left continuous at each point $l \in \mathcal{S}_1$ and right continuous at each point $m \in \mathcal{T}_1$.

(iv) A contravariant function $G : (\mathcal{S}_1, \mathcal{T}_1, d_1) \leftrightharpoons (\mathcal{S}_2, \mathcal{T}_2, d_2)$ is continuous $\Leftrightarrow$ it is continuous as a covariant map $G : (\mathcal{S}_1, \mathcal{T}_1, d_1) \rightrightarrows (\mathcal{S}_2, \mathcal{T}_2, d_2)$.

It follows from the above definition a covariant (or a contravariant) mapping $G : (\mathcal{S}_1, \mathcal{T}_1, d_1)$ to $(\mathcal{S}_2, \mathcal{T}_2, d_2)$ is continuous $\Leftrightarrow \{u_n\} \to v$ in $(\mathcal{S}_1, \mathcal{T}_1, d_1)$ implies $\{G(u_n)\} \to G(v)$ in $(\mathcal{S}_2, \mathcal{T}_2, d_2)$.

Definition 1.3.7. ([7]): Let $(\mathcal{S}, \mathcal{T}, d)$ be a bipolar metric space (BMS), $G : (\mathcal{S}, \mathcal{T}) \rightrightarrows (\mathcal{S}, \mathcal{T})$ be a covariant mapping if $G(\alpha) = \alpha$ for $\alpha \in \mathcal{S} \cup \mathcal{T}$ then α is called a fixed point of G.

Definition 1.3.8. ([6], [63]): Let $(\mathcal{S}, \mathcal{T}, d)$ be a bipolar metric space(BMS) and a pair $(\wp, \varpi)$ is called

(a) coupled fixed point of covariant mapping $\Omega : (\mathcal{S}^2, \mathcal{T}^2) \rightrightarrows (\mathcal{S}, \mathcal{T})$ if $\Omega(\wp, \varpi) = \wp$, $\Omega(\varpi, \wp) = \varpi$ for $(\wp, \varpi) \in \mathcal{S}^2 \cup \mathcal{T}^2$;

(b) coupled coincident point of $\Omega : (\mathcal{S}^2, \mathcal{T}^2) \rightrightarrows (\mathcal{S}, \mathcal{T})$ and $\Lambda : (\mathcal{S}, \mathcal{T}) \rightrightarrows (\mathcal{S}, \mathcal{T})$ if $\Omega(\wp, \varpi) = \Lambda\wp$, $\Omega(\varpi, \wp) = \Lambda\varpi$;

(c) coupled common point of $\Omega : (\mathcal{S}^2, \mathcal{T}^2) \rightrightarrows (\mathcal{S}, \mathcal{T})$ and $\Lambda : (\mathcal{S}, \mathcal{T}) \rightrightarrows (\mathcal{S}, \mathcal{T})$ if $\Omega(\wp, \varpi) = \Lambda\wp = \wp$, $\Omega(\varpi, \wp) = \Lambda\varpi = \varpi$;

(d) the pair (Ω, Λ) is weakly compatible if $\Lambda(\Omega(\wp, \varpi)) = \Omega(\Lambda\wp, \Lambda\varpi)$ and

$\Lambda(\Omega(\varpi, \wp)) = \Omega(\Lambda\varpi, \Lambda\wp)$ whenever $\Omega(\wp, \varpi) = \Lambda\wp$, $\Omega(\varpi, \wp) = \Lambda\varpi$

Definition 1.3.9. Let $(\mathcal{S}, \mathcal{T}, d)$ be a bipolar metric space (BMS),

$\Omega : (\mathcal{S} \times \mathcal{T}, \mathcal{T} \times \mathcal{S}) \rightrightarrows (\mathcal{S}, \mathcal{T})$ be a covariant mapping for $\wp \in \mathcal{S}, \varpi \in \mathcal{T}$

if $\Omega(\wp, \varpi) = \wp$, $\Omega(\varpi, \wp) = \varpi$ then $(\wp, \varpi)$ is called a coupled fixed point (CFP) of Ω.

1.4 Preliminaries of C^*-Algebra Valued Fuzzy Soft Metric Spaces

In 2018, Ravi P. Agarwal1 et.al [91] described C^*-algebra valued fuzzy soft metric spaces (C^*-AVFSMS) by applying the concept of C^*-algebra valued metric spaces [77] and fuzzy soft metric spaces [118] also established some fixed point results in C^*-algebra valued fuzzy soft metric spaces (C^*-AVFSMS). Subsequently to improve many authors established numerous results on C^*-algebra valued fuzzy soft metric spaces (C^*-AVFSMS) (see. [58], [61], [86], [115]).

Throughout discussion of C^*-algebra valued fuzzy soft metric spaces, U refers to an initial universe, Θ the set of all parameters for U and $P(\tilde{U})$ the set of all fuzzy set of U. (U, Θ) means the universal set U and parameter set Θ, $\tilde{C}$ refer to C^*-algebra.

Definition 1.4.1. ([77], [91]): A Banach algebra $\tilde{C}$ is said to be C^*-algebra if there is a conjugate linear involution map $*$ on $\tilde{C}$ (i.e $*: \tilde{C} \to \tilde{C}$ as $\tilde{a} \to \tilde{a}^*$) such that $\forall\, \tilde{a}, \tilde{b} \in \tilde{C}$ and $\alpha, \beta \in \mathcal{C}$, the following holds

(i) $\left(\alpha\tilde{a} + \beta\tilde{b}\right)^* = \overline{\alpha}\tilde{a}^* + \overline{\beta}\tilde{b}^*$

(ii) $(\tilde{a}\tilde{b})^* = \tilde{b}^*\tilde{a}^*$ and $(\tilde{a}^*)^* = \tilde{a}$

(iii) $||\tilde{a}^*\tilde{a}|| = ||\tilde{a}||^2$

(iv) $||\tilde{a}\tilde{b}|| \leq ||\tilde{a}||||\tilde{b}||$

Note: From (iii) it is easily follows that $||\tilde{a}^*|| = ||\tilde{a}||$ for each $\tilde{a} \in \tilde{C}$.

Discussion:

(i) An algebra $\tilde{C}$, together with a conjugate linear involution map $*: \tilde{C} \to \tilde{C}$ defined by $\tilde{a} \to \tilde{a}^*$ is called a $*$-algebra if

(1) $(\tilde{a}\tilde{b})^* = \tilde{b}^*\tilde{a}^*$

(2) $(\tilde{a}^*)^* = \tilde{a}$ for all $\tilde{a}, \tilde{b} \in \tilde{C}$

(ii) The pair $(\tilde{C}, \star)$ is called a unital $\star$-algebra if $\tilde{C}$ contains the identity element $\tilde{I}_{\tilde{C}}$.

(iii) By a Banach $*$-algebra, we mean a complete normed unital $\star$-algebra $(\tilde{C}, \star)$ such that the norm on $\tilde{C}$ is sub-multiplicative ($||\tilde{a}\tilde{b}|| \leq ||\tilde{a}||||\tilde{b}||$) and satisfies $||\tilde{a}|| = ||\tilde{a}^*||$ for all $\tilde{a} \in \tilde{C}$.

(iv) if for all $\tilde{a} \in \tilde{C}$, we have $||\tilde{a}^*\tilde{a}|| = ||\tilde{a}||^2$ in Banach $*$-algebra $(\tilde{C}, \star)$, then $\tilde{C}$ is known as C^*-algebra.

Note: A Banach algebra $\tilde{C}$ is said to be C^*-algebra if

(a) $*$-algebra,

(b) Unital $*$-algebra,

(c) Banach $*$-algebra,

(d) $||\tilde{a}^*\tilde{a}|| = ||\tilde{a}||^2 \; \forall \; \tilde{a} \in \tilde{C}$.

Definition 1.4.2. ([77], [91]): An element $\tilde{a} \in \tilde{C}$ is called a positive element if $\tilde{a} = \tilde{a}^*$ and its spectrum $\sigma(\tilde{a}) \subset R(C)^*$ is set of non-negative fuzzy soft real numbers, where $\sigma(\tilde{a}) = \{\lambda \in R(C)^* : \lambda\tilde{I} - \tilde{a}, \text{ is non-invertible}\}$. The set of all +ve elements denoted by $\tilde{C}_+$. If $\tilde{a} \in \tilde{C}$ is positive, we write it as $\tilde{a} \geq \tilde{0}_{\tilde{C}}$ where $\tilde{0}_{\tilde{C}}$ is zero element of $\tilde{C}$.

Note:

(a) Using positive elements, one can define partial ordering $\preceq$ or $\succeq$ on $\tilde{C}$ as follows;

$$\tilde{a} \preceq \tilde{b} \text{ if and only if } \tilde{0}_{\tilde{C}} \preceq \tilde{b} - \tilde{a}, \text{ or } \tilde{b} \succeq \tilde{a} \text{ if and only if } \tilde{b} - \tilde{a} \succeq \tilde{0}_{\tilde{C}}$$

Each positive element $\tilde{a}$ of a C^*-algebra $\tilde{C}$ has a unique positive square root.

(b) Further, $\tilde{C}_+ = \{\tilde{a} \in \tilde{C} : \tilde{0}_{\tilde{C}} \preceq \tilde{a}\}$ of positive element of $\tilde{C}$ and $(\tilde{a}\tilde{a}^*)^{\frac{1}{2}} = ||\tilde{a}||$.

A C^*-algebra-valued Fuzzy soft metric space is defined in the following .

Definition 1.4.3. ([91]): Let $C \subseteq \Theta$ and $\tilde{\Theta}$ be the absolute fuzzy soft set that is $F_\Theta(x) = \tilde{1}$ for all $x \in \Theta$. Let $\tilde{C}$ denote the C^*-algebra. The C^*-algebra valued fuzzy soft metric using fuzzy soft points is defined as a mapping $\tilde{d}_{c^*} : \tilde{\Theta} \times \tilde{\Theta} \to \tilde{C}$ satisfying the following conditions

(M_0) $\tilde{0}_{\tilde{C}} \preceq \tilde{d}(G_{x_1}, G_{x_2})$ for all $G_{x_1}, G_{x_2} \in \tilde{\Theta}$

(M_1) $\tilde{d}_{c^*}(G_{x_1}, G_{x_2}) = \tilde{0}_{\tilde{C}} \Leftrightarrow G_{x_1} = G_{x_2}$

(M_2) $\tilde{d}_{c^*}(G_{x_1}, G_{x_2}) = \tilde{d}_{c^*}(G_{x_2}, G_{x_1})$

(M_3) $\tilde{d}_{c^*}(G_{x_1}, G_{x_3}) \preceq \tilde{d}_{c^*}(G_{x_1}, G_{x_2}) + \tilde{d}_{c^*}(G_{x_2}, G_{x_3}) \ \forall \ G_{x_1}, G_{x_2}, G_{x_3} \in \tilde{\Theta}.$

The fuzzy soft set $\tilde{\Theta}$ with the C^* algebra valued fuzzy soft metric $\tilde{d}_{c^*}$ is called the C^*-algebra valued fuzzy soft metric space. It is denoted by $(\tilde{\Theta}, \tilde{C}, \tilde{d}_{c^*})$.

Definition 1.4.4. ([91]): A sequence $\{F_{x_n}\}$ in a C^*-algebra valued fuzzy soft metric space $(\tilde{\Theta}, \tilde{C}, \tilde{d}_{c^*})$ is said to converges to $F_{x'}$ in $\tilde{\Theta}$ with respect to $\tilde{C}$,

if $||\tilde{d}_{c^*}(F_{x_n}, F_{x'})||_{\tilde{C}} \to \tilde{0}_{\tilde{C}}$ as $n \to \infty$ that is for every $\tilde{0}_{\tilde{C}} \prec \tilde{\epsilon}$ there exists $\tilde{0}_{\tilde{C}} \prec \tilde{\delta}$ and a positive integer $N = N(\tilde{\epsilon})$ such that $||\tilde{d}_{c^*}(F_{x_n}, F_{x'})|| < \tilde{\delta}$

implies that $||\mu^a_{F_{x_n}}(s) - \mu^a_{F_{x'}}(s)|| < \tilde{\epsilon}$ whenever $n \geq N$. It is usually denoted as $\lim\limits_{n\to\infty} F_{x_n} = F_{x'}$.

Definition 1.4.5. ([91]): A sequence $\{F_{x_n}\}$ in a C^* - algebra valued fuzzy soft metric space $(\tilde{\Theta}, \tilde{C}, \tilde{d}_{c^*})$ is said to be cauchy sequence if for every $\tilde{0}_{\tilde{C}} \prec \tilde{\epsilon}$ there exist $\tilde{0}_{\tilde{C}} \prec \tilde{\delta}$ and a positive integer $N = N(\tilde{\epsilon})$ such that $||\tilde{d}_{c^*}(F_{x_n}, F_{x_m})|| < \tilde{\delta}$ implies that $||\mu^a_{F_{x_n}}(s) - \mu^a_{F_{x_m}}(s)|| < \tilde{\epsilon}$ whenever $n, m \geq N$. That is

$||\tilde{d}_{c^*}(F_{x_n}, F_{x_m})||_{\tilde{C}} \to \tilde{0}_{\tilde{C}}$ as $n, m \to \infty$.

Definition 1.4.6. ([91]): Let $(\tilde{\Theta}, \tilde{C}, \tilde{d}_{c^*})$ be a C^*-algebra valued fuzzy soft metric space is said to be complete, if every cauchy sequence in $\tilde{\Theta}$ converges to some fuzzy soft point of $\tilde{\Theta}$.

Example 1.4. ([91]): Let $C \subseteq R$ and $\Theta \subseteq R$, let $\tilde{\Theta}$ be absolute fuzzy soft set, that is $\tilde{\Theta}(x) = \tilde{1}$ for all $x \in \Theta$ and $\tilde{C} = M_2(R(C)^*)$, define $\tilde{d}_{c^*} : \tilde{\Theta} \times \tilde{\Theta} \to \tilde{C}$ by

$$\tilde{d}_{c^*}(F_{x_1}, F_{x_2}) = \begin{bmatrix} i & 0 \\ 0 & i \end{bmatrix}$$

where $i = \inf\{|\mu^a_{F_{x_1}}(s) - \mu^a_{F_{x_2}}(s)|/s \in C\}$ and $F_{x_1}, F_{x_2} \in \tilde{\Theta}$. Then $\tilde{d}_{c^*}$ is a C^* - algebra valued fuzzy soft metric and $(\tilde{\Theta}, \tilde{C}, \tilde{d}_{c^*})$ is a complete C^* - algebra valued fuzzy soft metric space.

Lemma 1.4.1. ([91]): A C^*-algebra valued fuzzy soft metric space $(\tilde{\Theta}, \tilde{C}, \tilde{d}_{c^*})$ is complete, if every cauchy sequence in $\tilde{\Theta}$ has a converges sub sequence.

Lemma 1.4.2. ([91]): Let $(\tilde{\Theta}, \tilde{C}, \tilde{d}_{c^*})$ be a C^*-algebra valued fuzzy soft metric space, then every C^*-algebra valued fuzzy soft convergent sequence is a C^*-algebra valued fuzzy soft cauchy sequence.

Definition 1.4.7. ([86]): Let $(\tilde{\Theta}, \tilde{C}, \tilde{d}_{c*})$ be a C^*-algebra valued fuzzy soft metric space. Let $S : \tilde{\Theta} \times \tilde{\Theta} \to \tilde{\Theta}$ be a mapping, then an element $(\psi_{\alpha_1}, \phi_{\alpha_1}) \in \tilde{\Theta} \times \tilde{\Theta}$ is called coupled fixed point of S if $S(\psi_{\alpha_1}, \phi_{\alpha_1}) = \psi_{\alpha_1}$ and $S(\phi_{\alpha_1}, \psi_{\alpha_1}) = \phi_{\alpha_1}$

Definition 1.4.8. ([86]): Let $\tilde{\Theta}$ be absolute fuzzy soft set and $S : \tilde{\Theta} \times \tilde{\Theta} \to \tilde{\Theta}$ and $f : \tilde{\Theta} \to \tilde{\Theta}$ be two mappings. An element $(\psi_{\alpha_1}, \phi_{\alpha_1}) \in \tilde{\Theta} \times \tilde{\Theta}$ is called

(i) a coupled coincidence point of S and f if $f\psi_{\alpha_1} = S(\psi_{\alpha_1}, \phi_{\alpha_1})$ and

$\quad f\phi_{\alpha_1} = S(\phi_{\alpha_1}, \psi_{\alpha_1})$

(ii) a common coupled fixed point of S and f if $\psi_{\alpha_1} = f\psi_{\alpha_1} = S(\psi_{\alpha_1}, \phi_{\alpha_1})$ and $\phi_{\alpha_1} = f\phi_{\alpha_1} = $

$\quad S(\phi_{\alpha_1}, \psi_{\alpha_1})$.

Definition 1.4.9. ([86]): Let $\tilde{\Theta}$ be absolute fuzzy soft set, $S : \tilde{\Theta} \times \tilde{\Theta} \to \tilde{\Theta}$ and $f : \tilde{\Theta} \to \tilde{\Theta}$ are two mappings, then $\{S, f\}$ is said to be ω-compatible if $f\left(S(\psi_{\alpha_1}, \phi_{\alpha_1})\right) = S(f\psi_{\alpha_1}, f\phi_{\alpha_1})$ and $f\left(S(\phi_{\alpha_1}, \psi_{\alpha_1})\right) = S(f\phi_{\alpha_1}, f\psi_{\alpha_1})$ whenever $f\psi_{\alpha_1} = S(\psi_{\alpha_1}, \phi_{\alpha_1})$ and $f\phi_{\alpha_1} = S(\phi_{\alpha_1}, \psi_{\alpha_1})$.

1.5 Preliminaries of Partial b-Metric Spaces

In 1993, Czerwik [29] extended results related to the b-metric spaces. In 1994, Matthews [72] introduced the concept of partial metric space in which the self-distance of any point of space may not be zero. In 2013, Shukla [107] generalized both the concept of b-metric and partial metric spaces by introducing the partial b-metric spaces. For more works on fixed, common fixed point theorems in partial b-metric spaces, we refer ([44], [79], [100]).

Definition 1.5.1. ([107]): Let $\Im$ be a nonempty set and $\kappa \geq 1$ be a given real number. A function $P_b : \Im \times \Im \to [0, \infty)$ is called a partial b- metric (PbMS) if for all $\alpha, \beta, \gamma \in \Im$ the following conditions are satisfied:

(P_b1) $\alpha = \beta$ if and only if $P_b(\alpha, \alpha) = P_b(\alpha, \beta) = P_b(\beta, \beta)$;

(P_b2) $P_b(\alpha, \alpha) \leq P_b(\alpha, \beta)$;

(P_b3) $P_b(\alpha, \beta) = P_b(\beta, \alpha)$;

(P_b4) $P_b(\alpha, \beta) \leq \kappa \left(P_b(\alpha, \gamma) + P_b(\gamma, \beta) - P_b(\gamma, \gamma) \right)$.

Then the pair $(\Im, P_b)$ is called a partial b-metric space (PbMS) and the number $\kappa \geq 1$ is called the coefficient of $(\Im, P_b)$.

Remark 1.3. The class of partial b-metric space $(\Im, P_b)$ is effectively larger than the class of partial metric space, since a partial metric space is a special case of a partial b-metric space $(\Im, P_b)$ when $\kappa = 1$.

Remark 1.4. The class of partial b-metric space $(\Im, P_b)$ is effectively larger than the class of b-metric space, since a b-metric space is a special case of a partial b-metric space $(\Im, P_b)$ when the self-distance $P(\alpha, \alpha) = 0$.

The following example shows that a partial b-metric on $\Im$ need not be a partial metric, nor a b-metric on $\Im$ see also ([79], [107]).

Example 1.5. ([107]): Let $\Im = [0, 1)$. Define a function $P_b : \Im \times \Im \to [0, \infty)$ such that $P_b(\alpha; \beta) = [\max\{\alpha, \beta\}]^2 + |\alpha - \beta|^2$, for all $\alpha, \beta \in \Im$. Then $(\Im, P_b)$ is called a partial b-metric space with the coefficient $\kappa = 2 > 1$. But, P_b is need not be a b-metric nor a partial metric on $\Im$.

Definition 1.5.2. ([98]) Let $\mathcal{T} : \Im^3 \to \Im$, $\int : \Im \to \Im$ and $\alpha : \Im^3 \to \mathbf{R}^+$ are 3 mappings, then we say that $\mathcal{T}$ and $\int$ are an α-admissible if $\forall\, \ell_1, \ell_2, \ell_3 \in \Im$, we have

$$\alpha(\int\ell_1, \int\ell_2, \int\ell_3) \geq 1 \text{ implies } \alpha(\mathcal{T}(\ell_1, \ell_2, \ell_3), \mathcal{T}(\ell_2, \ell_3, \ell_1), \mathcal{T}(\ell_3, \ell_1, \ell_2)) \geq 1.$$

Definition 1.5.3. ([79]): Every partial b-metric P_b defines a b-metric d_{P_b}, where

$d_{P_b}(\alpha, \beta) = 2P_b(\alpha, \beta) - P_b(\alpha, \alpha) - P_b(\beta, \beta)$, for all $\alpha, \beta \in \Im$

Definition 1.5.4. ([79]): A sequence $\{\alpha_n\}$ in a partial b-metric space $(\Im, P_b)$ is said to be:

(*i*) P_b -convergent to a point $\alpha \in \Im$ if $\lim_{n \to \infty} P_b(\alpha, \alpha_n) = P_b(\alpha, \alpha)$

(*ii*) a P_b -Cauchy sequence if $\lim_{n,m \to \infty} P_b(\alpha_n, \alpha_m)$ exists and is finite;

(*iii*) A partial b-metric space $(\Im, P_b)$ is said to be P_b-complete if every P_b-cauchy sequence $\{\alpha_n\}$

in $\Im$ is P_b converges to a point $\alpha \in \Im$ such that

$$\lim_{n,m \to \infty} P_b(\alpha_n, \alpha_m) = \lim_{n \to \infty} P_b(\alpha, \alpha_n) = P_b(\alpha, \alpha).$$

Lemma 1.5.1. ([79]): A sequence $\{\alpha_n\}$ is a P_b-cauchy sequence in a partial b-metric space $(\Im, P_b)$ if and only if it is a b-cauchy sequence in the b-metric space $(\Im, d_{P_b})$.

Lemma 1.5.2. ([79]): A partial b-metric space $(\Im, P_b)$ is P_b-complete if and only if the b-metric space $(\Im, d_{P_b})$ is b-complete. Moreover $\lim_{n,m \to \infty} d_{P_b}(\alpha_n, \alpha_m) = 0$ if and only if $\lim_{m \to \infty} P_b(\alpha_m, \alpha) = \lim_{n \to \infty} P_b(\alpha_n, \alpha) = P_b(\alpha, \alpha).$

CHAPTER 2

Fixed Point Theorems in S_b- Metric Spaces with Applications

Fixed Points Theorems in S_b- Metric Spaces with Applications

In this chapter, we establishes unique fixed point theorems for mappings in complete S_b-MS and introduces the concept of $(\alpha, \varphi, \mathcal{F})$-contraction in the context of S_b-metric spaces. Furthermore, we show how the results may be used and provided applications to Integral equations and Homotopy.

2.1 On certain fixed points for $(\alpha, \varphi, \mathcal{F})$-contraction on S_b-metric spaces

In this Section, we will demonstrate some basic fixed point theorems for self-mapping using novel contractive condition of the $(\alpha, \varphi, \mathcal{F})$-type in S_b-metric spaces.

Definition 2.1.1. Let $\Gamma : \mathcal{G} \to \mathcal{G}$ be a mapping and $(\mathcal{G}, S_b)$ be an S_b-metric space. Assume that $\mathcal{F} \in \mathcal{X}$, $\varphi \in \mathcal{L}$ in definition $(1.1.5)$ and $\alpha : \mathcal{G}^3 \to \mathbf{R}^+$ are functions such that for all $\ell, \zeta \in \mathcal{G}$ with $j = 3, 4, 5$, then we say that Γ is a $(\alpha, \varphi, \mathcal{F})$-contraction if

$$S_b(\Gamma\ell, \Gamma\ell, \Gamma\zeta) > 0 \Rightarrow \varphi\left(S_b(\ell, \ell, \zeta)\right) + \alpha(\ell, \ell, \zeta)\mathcal{F}\left(S_b\left(\Gamma\ell, \Gamma\ell, \Gamma\zeta\right)\right) \le \mathcal{F}\left(\frac{1}{2\kappa^4}M_S^j\left(\ell, \zeta\right)\right)$$

$$(2.1.1)$$

where

$$M_S^3\left(\ell,\varsigma\right) = \max \left\{ \begin{array}{c} S_b\left(\ell,\ell,\varsigma\right), \frac{S_b(\ell,\ell,\Gamma\ell)+S_b(\varsigma,\varsigma,\Gamma\varsigma)}{2\kappa^4}, \\[2mm] \frac{S_b(\ell,\ell,\Gamma\varsigma)+S_b(\varsigma,\varsigma,\Gamma\ell)}{2\kappa^4} \end{array} \right\}$$

$$M_S^4\left(\ell,\varsigma\right) = \max \left\{ \begin{array}{c} S_b\left(\ell,\ell,\varsigma\right), S_b\left(\ell,\ell,\Gamma\ell\right), \\[2mm] S_b\left(\varsigma,\varsigma,\Gamma\varsigma\right), \frac{S_b(\ell,\ell,\Gamma\varsigma)+S_b(\varsigma,\varsigma,\Gamma\ell)}{2\kappa^4} \end{array} \right\}$$

$$M_S^5\left(\ell,\varsigma\right) = \max \left\{ \begin{array}{c} S_b\left(\ell,\ell,\varsigma\right), S_b\left(\ell,\ell,\Gamma\ell\right), \\[2mm] S_b\left(\varsigma,\varsigma,\Gamma\varsigma\right), S_b\left(\ell,\ell,\Gamma\varsigma\right), S_b\left(\varsigma,\varsigma,\Gamma\ell\right) \end{array} \right\}$$

Theorem 2.1.1. A CS_bMS with the coefficient $\kappa > 1$ is defined as $(\mathcal{G}, S_b)$. Let $\Gamma : \mathcal{G} \to \mathcal{G}$ be a mapping of the type $(\alpha, \varphi, \mathcal{F})$-contraction with $j = 5$, where $\mathcal{F} \in \mathcal{X}$ and $\varphi \in \mathcal{L}$. Assume that each of the following statements is true.

(i_0) Γ is a α-admissible mapping,

(i_1) There exist $\ell_0 \in \mathcal{G}$ such that $\alpha(\ell_0, \ell_0, \Gamma\ell_0) \geq 1$.

(i_2) If $\{\ell_p\}$ is sequence in $\mathcal{G}$ with $\alpha(\ell_p, \ell_p, \ell_{p+1}) \geq 1$ for all positive integers p and $\ell_p \to \vartheta$ as $p \to \infty$, we have $\alpha(\ell_p, \ell_p, \vartheta) \geq 1$ for all $p \in N$.

Then, in $\mathcal{G}$, there is a unique fixed point of Γ.

Proof. According to the theory, there are $\varsigma_0 \in \mathcal{G}$ such that $\alpha(\varsigma_0, \varsigma_0, \Gamma\varsigma_0) \geq 1$. Create a sequence $\{\varsigma_p\}$ by setting $\varsigma_{p+1} = \Gamma\varsigma_p$ for all $p \in N$. If an integer p exists and $\varsigma_p = \Gamma\varsigma_p$, then ς_p is FP of Γ, and the proof is thus complete. We therefore suppose that there is no number p such that $\varsigma_p = \varsigma_{p+1}$. This means that $\alpha(\varsigma_0, \varsigma_0, \Gamma\varsigma_0) \geq 1$ also holds for $\alpha(\varsigma_0, \varsigma_0, \varsigma_1) \geq 1$. Since Γ is a α-admissible mapping, we obtain $\alpha(\varsigma_p, \varsigma_p, \varsigma_{p+1}) \geq 1$ for every $p \in N$.

Assuming that Eq. (2.1.1) and $S_b(\Gamma\varsigma_{p-1}, \Gamma\varsigma_{p-1}, \Gamma\varsigma_p) \geq 1$ for all $p \in N$, we have

$$
\begin{aligned}
\mathcal{F}\left(S_b(\zeta_p, \zeta_p, \zeta_{p+1})\right) &= \mathcal{F}\left(S_b(\Gamma\zeta_{p-1}, \Gamma\zeta_{p-1}, \Gamma\zeta_p)\right) \\
&\leq \alpha(\zeta_{p-1}, \zeta_{p-1}, \zeta_p)\mathcal{F}\left(S_b\left(\Gamma\zeta_{p-1}, \Gamma\zeta_{p-1}, \Gamma\zeta_p\right)\right) \\
&\leq \mathcal{F}\left(\frac{1}{2\kappa^4}M_S^j\left(\zeta_{p-1}, \zeta_p\right)\right) - \varphi\left(S_b(\zeta_{p-1}, \zeta_{p-1}, \zeta_p)\right) \\
&< \mathcal{F}\left(\frac{1}{2\kappa^4}M_S^j\left(\zeta_{p-1}, \zeta_p\right)\right).
\end{aligned}
\tag{2.1.2}
$$

Now, by simple computations, we have

$$
\begin{aligned}
M_S^j\left(\zeta_{p-1}, \zeta_p\right) &= \max \left\{
\begin{array}{c}
S_b\left(\zeta_{p-1}, \zeta_{p-1}, \zeta_p\right), S_b\left(\zeta_{p-1}, \zeta_{p-1}, \Gamma\zeta_{p-1}\right), \\
S_b\left(\zeta_p, \zeta_p, \Gamma\zeta_p\right), S_b\left(\zeta_{p-1}, \zeta_{p-1}, \Gamma\zeta_p\right), S_b\left(\zeta_p, \zeta_p, \Gamma\zeta_{p-1}\right)
\end{array}
\right\} \\
&= \max \left\{
\begin{array}{c}
S_b\left(\zeta_{p-1}, \zeta_{p-1}, \zeta_p\right), S_b\left(\zeta_{p-1}, \zeta_{p-1}, \zeta_p\right), \\
S_b\left(\zeta_p, \zeta_p, \zeta_{p+1}\right), S_b\left(\zeta_{p-1}, \zeta_{p-1}, \zeta_{p+1}\right), S_b\left(\zeta_p, \zeta_p, \zeta_p\right)
\end{array}
\right\} \\
&= \max \left\{
\begin{array}{c}
S_b\left(\zeta_{p-1}, \zeta_{p-1}, \zeta_p\right), \\
S_b\left(\zeta_p, \zeta_p, \zeta_{p+1}\right), S_b\left(\zeta_{p-1}, \zeta_{p-1}, \zeta_{p+1}\right)
\end{array}
\right\}.
\end{aligned}
$$

From Eq. (2.1.2), we have

$$
\mathcal{F}\left(S_b(\zeta_p, \zeta_p, \zeta_{p+1})\right) < \mathcal{F}\left(\max\left\{
\begin{array}{c}
\frac{1}{2\kappa^4}S_b\left(\zeta_{p-1}, \zeta_{p-1}, \zeta_p\right), \\
\frac{1}{2\kappa^4}S_b\left(\zeta_p, \zeta_p, \zeta_{p+1}\right), \frac{1}{2\kappa^4}S_b\left(\zeta_{p-1}, \zeta_{p-1}, \zeta_{p+1}\right)
\end{array}
\right\}\right).
$$

But

$$
\begin{aligned}
\frac{1}{2\kappa^4}S_b\left(\zeta_{p-1}, \zeta_{p-1}, \zeta_{p+1}\right) &\leq \frac{1}{2\kappa^4}\left(2\kappa S_b\left(\zeta_{p-1}, \zeta_{p-1}, \zeta_p\right) + \kappa^2 S_b\left(\zeta_p, \zeta_p, \zeta_{p+1}\right)\right) \\
&\leq \max\{\frac{1}{\kappa^3}S_b\left(\zeta_{p-1}, \zeta_{p-1}, \zeta_p\right), \frac{1}{2\kappa^2}S_b\left(\zeta_p, \zeta_p, \zeta_{p+1}\right)\}.
\end{aligned}
$$

Therefore,

$$\mathcal{F}\left(S_b(\zeta_p, \zeta_p, \zeta_{p+1})\right) \le \mathcal{F}\left(\max\{\frac{1}{\kappa^3}S_b\left(\zeta_{p-1}, \zeta_{p-1}, \zeta_p\right), \frac{1}{2\kappa^2}S_b\left(\zeta_p, \zeta_p, \zeta_{p+1}\right)\}\right)$$

we get a contradiction if $\frac{1}{2\kappa^2}S_b\left(\zeta_p, \zeta_p, \zeta_{p+1}\right)$ is the maximum. Hence

$$\mathcal{F}\left(S_b(\zeta_p, \zeta_p, \zeta_{p+1})\right) < \mathcal{F}\left(\frac{1}{\kappa^3}S_b\left(\zeta_{p-1}, \zeta_{p-1}, \zeta_p\right)\right)$$

$$\Rightarrow \quad S_b(\zeta_p, \zeta_p, \zeta_{p+1}) < \frac{1}{\kappa^3}S_b\left(\zeta_{p-1}, \zeta_{p-1}, \zeta_p\right).$$

This demonstrates that the $\{\zeta_p\}$ sequence of nonnegative real numbers is a decreasing sequence. We assert that $\lim\limits_{p\to\infty} S_b(\zeta_p, \zeta_p, \zeta_{p+1}) = 0$. If possible, Assume that $\lim\limits_{p\to\infty} S_b(\zeta_p, \zeta_p, \zeta_{p+1}) = \gamma$ for some $\gamma > 0$. Therefore, for every $p \in N$, we have $S_b(\zeta_p, \zeta_p, \zeta_{p+1}) \ge \gamma$. By using condition (a) and Eq. (2.1.2), we have

$$\begin{aligned}
\mathcal{F}(\gamma) \le \mathcal{F}\left(S_b(\zeta_p, \zeta_p, \zeta_{p+1})\right) \ &< \ \mathcal{F}\left(\frac{1}{\kappa^3}S_b\left(\zeta_{p-1}, \zeta_{p-1}, \zeta_p\right)\right) \\
&< \ \mathcal{F}\left(\frac{1}{(\kappa^3)^2}S_b\left(\zeta_{p-2}, \zeta_{p-2}, \zeta_{p-1}\right)\right) \\
&\vdots \\
&< \ \mathcal{F}\left(\frac{1}{(\kappa^3)^p}S_b\left(\zeta_0, \zeta_0, \zeta_1\right)\right).
\end{aligned}$$

As $\lim\limits_{p\to\infty} \mathcal{F}\left(\frac{1}{(\kappa^3)^p}S_b\left(\zeta_0, \zeta_0, \zeta_1\right)\right) = -\infty$, so we can find some $q \in N$ such that $\mathcal{F}\left(\frac{1}{(\kappa^3)^p}S_b\left(\zeta_0, \zeta_0, \zeta_1\right)\right) < \mathcal{F}(\gamma)$ for all $p > q$, which contradicts the above equation. Therefore, we must have $\lim\limits_{p\to\infty} S_b(\zeta_p, \zeta_p, \zeta_{p+1}) = 0$. As of right now, we have established that Cauchy sequences in $(\mathcal{G}, S_b)$ exist. On the other hand, we assume that $\{\zeta_p\}$ is not Cauchy. The sequence of natural integers $\{q_k\}$ and $\{p_k\}$ exists when

$\epsilon > 0$ and monotonically increases such that $p_k > q_k$,

$$S_b\left(\zeta_{q_k}, \zeta_{q_k}, \varsigma_{p_k}\right) \geq \epsilon \tag{2.1.3}$$

and

$$S_b\left(\zeta_{q_k}, \zeta_{q_k}, \varsigma_{p_k-1}\right) < \epsilon. \tag{2.1.4}$$

From Lemma $(1.2.1)$, Eq. $(2.1.3)$ and Eq. $(2.1.4)$, we have

$$\begin{aligned}
\epsilon &\leq S_b\left(\zeta_{q_k}, \zeta_{q_k}, \varsigma_{p_k}\right) \\
&\leq 2\kappa S_b\left(\zeta_{q_k}, \zeta_{q_k}, \zeta_{q_k+1}\right) + \kappa^2 S_b\left(\zeta_{q_k+1}, \zeta_{q_k+1}, \varsigma_{p_k}\right).
\end{aligned}$$

So that

$$\frac{\epsilon}{\kappa^2} \leq \frac{2}{\kappa} S_b\left(\zeta_{q_k}, \zeta_{q_k}, \zeta_{q_k+1}\right) + S_b\left(\zeta_{q_k+1}, \zeta_{q_k+1}, \varsigma_{p_k}\right).$$

We obtain that by setting $k \to \infty$ and applying $\mathcal{F}$ on both sides.

$$\begin{aligned}
\mathcal{F}\left(\frac{\epsilon}{\kappa^2}\right) &\leq \lim_{k\to\infty} \mathcal{F}\left(S_b\left(\zeta_{q_k+1}, \zeta_{q_k+1}, \varsigma_{p_k}\right)\right) \\
&= \lim_{k\to\infty} \mathcal{F}\left(S_b\left(\Gamma\zeta_{q_k}, \Gamma\zeta_{q_k}, \Gamma\varsigma_{p_k-1}\right)\right) \\
&\leq \lim_{k\to\infty} \alpha(\zeta_{q_k}, \zeta_{q_k}, \varsigma_{p_k-1})\mathcal{F}\left(S_b\left(\Gamma\zeta_{q_k}, \Gamma\zeta_{q_k}, \Gamma\varsigma_{p_k-1}\right)\right) \\
&\leq \lim_{k\to\infty} \mathcal{F}\left(\frac{1}{2\kappa^4} M_S^j\left(\zeta_{q_k}, \varsigma_{p_k-1}\right)\right) - \lim_{n\to\infty} \varphi\left(S_b(\zeta_{q_k}, \zeta_{q_k}, \varsigma_{p_k-1})\right) \\
&\leq \lim_{k\to\infty} \mathcal{F}\left(\frac{1}{2\kappa^4} M_S^j\left(\zeta_{q_k}, \varsigma_{p_k-1}\right)\right) - \lim_{n\to\infty} \varphi\left(\epsilon\right) \\
&< \lim_{k\to\infty} \mathcal{F}\left(\frac{1}{2\kappa^4} M_S^j\left(\zeta_{q_k}, \varsigma_{p_k-1}\right)\right). \tag{2.1.5}
\end{aligned}$$

Now, by simple computations, we have

$$
\lim_{k\to\infty} M_S^j\left(\zeta_{q_k},\zeta_{p_k-1}\right) = \lim_{k\to\infty} \max \left\{ \begin{array}{c} S_b\left(\zeta_{q_k},\zeta_{q_k},\zeta_{p_k-1}\right), S_b\left(\zeta_{q_k},\zeta_{q_k},\Gamma\zeta_{q_k}\right), \\ S_b\left(\zeta_{p_k-1},\zeta_{p_k-1},\Gamma\zeta_{p_k-1}\right), S_b\left(\zeta_{q_k},\zeta_{q_k},\Gamma\zeta_{p_k-1}\right), \\ S_b\left(\zeta_{p_k-1},\zeta_{p_k-1},\Gamma\zeta_{q_k}\right) \end{array} \right\}
$$

$$
= \lim_{k\to\infty} \max \left\{ \begin{array}{c} S_b\left(\zeta_{q_k},\zeta_{q_k},\zeta_{p_k-1}\right), S_b\left(\zeta_{q_k},\zeta_{q_k},\zeta_{q_k+1}\right), \\ S_b\left(\zeta_{p_k-1},\zeta_{p_k-1},\zeta_{p_k}\right), S_b\left(\zeta_{q_k},\zeta_{q_k},\zeta_{p_k}\right), \\ S_b\left(\zeta_{p_k-1},\zeta_{p_k-1},\zeta_{p_k+1}\right) \end{array} \right\}
$$

$$
= \lim_{k\to\infty} \max \left\{ \begin{array}{c} \epsilon, 0, S_b\left(\zeta_{q_k},\zeta_{q_k},\zeta_{p_k}\right), \\ S_b\left(\zeta_{p_k-1},\zeta_{p_k-1},\zeta_{p_k+1}\right) \end{array} \right\}
$$

$$
\leq \lim_{k\to\infty} \max \left\{ \begin{array}{c} \epsilon, 0, 2\kappa S_b\left(\zeta_{q_k},\zeta_{q_k},\zeta_{p_k-1}\right) + \kappa^2 S_b\left(\zeta_{p_k-1},\zeta_{p_k-1},\zeta_{p_k}\right), \\ 2\kappa S_b\left(\zeta_{p_k-1},\zeta_{p_k-1},\zeta_{q_k}\right) + \kappa^2 S_b\left(\zeta_{q_k},\zeta_{q_k},\zeta_{p_k+1}\right) \end{array} \right\}
$$

$$
\leq \max\{\epsilon, 0, 2\kappa\epsilon, 2\kappa^2\epsilon\} = 2\kappa^2\epsilon.
$$

Therefore, from Eq. $(2.1.5)$ and condition (e), we deduce

$$
\mathcal{F}(\frac{\epsilon}{\kappa^2}) < \lim_{k\to\infty} \mathcal{F}\left(\frac{1}{2\kappa^4} M_S^j\left(\zeta_{q_k},\zeta_{p_k-1}\right) \right) < \mathcal{F}(\frac{\epsilon}{\kappa^2})
$$

which is incongruous. Hence a S_b-CS called $\{\zeta_p\}$ exists in CS_bMS $(\mathcal{G},S_b)$. The sequences $\{\zeta_p\}$ are convergent to $\vartheta \in (\mathcal{G},S_b)$ according to the completeness of $(\mathcal{G},S_b)$.

$$
\lim_{p\to\infty} \Gamma\zeta_p = \vartheta = \lim_{p\to\infty} \Gamma\zeta_{p+1}. \tag{2.1.6}
$$

Assume that Γ is α-admissible mapping, there is a sub sequence $\{\zeta_{p_k}\}$ of $\{\zeta_p\}$ such that $\alpha(\zeta_{p_k},\zeta_{p_k},\zeta_{p_k+1}) \geq 1$ for all $k \in N$ and we have $\alpha(\vartheta,\vartheta,\zeta_{p_k+1}) \geq 1$. At this stage, we must demonstrate that ϑ is a fixed point of Γ, Lemma (1.2.3) says that if $\Gamma\vartheta \neq \vartheta$, then we have that.

$$\frac{1}{2\kappa}S_b(\Gamma\vartheta,\Gamma\vartheta,\vartheta) \leq \liminf_{p\to\infty} S_b\left(\Gamma\vartheta,\Gamma\vartheta,\Gamma\zeta_{p+1}\right).$$

Again, by the property of $\mathcal{F}$ and Eq. (2.1.1), we obtain

$$
\begin{aligned}
\mathcal{F}\left(\frac{1}{2\kappa}S_b(\Gamma\vartheta,\Gamma\vartheta,\vartheta)\right) &\leq \liminf_{p\to\infty}\mathcal{F}\left(S_b\left(\Gamma\vartheta,\Gamma\vartheta,\Gamma\zeta_{p+1}\right)\right) \\
&\leq \liminf_{p\to\infty}\alpha\left(\vartheta,\vartheta,\zeta_{p+1}\right)\mathcal{F}\left(S_b\left(\Gamma\vartheta,\Gamma\vartheta,\Gamma\zeta_{p+1}\right)\right) \\
&\leq \liminf_{k\to\infty}\mathcal{F}\left(\frac{1}{2\kappa^4}M_S^j\left(\vartheta,\zeta_{p+1}\right)\right) - \liminf_{n\to\infty}\varphi\left(S_b(\vartheta,\vartheta,\zeta_{p+1})\right) \\
&< \liminf_{k\to\infty}\mathcal{F}\left(\frac{1}{2\kappa^4}M_S^j\left(\vartheta,\zeta_{p+1}\right)\right) \tag{2.1.7}
\end{aligned}
$$

where

$$
\begin{aligned}
\liminf_{k\to\infty} M_S^j\left(\vartheta,\zeta_{p+1}\right) &= \liminf_{k\to\infty}\max\left\{\begin{array}{c} S_b\left(\vartheta,\vartheta,\zeta_{p+1}\right),S_b\left(\vartheta,\vartheta,\Gamma\vartheta\right), \\ S_b\left(\zeta_{p+1},\zeta_{p+1},\Gamma\zeta_{p+1}\right),S_b\left(\vartheta,\vartheta,\Gamma\zeta_{p+1}\right), \\ S_b\left(\zeta_{p+1},\zeta_{p+1},\Gamma\vartheta\right) \end{array}\right\} \\
&\leq \limsup_{k\to\infty}\max\left\{\begin{array}{c} S_b\left(\vartheta,\vartheta,\zeta_{p+1}\right),S_b\left(\vartheta,\vartheta,\Gamma\vartheta\right), \\ S_b\left(\zeta_{p+1},\zeta_{p+1},\Gamma\zeta_{p+1}\right),S_b\left(\vartheta,\vartheta,\Gamma\zeta_{p+1}\right), \\ S_b\left(\zeta_{p+1},\zeta_{p+1},\Gamma\vartheta\right) \end{array}\right\} \\
&\leq \max\{0,S_b\left(\vartheta,\vartheta,\Gamma\vartheta\right)\} = \kappa S_b\left(\Gamma\vartheta,\Gamma\vartheta,\vartheta\right).
\end{aligned}
$$

From Eq. (2.1.7), we get that

$$\mathcal{F}\left(\frac{1}{2\kappa}S_b(\Gamma\vartheta,\Gamma\vartheta,\vartheta)\right) < \mathcal{F}\left(\frac{1}{2\kappa^3}S_b\left(\Gamma\vartheta,\Gamma\vartheta,\vartheta\right)\right).$$

This is incongruous. ϑ is hence a fixed point of Γ. Assume that there is a fixed point in Γ called ϑ' that is such that $\vartheta \neq \vartheta'$.

Consider

$$
\begin{aligned}
\mathcal{F}\left(S_b(\vartheta, \vartheta, \vartheta')\right) &= \mathcal{F}\left(S_b(\Gamma\vartheta, \Gamma\vartheta, \Gamma\vartheta')\right) \\
&\leq \alpha(\vartheta, \vartheta, \vartheta')\mathcal{F}\left(S_b(\Gamma\vartheta, \Gamma\vartheta, \Gamma\vartheta')\right) \\
&\leq \mathcal{F}\left(\frac{1}{2\kappa^4}M_S^j(\vartheta, \vartheta')\right) - \varphi\left(S_b(\vartheta, \vartheta, \vartheta')\right) \\
&< \mathcal{F}\left(\frac{1}{2\kappa^4}M_S^j(\vartheta, \vartheta')\right) \\
&< \mathcal{F}\left(\frac{1}{2\kappa^4}\max\{0, S_b(\vartheta, \vartheta, \vartheta'), S_b(\vartheta', \vartheta', \vartheta)\}\right) \\
&< \mathcal{F}\left(\frac{1}{2\kappa^3}S_b(\vartheta, \vartheta, \vartheta')\right)
\end{aligned}
$$

This is incongruous. Consequently, $\vartheta = \vartheta'$. Therefore, the unique fixed point of Γ is ϑ. $\qquad\square$

Theorem 2.1.2. A CS_bMS with the coefficient $\kappa > 1$ is defined as $(\mathcal{G}, S_b)$. Let $\Gamma : \mathcal{G} \to \mathcal{G}$ be a $(\alpha, \varphi, \mathcal{F})$-contraction type mapping with $j = 4$ or 3, assuming that all the requirements in Theorem (2.1.1) are true. Then, in $\mathcal{G}$, there is a UFP of Γ.

Proof. If we substitute $M_S^4(\ell, \varsigma)$ or $M_S^3(\ell, \varsigma)$ for $M_S^5(\ell, \varsigma)$ in Theorem (2.1.1), then follows in a manner similar to Theorem (2.1.1). $\qquad\square$

Theorem 2.1.3. If $(\mathcal{G}, S_b)$ is a CS_bMS with coefficient $\kappa > 1$, then suppose that a self map $\Gamma : \mathcal{G} \to \mathcal{G}$ meets the condition.

$$
S_b(\Gamma\ell, \Gamma\ell, \Gamma\varsigma) > 0 \Rightarrow \varphi\left(S_b(\ell, \ell, \varsigma)\right) + \mathcal{F}\left(S_b(\Gamma\ell, \Gamma\ell, \Gamma\varsigma)\right) \leq \mathcal{F}\left(\frac{1}{2\kappa^4}M_S^j(\ell, \varsigma)\right)
$$

where $\mathcal{F} \in \mathcal{X}$ and $\varphi \in \mathcal{L}$, $j = 5, 4$ or 3. Then, in $\mathcal{G}$, there is a UFP of Γ.

Proof. The proof follows from Theorems (2.1.1) and (2.1.2) by taking

$$\alpha\left(\ell,\ell,\zeta\right)=1.$$ $\qquad\square$

Theorem 2.1.4. If $(\mathcal{G}, S_b)$ is a CS_bMS with coefficient $\kappa > 1$, then suppose that a self map $\Gamma : \mathcal{G} \to \mathcal{G}$ meets the condition.

$$S_b(\Gamma\ell, \Gamma\ell, \Gamma\zeta) > 0 \Rightarrow \tau + \mathcal{F}\left(S_b\left(\Gamma\ell, \Gamma\ell, \Gamma\zeta\right)\right) \leq \mathcal{F}\left(\frac{1}{2\kappa^4} M_S^j\left(\ell,\zeta\right)\right)$$

where $\mathcal{F} \in \mathcal{X}$ with $\tau > 0$, $j = 5, 4$ or 3. Then, in $\mathcal{G}$, there is a UFP of Γ.

Proof. The proof follows from Theorems (2.1.1), (2.1.2) and (2.1.3) by taking $\varphi(\tau) = \tau$ where $\tau > 0$. $\qquad\square$

Corollary 2.1.5. Let $(\mathcal{G}, S_b)$ be a CS_bMS with a coefficient $\kappa > 1$. Let $\Gamma : \mathcal{G} \to \mathcal{G}$ be a satisfying.

$$S_b(\Gamma u, \Gamma u, \Gamma p) \leq \lambda M_S^j\left(u, p\right)$$

for all $u, p \in \mathcal{G}$ with $j = 5, 4$ or 3 and $\lambda \in [0, \frac{1}{2\kappa^4})$. Then, in $\mathcal{G}$, there is a UFP of Γ.

Proof. Similar proof follow from Theorems 2.1.4 by taking $\mathcal{F}(\tau) = \tau$ and omitting remanining conditions. $\qquad\square$

Example 2.1. Let $S_b : \mathcal{G}^3 \to \mathbb{R}^+$ be a mapping defined as

$S_b(\nabla_1, \nabla_2, \nabla_3) = (|\nabla_2 + \nabla_3 - 2\nabla_1| + |\nabla_2 - \nabla_3|)^2$ where $\mathcal{G} = [0, \infty)$. So clearly $(\mathcal{G}, S_b)$ is CS_bMS with $\kappa = 2$. Define $\Gamma : \mathcal{G} \to \mathcal{G}$ by $\Gamma(a) = \frac{a}{3\sqrt{8}}$.

Let $\varphi : (0, \infty) \to (0, \infty)$ and $\mathcal{F} : R^+ \to R$ as $\varphi(t) = \frac{t}{4\kappa^4}$ and $\mathcal{F}(t) = t$ and

$$\alpha : \mathcal{G}^3 \to R^+ \text{ as } \alpha(\imath, \imath, \jmath) = \begin{cases} 1 & \imath, \jmath \in [0, 1] \\ \frac{1}{2} & \text{otherwise.} \end{cases}$$

Let $\imath, \jmath \in \mathcal{G}$, if $\alpha\left(\imath, \imath, \jmath\right) \geq 1$, then $\imath, \jmath \in [0, 1]$. On the other hand, $\Gamma(\imath) \leq 1$ for every $\imath, \jmath \in [0, 1]$.

As a result, $\alpha\left(\Gamma\imath, \Gamma\imath, \Gamma\jmath\right) \geq 1$. As a result, the prediction is correct. In support of the preceding argument, $\alpha(0,0,0) > 1$. If $\{\imath_p\}$ and $\{\jmath_p\}$ are a sequence in $\mathcal{G}$ such that $\alpha(\imath_p, \imath_p, \jmath_p) > 1$ and $\imath_p \to \imath, \jmath_p \to \jmath \in \mathcal{G}$ for all $p \in N \cup \{0\}$, then $\imath_p, \jmath_p \subseteq [0,1]$ and hence $\imath, \jmath \in [0,1]$ which implies $\alpha(\imath, \imath, \jmath) \geq 1$. Let $\imath, \jmath, \in [0, \infty)$, we have

$$
\begin{aligned}
\mathcal{F}\left(S_b(\Gamma(\imath), \Gamma(\imath), \Gamma(\jmath))\right) &= S_b(\Gamma(\imath), \Gamma(\imath), \Gamma(\jmath)) \\
&= 4|\Gamma\imath - \Gamma\jmath|^2 = 4\left|\frac{\imath}{3\sqrt{8}} - \frac{\jmath}{3\sqrt{8}}\right|^2 \\
&\leq \frac{1}{64} S_b(\imath, \imath, \jmath) \leq \frac{1}{2\kappa^4} S_b(\imath, \imath, \jmath) - \frac{1}{4\kappa^4} S_b(\imath, \imath, \jmath) \\
&\leq \frac{1}{2\kappa^4} \max\left\{
\begin{array}{c}
S_b(\imath, \imath, \jmath), \, S_b(\imath, \imath, \Gamma\imath), \\
S_b(\jmath, \jmath, \Gamma\jmath), \, S_b(\imath, \imath, \Gamma\jmath), \, S_b(\jmath, \jmath, \Gamma\imath)
\end{array}
\right\} \\
&\quad - \frac{1}{4\kappa^4} S_b(\imath, \imath, \jmath) \\
&\leq \frac{1}{2\kappa^4} M_S^5(\imath, \jmath) - \frac{1}{4\kappa^4} S_b(\imath, \imath, \jmath) \\
&\leq \mathcal{F}\left(\frac{1}{2\kappa^4} M_S^j(\imath, \jmath)\right) - \varphi\left(S_b(\imath, \imath, \jmath)\right).
\end{aligned}
$$

As a result, the Theorem $(2.1.1)$'s presumptions are all met, and 0 is the only fixed point of Γ.

2.2 Application to Integral Equation

As an application of Theorem $(2.1.3)$, we investigate the existence of a unique solution to an IVP in this section.

$$
\alpha(t) = \mathcal{A}(t) + 2\kappa^4 \int_0^t K(t, \lambda)\mathfrak{h}(\lambda, \alpha(\lambda))d\lambda \text{ for all } t \in [0,1]. \tag{2.2.1}
$$

Let $\oplus = \{\mathcal{H}/\mathcal{H} : [0, \infty) \to [0, \infty)\}$ be an family of non-decreasing functions and $\mathcal{B} = \{\mathcal{F}/\mathcal{F} : R^+ \to R\}$ be a family of increasing functions satisfying

$$(\mathcal{H}(t))^\theta \leq \mathcal{F}(t^\theta) - 2\kappa^4 t^\theta \text{ for all } \theta \geq 1 \text{ and } t \geq 0.$$

Eq. (2.2.1) will be examined under the ensuing presumptions:

(i_0) $\mathcal{A} : [0, 1] \to [\frac{\alpha_0}{2\kappa^4}, \infty)$ is a continuous function;

(i_1) $\mathfrak{h} : I \times [\frac{\alpha_0}{2\kappa^4}, \infty) \to [\frac{\alpha_0}{2\kappa^4}, \infty)$ is a continuous function, $\mathfrak{h}(t, \alpha) \geq 0$ and $\exists\ \mathcal{H} \in \oplus$ such that $\forall$

$\alpha, \beta \in [\frac{\alpha_0}{2\kappa^4}, \infty)$,

$|\mathfrak{h}(t, \alpha) - \mathfrak{h}(t, \beta)| \leq \mathcal{H}(|\alpha - \beta|)$ with $\mathcal{H}(t_p) \to \frac{1}{2^{\theta-1}}$ as $p \to \infty$ implies

$\lim\limits_{p \to \infty} t_p = 0$

(i_2) $\mathcal{K} : [0, 1] \times [0, 1] \to R$ is a continuous function in $t \in [0, 1]$ and is measurable in each $\lambda \in [0, 1]$,

for every t in such a way that $\mathcal{K}(t, \alpha) \geq 0$

and $\int\limits_0^t \mathcal{K}(t, \lambda)d\lambda \leq \frac{1}{\sqrt{2^{3+\frac{3}{\theta}}}}$.

Consider the space of continuous functions $\mathcal{G} = C\left(I, [\frac{\alpha_0}{2\kappa^4}, \infty)\right)$ and define the function $S_b(\nabla_1, \nabla_2, \nabla_3) = (|\nabla_2 + \nabla_3 - 2\nabla_1| + |\nabla_2 - \nabla_3|)^2$ for $\nabla_1, \nabla_2, \nabla_3 \in \mathcal{G}$. Then $(\mathcal{G}, S_b)$ is a CS_bMS with $\kappa = 2$.

Theorem 2.2.1. Equation (2.2.1) has a unique solution in $C\left(I, [\frac{\alpha_0}{2\kappa^4}, \infty)\right)$ under assumptions $(i_0) - (i_2)$.

Proof. Define $\Gamma : \mathcal{G} \to \mathcal{G}$ by $\Gamma(\alpha)(t) = \frac{\mathcal{A}(t)}{2\kappa^4} + \int\limits_0^t \mathcal{K}(t, \lambda)\mathfrak{h}(\tau, \alpha(\lambda))d\lambda, t \in [0, 1]$

Now, for $\rho, \mu \in \mathcal{G}$

$$\mathcal{F}\left(S_b(\Gamma(\rho)(t), \Gamma(\rho)(t), \Gamma(\mu)(t))\right) = S_b(\Gamma(\rho)(t), \Gamma(\rho)(t), \Gamma(\mu)(t))$$

$$= (2|(\Gamma(\rho)(t) - \Gamma(\mu)(t)|)^2$$

$$= 4|\int_0^t \mathcal{K}(t,\lambda)\mathfrak{h}(\tau,\rho(\lambda))d\lambda - \int_0^t \mathcal{K}(t,\lambda)\mathfrak{h}(\tau,\mu(\lambda))d\lambda|^2$$

$$\leq \left(2\int_0^t \mathcal{K}(t,\lambda)|\mathfrak{h}(\tau,\rho(\lambda)) - \mathfrak{h}(\tau,\mu(\lambda))|d\lambda\right)^2$$

$$\leq \frac{1}{2^{\frac{3\theta+3}{\theta}}}(\mathcal{H}(2|\rho - \mu|))^2$$

$$\leq \frac{1}{2^{\frac{3\theta+3}{\theta}}}\left(\mathcal{F}(2|\rho - \mu|)^2 - 2\kappa^4(2|\rho - \mu|)^2\right)$$

$$\leq \frac{1}{2^{\frac{3\theta+3}{\theta}}}\left(\mathcal{F}(S_b(\rho,\rho,\mu)) - 2\kappa^4 S_b(\rho,\rho,\mu)\right)$$

$$\leq \mathcal{F}(\frac{1}{2\kappa^4}S_b(\rho,\rho,\mu)) - \frac{1}{2}S_b(\rho,\rho,\mu)$$

$$\leq \mathcal{F}\left(\frac{1}{2\kappa^4}M_S^j(\rho,\mu)\right) - \varphi\left(S_b(\rho,\rho,\mu)\right)$$

in which $\frac{\theta+1}{\theta} = \kappa$, $\mathcal{F}(t) = t$, and $\varphi(t) = \frac{t}{2}$. According to Theorem 2.1.3, equation (2.2.1) has a unique solution in $C\left(I, [\frac{\alpha_0}{2\kappa^4}, \infty)\right)$. $\qquad\square$

2.3 Application to Homotopy

This section investigates the existence of a unique solution to Homotopy.

Theorem 2.3.1. If $(\mathcal{G}, S_b)$ is a CS_bMS, then Δ and $\overline{\Delta}$ are open and closed subsets of $\mathcal{G}$, respectively, such that $\Delta \subseteq \overline{\Delta}$. Let $\mathfrak{H}_b : \overline{\Delta} \times [0,1] \to \mathcal{G}$ be an operator meeting the requirements listed below.

(τ_0) $\alpha \neq \mathfrak{H}_b(\alpha, s)$, for each $\alpha \in \partial\Delta$ and $s \in [0,1]$ (Here $\partial\Delta$ is boundary of Δ in $\mathcal{G}$)

(τ_1) $S_b(\mathfrak{H}_b(\alpha, s), \mathfrak{H}_b(\alpha, s), \mathfrak{H}_b(\beta, s)) \geq 0$ implies

$$\tau + \mathcal{F}\left(2\kappa^4 S_b(\mathfrak{H}_b(\alpha, s), \mathfrak{H}_b(\alpha, s), \mathfrak{H}_b(\beta, s))\right) \leq \mathcal{F}\left(S_b(\alpha, \alpha, \beta)\right)$$

for all $\alpha, \beta \in \overline{\Delta}$ with $\tau > 0$ and $s \in [0, 1]$,

(τ_2) $\exists\, M_b \geq 0 \ni S_b(\mathfrak{H}_b(\alpha, s), \mathfrak{H}_b(\alpha, s), \mathfrak{H}_b(\alpha, t)) \leq M_b|s - t|$ for every $\alpha \in \overline{\Delta}$ and $s, t \in [0, 1]$.

Then $\mathfrak{H}_b(., 1)$ has a FP $\iff$ $\mathfrak{H}_b(., 0)$ has a FP.

Proof. Take into account the set $A = \{s \in [0, 1] : \alpha = \mathfrak{H}_b(\alpha, s)$ for some $\alpha \in \Delta\}$. Due to the fact that $\mathfrak{H}_b(, 0)$ has a FP in Δ, we have that $0 \in A$. The set A is not empty as a result. We will prove that $A = [0, 1]$ by establishing that A is both open and closed in $[0, 1]$. $\mathfrak{H}_b(, 1)$ has a FP in Δ as a result. The first thing we do is show that $A \subseteq [0, 1]$ is closed. To observe this, assign $s_p \to s \in [0, 1]$ as $p \to \infty$ and let $\{s_p\}_{p=1}^{\infty} \subseteq A$. We must show that s is in A. Given that s_p in A for $p = 0, 1, 2, ...$, there is α_p in Δ with $\alpha_{p+1} = \mathfrak{H}_b(\alpha_p, s_p)$. The proof is successful if $n \in N$ exist such that $S_b(\alpha_p, \alpha_p, \mathfrak{H}_b(\alpha_p, s_p)) = 0$. So, we assume that

$$
\begin{aligned}
0 \;<\; & S_b(\alpha_p, \alpha_p, \mathfrak{H}_b(\alpha_p, s_p)) \\
=\; & S_b(\mathfrak{H}_b(\alpha_{p-1}, s_{p-1}), \mathfrak{H}_b(\alpha_{p-1}, s_{p-1}), \mathfrak{H}_b(\alpha_p, s_p)) \;\; \forall\; p \in N.
\end{aligned}
$$

For any $p \in N$, we have

$$
\begin{aligned}
S_b(\alpha_p, \alpha_p, \alpha_{p+1}) \;=\; & S_b\left(\mathfrak{H}_b(\alpha_{p-1}, s_{p-1}), \mathfrak{H}_b(\alpha_{p-1}, s_{p-1}), \mathfrak{H}_b(\alpha_p, s_p)\right) \\
\leq\; & 2\kappa S_b\left(\mathfrak{H}_b(\alpha_{p-1}, s_{p-1}), \mathfrak{H}_b(\alpha_{p-1}, s_{p-1}), \mathfrak{H}_b(\alpha_p, s_{p-1})\right) \\
& +\kappa^2 S_b\left(\mathfrak{H}_b(\alpha_p, s_{p-1}), \mathfrak{H}_b(\alpha_p, s_{p-1}), \mathfrak{H}_b(\alpha_p, s_p)\right) \\
\leq\; & 2\kappa S_b\left(\mathfrak{H}_b(\alpha_{p-1}, s_{p-1}), \mathfrak{H}_b(\alpha_{p-1}, s_{p-1}), \mathfrak{H}_b(\alpha_p, s_{p-1})\right) \\
& +\kappa^2 M_b|s_p - s_{p-1}|.
\end{aligned}
$$

Letting $p \to \infty$, we obtain

$$\lim_{p \to \infty} S_b(\alpha_p, \alpha_p, \alpha_{p+1}) \leq \lim_{p \to \infty} 2\kappa S_b\left(\mathfrak{H}_b(\alpha_{p-1}, s_{p-1}), \mathfrak{H}_b(\alpha_{p-1}, s_{p-1}), \mathfrak{H}_b(\alpha_p, s_{p-1})\right).$$

Since $\mathcal{F}$ is continuous and increasing function, we obtain

$$
\begin{aligned}
&\lim_{p \to \infty} \mathcal{F}\left(\kappa^3 S_b(\alpha_p, \alpha_p, \alpha_{p+1})\right) \\
=\ &\lim_{p \to \infty} \mathcal{F}\left(2\kappa^4 S_b\left(\mathfrak{H}_b(\alpha_{p-1}, s_{p-1}), \mathfrak{H}_b(\alpha_{p-1}, s_{p-1}), \mathfrak{H}_b(\alpha_p, s_{p-1})\right)\right) \\
\leq\ &\lim_{p \to \infty} \left(\mathcal{F}\left(S_b(\alpha_{p-1}, \alpha_{p-1}, \alpha_p)\right) - \tau\right) \\
\leq\ &\lim_{p \to \infty} \left(\mathcal{F}\left(S_b(\alpha_{n-2}, \alpha_{n-2}, \alpha_{p-1})\right) - 2\tau\right) \\
&\ \ \vdots \\
\leq\ &\lim_{p \to \infty} \left(\mathcal{F}\left(S_b(\alpha_0, \alpha_0, \alpha_1)\right) - p\tau\right).
\end{aligned}
\tag{2.3.1}
$$

In above inequality Eq. (2.3.1), we have

$$\lim_{p \to \infty} \mathcal{F}\left(\kappa^3 S_b(\alpha_p, \alpha_p, \alpha_{p+1})\right) = -\infty$$

which together with Definition (1.1.5)(b), gives $\lim_{p \to \infty} S_b(\alpha_p, \alpha_p, \alpha_{p+1}) = 0$. It is now time to demonstrate the S_b-CS $\{\alpha_p\}$ in $(\mathcal{G}, S_b)$. On the other hand, Assume $\{\alpha_p\}$ is not a S_b-CS. Natural numbers $\{q_k\}$ and $\{p_k\}$ can be arranged in a monotone increasing sequence with $\epsilon > 0$ such that $p_k > q_k$,

$$S_b\left(\alpha_{q_k}, \alpha_{q_k}, \alpha_{p_k}\right) \geq \epsilon \tag{2.3.2}$$

and

$$S_b\left(\alpha_{q_k}, \alpha_{q_k}, \alpha_{p_k-1}\right) < \epsilon. \tag{2.3.3}$$

From Eq. (2.3.2) and Eq. (2.3.3), we have

$$
\begin{aligned}
\epsilon \ \leq \ & S_b\left(\alpha_{q_k}, \alpha_{q_k}, \alpha_{p_k}\right) \\[4pt]
\leq \ & 2\kappa S_b\left(\alpha_{q_k}, \alpha_{q_k}, \alpha_{q_{k+1}}\right) + \kappa^2 S_b\left(\alpha_{q_{k+1}}, \alpha_{q_{k+1}}, \alpha_{p_k}\right) \\[4pt]
\leq \ & 2\kappa S_b\left(\alpha_{q_k}, \alpha_{q_k}, \alpha_{q_{k+1}}\right) + \kappa^2 S_b\left(\mathfrak{H}_b(\alpha_{q_k}, s_{q_k}), \mathfrak{H}_b(\alpha_{q_k}, s_{q_k}), \mathfrak{H}_b(\alpha_{p_{k-1}}, s_{p_{k-1}})\right) \\[4pt]
\leq \ & 2\kappa S_b\left(\alpha_{q_k}, \alpha_{q_k}, \alpha_{q_{k+1}}\right) + 2\kappa^3 S_b\left(\mathfrak{H}_b(\alpha_{q_k}, s_{q_k}), \mathfrak{H}_b(\alpha_{q_k}, s_{q_k}), \mathfrak{H}_b(\alpha_{p_{k-1}}, s_{q_k})\right) \\[4pt]
& + \kappa^4 S_b\left(\mathfrak{H}_b(\alpha_{p_{k-1}}, s_{q_k}), \mathfrak{H}_b(\alpha_{p_{k-1}}, s_{q_k}), \mathfrak{H}_b(\alpha_{p_{k-1}}, s_{p_{k-1}})\right).
\end{aligned}
$$

So that

$$
\begin{aligned}
\kappa\epsilon \ \leq \ & 2\kappa^2 S_b\left(\alpha_{q_k}, \alpha_{q_k}, \alpha_{q_{k+1}}\right) + 2\kappa^4 S_b\left(\mathfrak{H}_b(\alpha_{q_k}, s_{q_k}), \mathfrak{H}_b(\alpha_{q_k}, s_{q_k}), \mathfrak{H}_b(\alpha_{p_{k-1}}, s_{q_k})\right) \\[4pt]
& + \kappa^5\left|s_{q_k} - s_{p_{k-1}}\right|.
\end{aligned}
$$

We obtain that by setting $k \to \infty$ and applying $\mathcal{F}$ on both sides.

$$
\begin{aligned}
\mathcal{F}(\kappa\epsilon) \ \leq \ & \lim_{k\to\infty} \mathcal{F}\left(2\kappa^4 S_b\left(\mathfrak{H}_b(\alpha_{q_k}, s_{q_k}), \mathfrak{H}_b(\alpha_{q_k}, s_{q_k}), \mathfrak{H}_b(\alpha_{p_{k-1}}, s_{q_k})\right)\right) \\[4pt]
\leq \ & \lim_{k\to\infty} \mathcal{F}\left(S_b(\alpha_{q_k}, \alpha_{q_k}, \alpha_{p_{k-1}})\right) - \tau \\[4pt]
\leq \ & \mathcal{F}(\epsilon) - \tau.
\end{aligned}
$$

This leads to the conclusion that $\tau + \mathcal{F}(\kappa\epsilon) \leq \mathcal{F}(\epsilon)$. It contradicts itself. In the S_b-metric space $(\mathcal{G}, S_b)$, the sequence $\{\alpha_p\}$ is a S_b-Cauchy sequence. The sequence $\{\alpha_p\} \to \nu \in (\mathcal{G}, S_b)$ comes from the completeness of $(\mathcal{G}, S_b)$.

$$
\lim_{p\to\infty} \alpha_{p+1} = \nu = \lim_{p\to\infty} \alpha_p.
$$

We can prove $\nu = \mathfrak{H}_b(\nu, s)$.Suppose that $S_b(\mathfrak{H}_b(\nu, s), \mathfrak{H}_b(\nu, s), \nu) > 0$.

From Lemma $(1.2.3)(\mathrm{i})$, we have

$$
\begin{aligned}
\mathcal{F}\left(\kappa^3 S_b(\mathfrak{H}_b(\nu, s), \mathfrak{H}_b(\nu, s), \nu)\right) &\leq \lim_{p \to \infty} \inf \mathcal{F}\left(2\kappa^4 S_b(\mathfrak{H}_b(\nu, s), \mathfrak{H}_b(\nu, s), \mathfrak{H}_b(\alpha_p, s))\right) \\
&\leq \lim_{p \to \infty} \mathcal{F}\left(S_b(\nu, \nu, \alpha_p)\right) - \tau.
\end{aligned}
$$

This is

$$
\mathcal{F}\left(\kappa^3 S_b(\mathfrak{H}_b(\nu, s), \mathfrak{H}_b(\nu, s), \nu)\right) = -\infty \text{ as } \tau \to \infty.
$$

Accordingly, $\nu = \mathfrak{H}_b(\nu, s)$ indicates that $S_b(\mathfrak{H}_b(\nu, s), \mathfrak{H}_b(\nu, s), \nu) = 0$. So, s in A. It is obvious that A is closed in $[0, 1]$. Let $s_0 \in A$, then α_0 exists in Δ such that $\alpha_0 = \mathfrak{H}_b(\alpha_0, s_0)$. Because Δ is open, $\delta > 0$ must exist for $B_{S_b}(\alpha_0, \delta) \subseteq \Delta$. Select the value of $s \in (s_0 - \epsilon, s_0 + \epsilon)$ such that $|s - s_0| \leq \frac{1}{M^p} < \epsilon$. Consequently, for $\overline{B_b(\alpha_0, \delta)} = \{\alpha \in \mathcal{G} : S_b(\alpha, \alpha, \alpha_0) \leq \delta + \kappa^2 S_b(\alpha_0, \alpha_0, \alpha_0)\}$.

Now

$$
\begin{aligned}
S_b\left(\mathfrak{H}_b(\alpha, s), \mathfrak{H}_b(\alpha, s), \alpha_0)\right) &= S_b\left(\mathfrak{H}_b(\alpha, s), \mathfrak{H}_b(\alpha, s), \mathfrak{H}_b(\alpha_0, s_0)\right) \\
&\leq 2\kappa S_b\left(\mathfrak{H}_b(\alpha, s), \mathfrak{H}_b(\alpha, s), \mathfrak{H}_b(\alpha, s_0)\right) \\
&\quad + \kappa^2 S_b\left(\mathfrak{H}_b(\alpha, s_0), \mathfrak{H}_b(\alpha, s_0), \mathfrak{H}_b(\alpha_0, s_0)\right) \\
&\leq 2\kappa M|s - s_0| + \kappa^2 S_b\left(\mathfrak{H}_b(\alpha, s_0), \mathfrak{H}_b(\alpha, s_0), \mathfrak{H}_b(\alpha_0, s_0)\right).
\end{aligned}
$$

If p is allowed to reach ∞ and $\mathcal{F}$ is applied on both sides, then

$$
\begin{aligned}
\mathcal{F}\left(S_b\left(\mathfrak{H}_b(\alpha, s), \mathfrak{H}_b(\alpha, s), \alpha_0)\right)\right) &\leq \mathcal{F}\left(2\kappa^2 S_b\left(\mathfrak{H}_b(\alpha, s), \mathfrak{H}_b(\alpha, s), \alpha_0\right)\right) \\
&\leq \mathcal{F}\left(2\kappa^4 S_b\left(\mathfrak{H}_b(\alpha, s_0), \mathfrak{H}_b(\alpha, s_0), \mathfrak{H}_b(\alpha_0, s_0)\right)\right) \\
&\leq \mathcal{F}\left(S_b(\alpha, \alpha, \alpha_0)\right) - \tau \leq \mathcal{F}(S_b(\alpha, \alpha, \alpha_0)).
\end{aligned}
$$

Therefore,

$$S_b\left(\mathfrak{H}_b(\alpha,s),\mathfrak{H}_b(\alpha,s),\alpha_0)\right) \leq S_b(\alpha,\alpha,\alpha_0) \leq \delta + \kappa^2 S_b(\alpha_0,\alpha_0,\alpha_0).$$

Thus for each fixed $s \in (s_0 - \epsilon, s_0 + \epsilon)$, $\mathfrak{H}_b(.;s) : \overline{B_b(\alpha_0,\delta)} \to \overline{B_b(\alpha_0,\delta)}$. Then, all of the criteria of Theorem $(2.3.1)$ are satisfied. As a result, we conclude that $\mathfrak{H}_b(.;s)$ has a FP in $\overline{\Delta}$. However, this must be in Δ. As a result, $s \in A$ for $s \in (s_0 - \epsilon, s_0 + \epsilon)$. As a result, $(s_0 - \epsilon, s_0 + \epsilon) \subseteq A$. Clearly, A is open in the range $[0,1]$.

A similar method can be used to demonstrate the inverse. $\square$

2.4   Conclusion

In this chapter, contractive mappings of the $(\alpha, \varphi, \mathcal{F})$ type are used to show certain fixed point results in the context of S_b-metric space, along with appropriate example that illustrate the key findings. Applications to integral equations and homotopy are also offered.

Coupled Fixed Point Theorems in Bipolar Metric Spaces with Applications

CHAPTER 3

Coupled Fixed Point Theorems in Bipolar Metric Spaces with Applications

This chapter's goal is to prove CCFP theorems via C-class functions in bipolar metric spaces. We illustrated certain applications to integral equations and homotopy.

3.1 Existence fixed point solutions for C-class functions in Bipolar metric spaces

In this section, two covariant mappings that meet new type contractive criteria in bipolar metric spaces and given some common coupled fixed point theorems via C-class functions.

Theorem 3.1.1. Let $(\mathcal{S}, \mathcal{T}, d)$ be a CBMS. Suppose that $\Gamma : (\mathcal{S}^2, \mathcal{T}^2) \rightrightarrows (\mathcal{S}, \mathcal{T})$ and $\Lambda : (\mathcal{S}, \mathcal{T}) \rightrightarrows (\mathcal{S}, \mathcal{T})$ be two covariant mappings satiesfies

$$\psi_\star \left(d(\Gamma(u, v), \Gamma(p, q)) \right) \leq \Delta \left(\psi_\star \left(M(u, v, p, q) \right), \phi_\star \left(M(u, v, p, q) \right) \right)$$

$$(3.1.1)$$

where, $M(u, v, p, q) = \ell \max \left\{ d\left(\Lambda u, \Lambda p \right), d\left(\Lambda v, \Lambda q \right) \right\}$ for all $u, v \in \mathcal{S}$ and $p, q \in \mathcal{T}$ and $\Delta \in C$, $\psi_\star \in \mathfrak{F}$, $\phi_\star \in \mathfrak{G}$ with $\ell \in (0, 1)$

(ξ_0) $\Gamma(\mathcal{S}^2 \cup \mathcal{T}^2) \subseteq \Lambda(\mathcal{S} \cup \mathcal{T})$ and $\Lambda(\mathcal{S} \cup \mathcal{T})$ is a complete subspace of $\mathcal{S} \cup \mathcal{T}$,

(ξ_1) pair (Γ, Λ) is ω-compatible.

Then there is a UCCFP of Γ and Λ in $\mathcal{S} \cup \mathcal{T}$.

Proof. Let $x_0, y_0 \in \mathcal{S}$ and $p_0, q_0 \in \mathcal{T}$ be arbitrary, and from condition (ξ_0), we construct the bisequences $(\{\alpha_\kappa\}, \{\zeta_\kappa\}), (\{\beta_\kappa\}, \{\eta_\kappa\})$ in $(\mathcal{S}, \mathcal{T})$ as

$$\Gamma\left(x_\kappa, y_\kappa\right) = \Lambda x_{\kappa+1} = \alpha_\kappa, \quad \Gamma\left(p_\kappa, q_\kappa\right) = \Lambda p_{\kappa+1} = \zeta_\kappa$$
$$\Gamma\left(y_\kappa, x_\kappa\right) = \Lambda y_{\kappa+1} = \beta_\kappa, \quad \Gamma\left(q_\kappa, p_\kappa\right) = \Lambda q_{\kappa+1} = \eta_\kappa$$

where $\kappa = 0, 1, 2, \ldots$.

Then from Eq. (3.1.1), we can get

$$
\begin{aligned}
\psi_\star\left(d(\alpha_\kappa, \zeta_{\kappa+1})\right) &= \psi_\star\left(d(\Gamma\left(x_\kappa, y_\kappa\right), \Gamma\left(p_{\kappa+1}, q_{\kappa+1}\right))\right) \\
&\leq \Delta\left(\psi_\star\left(M(x_\kappa, y_\kappa, p_{\kappa+1}, q_{\kappa+1})\right), \phi_\star\left(M(x_\kappa, y_\kappa, p_{\kappa+1}, q_{\kappa+1})\right)\right)
\end{aligned}
$$

$$(3.1.2)$$

where,

$$
\begin{aligned}
M(x_\kappa, y_\kappa, p_{\kappa+1}, q_{\kappa+1}) &= \ell \max\left\{ d\left(\Lambda x_\kappa, \Lambda p_{\kappa+1}\right), d\left(\Lambda y_\kappa, \Lambda q_{\kappa+1}\right) \right\} \\
&= \ell \max\left\{ d\left(\alpha_{\kappa-1}, \zeta_\kappa\right), d\left(\beta_{\kappa-1}, \eta_\kappa\right) \right\}.
\end{aligned}
$$

From Eq. (3.1.2), deduce that

$$\psi_\star\left(d(\alpha_\kappa, \zeta_{\kappa+1})\right)$$

$$\leq \Delta \left(\psi_\star \left(\ell \max \left\{ \begin{array}{l} d\left(\alpha_{\kappa-1}, \zeta_\kappa\right), \\ d\left(\beta_{\kappa-1}, \eta_\kappa\right) \end{array} \right\} \right), \phi_\star \left(\ell \max \left\{ \begin{array}{l} d\left(\alpha_{\kappa-1}, \zeta_\kappa\right), \\ d\left(\beta_{\kappa-1}, \eta_\kappa\right) \end{array} \right\} \right) \right)$$

$$\leq \psi_\star \left(\ell \max \left\{ d\left(\alpha_{\kappa-1}, \zeta_\kappa\right), d\left(\beta_{\kappa-1}, \eta_\kappa\right) \right\} \right).$$

By using definition (1.3.3) of (ψ_0), we have

$$d(\alpha_\kappa, \zeta_{\kappa+1}) \leq \ell \max \left\{ d\left(\alpha_{\kappa-1}, \zeta_\kappa\right), d\left(\beta_{\kappa-1}, \eta_\kappa\right) \right\}. \tag{3.1.3}$$

Similarly, we can prove

$$d\left(\beta_\kappa, \eta_{\kappa+1}\right) \leq \ell \max \left\{ d\left(\alpha_{\kappa-1}, \zeta_\kappa\right), d\left(\beta_{\kappa-1}, \eta_\kappa\right) \right\}. \tag{3.1.4}$$

Combining Eq. (3.1.3) and Eq. (3.1.4), we have

$$\max \left\{ d\left(\alpha_\kappa, \zeta_{\kappa+1}\right), d\left(\beta_\kappa, \eta_{\kappa+1}\right) \right\} \leq \ell \max \left\{ d\left(\alpha_{\kappa-1}, \zeta_\kappa\right), d\left(\beta_{\kappa-1}, \eta_\kappa\right) \right\}$$

$$\leq \ell^2 \max \left\{ d\left(\alpha_{\kappa-2}, \zeta_{\kappa-1}\right), d\left(\beta_{\kappa-2}, \eta_{\kappa-1}\right) \right\}$$

$$\vdots$$

$$\leq \ell^\kappa \max \left\{ \begin{array}{l} d\left(\alpha_0, \zeta_1\right), \\ d\left(\beta_0, \eta_1\right) \end{array} \right\} \to 0 \text{ as } \kappa \to \infty. \tag{3.1.5}$$

On the other hand, we have

$$\psi_\star \left(d(\alpha_{\kappa+1}, \zeta_\kappa) \right) = \psi_\star \left(d(\Gamma\left(x_{\kappa+1}, y_{\kappa+1}\right), \Gamma\left(p_\kappa, q_\kappa\right)) \right)$$

$$\leq \Delta \left(\psi_\star \left(M(x_{\kappa+1}, y_{\kappa+1}, p_\kappa, q_\kappa) \right), \phi_\star \left(M(x_{\kappa+1}, y_{\kappa+1}, p_\kappa, q_\kappa) \right) \right)$$

$$\leq \ \psi_\star \left(\ell \max \left\{ \ d\left(\alpha_\kappa, \zeta_{\kappa-1}\right), d\left(\beta_\kappa, \eta_{\kappa-1}\right) \ \right\} \right).$$

By using definition $(1.3.3)$ of (ψ_0), we have

$$d(\alpha_{\kappa+1}, \zeta_\kappa) \leq \ell \max \left\{ \ d\left(\alpha_\kappa, \zeta_{\kappa-1}\right), d\left(\beta_\kappa, \eta_{\kappa-1}\right) \ \right\}. \tag{3.1.6}$$

Because of

$$\begin{aligned}
M(x_{\kappa+1}, y_{\kappa+1}, p_\kappa, q_\kappa) &= \ell \max \left\{ \ d\left(\Lambda x_{\kappa+1}, \Lambda p_\kappa\right), d\left(\Lambda y_{\kappa+1}, \Lambda q_\kappa\right) \ \right\} \\
&= \ell \max \left\{ \ d\left(\alpha_\kappa, \zeta_{\kappa-1}\right), d\left(\beta_\kappa, \eta_{\kappa-1}\right) \ \right\}.
\end{aligned}$$

Similarly, we can prove

$$d\left(\beta_{\kappa+1}, \eta_\kappa\right) \leq \ell \max \left\{ \ d\left(\alpha_\kappa, \zeta_{\kappa-1}\right), d\left(\beta_\kappa, \eta_{\kappa-1}\right) \ \right\}. \tag{3.1.7}$$

Combining Eq. $(3.1.6)$ and Eq. $(3.1.7)$, we have

$$\begin{aligned}
\max \left\{ \ d\left(\alpha_{\kappa+1}, \zeta_\kappa\right), d\left(\beta_{\kappa+1}, \eta_\kappa\right) \ \right\} &\leq \ell \max \left\{ \ d\left(\alpha_\kappa, \zeta_{\kappa-1}\right), d\left(\beta_\kappa, \eta_{\kappa-1}\right) \ \right\} \\
&\leq \ell^2 \max \left\{ \ d\left(\alpha_{\kappa-1}, \zeta_{\kappa-2}\right), d\left(\beta_{\kappa-1}, \eta_{\kappa-2}\right) \ \right\} \\
&\ \ \vdots \\
&\leq \ell^\kappa \max \left\{ \begin{array}{l} d\left(\alpha_1, \zeta_0\right), \\[4pt] d\left(\beta_1, \eta_0\right) \end{array} \right\} \to 0 \text{ as } \kappa \to \infty.
\end{aligned}$$

$$\tag{3.1.8}$$

Moreover,

$$
\begin{aligned}
\psi_\star\left(d(\alpha_\kappa,\zeta_\kappa)\right) &= \psi_\star\left(d(\Gamma\left(x_\kappa,y_\kappa\right),\Gamma\left(p_\kappa,q_\kappa\right))\right) \\
&\leq \Delta\left(\psi_\star\left(M(x_\kappa,y_\kappa,p_\kappa,q_\kappa)\right),\phi_\star\left(M(x_\kappa,y_\kappa,p_\kappa,q_\kappa)\right)\right) \\
&\leq \psi_\star\left(\ell\max\left\{\, d\left(\alpha_{\kappa-1},\zeta_{\kappa-1}\right),d\left(\beta_{\kappa-1},\eta_{\kappa-1}\right)\,\right\}\right).
\end{aligned}
$$

By using definition $(1.3.3)$ of (ψ_0), we have

$$
d(\alpha_\kappa,\zeta_\kappa)\leq \ell\max\left\{\, d\left(\alpha_{\kappa-1},\zeta_{\kappa-1}\right),d\left(\beta_{\kappa-1},\eta_{\kappa-1}\right)\,\right\}. \tag{3.1.9}
$$

Because of

$$
\begin{aligned}
M(x_\kappa,y_\kappa,p_\kappa,q_\kappa) &= \ell\max\left\{\, d\left(\Lambda x_\kappa,\Lambda p_\kappa\right),d\left(\Lambda y_\kappa,\Lambda q_\kappa\right)\,\right\} \\
&= \ell\max\left\{\, d\left(\alpha_{\kappa-1},\zeta_{\kappa-1}\right),d\left(\beta_{\kappa-1},\eta_{\kappa-1}\right)\,\right\}.
\end{aligned}
$$

Similarly, we can prove

$$
d\left(\beta_\kappa,\eta_\kappa\right) \leq \ell\max\left\{\, d\left(\alpha_{\kappa-1},\zeta_{\kappa-1}\right),d\left(\beta_{\kappa-1},\eta_{\kappa-1}\right)\,\right\}. \tag{3.1.10}
$$

Combining Eq. $(3.1.9)$ and Eq. $(3.1.10)$, we have

$$
\begin{aligned}
\max\left\{\, d\left(\alpha_\kappa,\zeta_\kappa\right),d\left(\beta_\kappa,\eta_\kappa\right)\,\right\} &\leq \ell\max\left\{\, d\left(\alpha_{\kappa-1},\zeta_{\kappa-1}\right),d\left(\beta_{\kappa-1},\eta_{\kappa-1}\right)\,\right\} \\
&\leq \ell^2\max\left\{\, d\left(\alpha_{\kappa-2},\zeta_{\kappa-2}\right),d\left(\beta_{\kappa-2},\eta_{\kappa-2}\right)\,\right\} \\
&\;\;\vdots
\end{aligned}
$$

$$\leq \ell^{\kappa} \max \left\{ \begin{array}{c} d\left(\alpha_0, \zeta_0\right), \\ \\ d\left(\beta_0, \eta_0\right) \end{array} \right\} \to 0 \text{ as } \kappa \to \infty.$$

$$(3.1.11)$$

For each $\kappa, \delta \in \mathbf{N}$ with $\kappa < \delta$. Then, from Eq. (3.1.5), Eq. (3.1.8), and

Eq. (3.1.11) and using property (B_4), we have

$$
\begin{aligned}
d\left(\alpha_{\kappa}, \zeta_{\delta}\right) + d\left(\beta_{\kappa}, \eta_{\delta}\right) \;\leq\;& \left(d\left(\alpha_{\kappa}, \zeta_{\kappa+1}\right) + d\left(\beta_{\kappa}, \eta_{\kappa+1}\right)\right) \\
& + \left(d\left(\alpha_{\kappa+1}, \zeta_{\kappa+1}\right) + d\left(\beta_{\kappa+1}, \eta_{\kappa+1}\right)\right) \\
& + \cdots + \left(d\left(\alpha_{\delta-1}, \zeta_{\delta-1}\right) + d\left(\beta_{\delta-1}, \eta_{\delta-1}\right)\right) \\
& + \left(d\left(\alpha_{\delta-1}, \zeta_{\delta}\right) + d\left(\beta_{\delta-1}, \eta_{\delta}\right)\right) \\
\leq\;& 2\left(\ell^{\kappa} + \ell^{\kappa+1} + \cdots + \ell^{\delta-1}\right) \max \left\{ \begin{array}{c} d\left(\alpha_0, \zeta_1\right), \\ \\ d\left(\beta_0, \eta_1\right) \end{array} \right\} \\
& + 2\left(\ell^{\kappa+1} + \ell^{\kappa+2} + \cdots + \ell^{\delta-1}\right) \max \left\{ \begin{array}{c} d\left(\alpha_0, \zeta_0\right), \\ \\ d\left(\beta_0, \eta_0\right) \end{array} \right\} \\
\leq\;& \frac{2\ell^{\kappa}}{1-\ell} \max \left\{ \begin{array}{c} d\left(\alpha_0, \zeta_1\right), \\ \\ d\left(\beta_0, \eta_1\right) \end{array} \right\} \\
& + \frac{2\ell^{\kappa+1}}{1-\ell} \max \left\{ \begin{array}{c} d\left(\alpha_0, \zeta_1\right), \\ \\ d\left(\beta_0, \eta_1\right) \end{array} \right\} \to 0 \text{ as } \kappa \to \infty.
\end{aligned}
$$

Similarly, we can prove that $\left(d\left(\alpha_{\delta}, \zeta_{\kappa}\right) + d\left(\beta_{\delta}, \eta_{\kappa}\right)\right) \to 0$ as $\kappa, \delta \to \infty$. Then the bisequence $\left(\alpha_{\kappa}, \zeta_{\delta}\right)$ and $\left(\beta_{\kappa}, \eta_{\delta}\right)$ are Cauchy bisequences in $(\mathcal{S}, \mathcal{T})$. Suppose $\Lambda(\mathcal{S} \cup \mathcal{T})$ is complete subspace of $(\mathcal{S}, \mathcal{T}, d)$, then the sequences $\{\alpha_{\kappa}\}, \{\beta_{\kappa}\}$ and $\{\zeta_{\kappa}\}, \{\eta_{\kappa}\} \subseteq f(\mathcal{S} \cup \mathcal{T})$ are convergence in complete bipolar metric spaces $(\Lambda(\mathcal{S}), \Lambda(\mathcal{T}), d)$. Therefore, there exist $a, b \in \Lambda(\mathcal{S})$ and $l, m \in \Lambda(\mathcal{T})$ such that

$$\lim_{\kappa \to \infty} \alpha_\kappa = l \quad \lim_{\kappa \to \infty} \beta_\kappa = m \quad \lim_{\kappa \to \infty} \zeta_\kappa = a \quad \lim_{\kappa \to \infty} \eta_\kappa = b. \qquad (3.1.12)$$

Since $\Lambda : \mathcal{S} \cup \mathcal{T} \to \mathcal{S} \cup \mathcal{T}$ and $a, b \in \Lambda(\mathcal{S})$ and $l, m \in \Lambda(\mathcal{T})$, there exist $x, y \in \mathcal{S}$ and $p, q \in \mathcal{T}$ such that $\Lambda x = a, \Lambda y = b$ and $\Lambda p = l, \Lambda q = m$. Hence

$$\lim_{\kappa \to \infty} \alpha_\kappa = l = \Lambda p \quad \lim_{\kappa \to \infty} \beta_\kappa = m = \Lambda q \quad \lim_{\kappa \to \infty} \zeta_\kappa = a = \Lambda x \quad \lim_{\kappa \to \infty} \eta_\kappa = b = \Lambda y.$$

Claim that $\Gamma(x, y) = l, \Gamma(y, x) = m$ and $\Gamma(p, q) = a, \Gamma(q, p) = b$.

By using Eq. $(3.1.1)$, (B_4), definition $1.3.3$ of (ψ_1) and (ψ_2), we have

$$\begin{aligned}
\psi_\star\left(d(\Gamma(x, y), l)\right) \leq\ & \psi_\star\left(d(\Gamma(x, y), \zeta_{\kappa+1})\right) + \psi_\star\left(d(\alpha_{\kappa+1}, \zeta_{\kappa+1})\right) + \psi_\star\left(d(\alpha_{\kappa+1}, l)\right) \\
\leq\ & \psi_\star\left(d(\Gamma(x, y), \Gamma(p_{\kappa+1}, q_{\kappa+1}))\right) + \psi_\star\left(d(\alpha_{\kappa+1}, \zeta_{\kappa+1})\right) + \psi_\star\left(d(\alpha_{\kappa+1}, l)\right) \\
\leq\ & \Delta\left(\psi_\star\left(M(x, y, p_{\kappa+1}, q_{\kappa+1})\right), \phi_\star\left(M(x, y, p_{\kappa+1}, q_{\kappa+1})\right)\right) \\
& + \psi_\star\left(d(\alpha_{\kappa+1}, \zeta_{\kappa+1})\right) + \psi_\star\left(d(\alpha_{\kappa+1}, l)\right) \\
\leq\ & \psi_\star\left(\ell \max\left\{ d\left(\Lambda x, \zeta_\kappa\right), d\left(\Lambda y, \eta_\kappa\right) \right\}\right) \\
& + \psi_\star\left(d(\alpha_{\kappa+1}, \zeta_{\kappa+1})\right) + \psi_\star\left(d(\alpha_{\kappa+1}, l)\right) \to 0 \text{ as } \kappa \to \infty.
\end{aligned}$$

It follows that $\psi_\star\left(d(\Gamma(x, y), l)\right) = 0$ implies that $d(\Gamma(x, y), l) = 0$, which deduce that $\Gamma(x, y) = l$. Similarly, we may demonstrate that $\Gamma(y, x) = m$ and $\Gamma(p, q) = a$, $\Gamma(q, p) = b$. Therefore, it follows that $\Gamma(x, y) = l = \Lambda p, \Gamma(y, x) = m = \Lambda q$ and $\Gamma(p, q) = a = \Lambda x, \Gamma(q, p) = b = \Lambda y$.

Since $\{\Gamma, \Lambda\}$ is ω-compatible pair, we have $\Gamma(l, m) = \Lambda l, \Gamma(m, l) = \Lambda m$ and $\Gamma(a, b) = \Lambda a, \Gamma(b, a) =$

Λb. Now we prove that $\Lambda l = l$, $\Lambda m = m$ and $\Lambda a = a$, $\Lambda b = b$. Now we have

$$
\begin{aligned}
\psi_\star \left(d(\Lambda a, \zeta_\kappa) \right) &\leq \psi_\star \left(d(\Gamma(a, b), \Gamma(p_\kappa, q_\kappa)) \right) \\
&\leq \Delta \left(\psi_\star \left(M(a, b, p_\kappa, q_\kappa) \right), \phi_\star \left(M(a, b, p_\kappa, q_\kappa) \right) \right) \\
&\leq \psi_\star \left(\ell \max \left\{ d\left(\Lambda a, \zeta_{\kappa-1} \right), d\left(\Lambda b, \eta_{\kappa-1} \right) \right\} \right).
\end{aligned}
$$

By using (ψ_0), we have

$$
d(\Lambda a, \zeta_\kappa) \leq \ell \max \left\{ d\left(\Lambda a, \zeta_{\kappa-1} \right), d\left(\Lambda b, \eta_{\kappa-1} \right) \right\}.
$$

Letting $\kappa \to \infty$, we have

$$
d(\Lambda a, a) \leq \ell \max \left\{ d\left(\Lambda a, a \right), d\left(\Lambda b, b \right) \right\}
$$

and

$$
\begin{aligned}
\psi_\star \left(d(\Lambda b, \eta_\kappa) \right) &\leq \psi_\star \left(d(\Gamma(b, a), \Gamma(q_\kappa, p_\kappa)) \right) \\
&\leq \Delta \left(\psi_\star \left(M(b, a, q_\kappa, p_\kappa) \right), \phi_\star \left(M(b, a, q_\kappa, p_\kappa) \right) \right) \\
&\leq \psi_\star \left(\ell \max \left\{ d\left(\Lambda b, \eta_{\kappa-1} \right), d\left(\Lambda a, \zeta_{\kappa-1} \right) \right\} \right).
\end{aligned}
$$

By using (ψ_0), we have

$$
d(\Lambda b, \eta_\kappa) \leq \ell \max \left\{ d\left(\Lambda b, \eta_{\kappa-1}, d\left(\Lambda a, \zeta_{\kappa-1} \right) \right) \right\}.
$$

Letting $\kappa \to \infty$, we have

$$d(\Lambda b, b) \leq \ell \max \left\{ d\left(\Lambda b, b\right), d\left(\Lambda a, a\right) \right\}.$$

Therefore,

$$\max \left\{ d\left(\Lambda a, a\right), d\left(\Lambda b, b\right) \right\} \leq \ell \max \left\{ d\left(\Lambda a, a\right), d\left(\Lambda b, b\right) \right\}$$

which implies that $d\left(\Lambda a, a\right) = 0$ and $d\left(\Lambda b, b\right) = 0$ and hence $\Lambda a = a$ and $\Lambda b = b$. Therefore, $\Gamma(a, b) = \Lambda a = a$, $\Gamma(b, a) = \Lambda b = b$.

Similarly, we can prove $\Gamma(l, m) = \Lambda l = l$, $\Gamma(m, l) = \Lambda m = m$. Therefore,

$$\Gamma(p, q) = \Lambda x = a = \Lambda a = \Gamma(a, b) \quad \Gamma(x, y) = \Lambda p = l = \Lambda l = \Gamma(l, m)$$

$$\Gamma(q, p) = \Lambda y = b = \Lambda b = \Gamma(b, a) \quad \Gamma(y, x) = \Lambda q = m = \Lambda m = \Gamma(m, l).$$

On the other hand, from Eq. (3.1.12), we get

$$d\left(\Lambda p, \Lambda x\right) = d(l, a) = d\left(\lim_{\kappa \to \infty} \alpha_\kappa, \lim_{\kappa \to \infty} \zeta_\kappa \right) = \lim_{\kappa \to \infty} d(\alpha_\kappa, \zeta_\kappa) = 0$$

and

$$d\left(\Lambda q, \Lambda y\right) = d(m, b) = d\left(\lim_{\kappa \to \infty} \beta_\kappa, \lim_{\kappa \to \infty} \eta_\kappa \right) = \lim_{\kappa \to \infty} d(\beta_\kappa, \eta_\kappa) = 0.$$

Thus $a = l, b = m$. Therefore, $(a, b) \in \mathcal{S}^2 \cap \mathcal{T}^2$ is a CCFP of Γ and Λ. We shall demonstrate the distinctiveness in the following sections. Assume there is still another CFP (a', b') of Γ, Λ. Then from Eq. $(3.1.1)$, we have

$$
\begin{aligned}
\psi_\star\left(d(a, a')\right) &= \psi_\star\left(d(\Gamma(a, b), \Gamma(a', b'))\right) \\[2mm]
&\leq \Delta\left(\psi_\star\left(M(a, b, a', b')\right), \phi_\star\left(M(a, b, a', b')\right)\right) \\[2mm]
&\leq \psi_\star\left(\ell \max\left\{ d\left(\Lambda a, \Lambda a'\right), d\left(\Lambda b, \Lambda b'\right) \right\}\right) \\[2mm]
&\leq \psi_\star\left(\ell \max\left\{ d\left(a, a'\right), d\left(b, b'\right) \right\}\right)
\end{aligned}
$$

by the property of definition $(1.3.3)$ (ψ_0), we have

$$
d(a, a') \leq \ell \max\left\{ d\left(a, a'\right), d\left(b, b'\right) \right\}.
$$

Therefore, we have

$$
\max\left\{ d\left(a, a'\right), d\left(b, b'\right) \right\} \leq \ell \max\left\{ d\left(a, a'\right), d\left(b, b'\right) \right\}
$$

hence, we get $a = a', b = b'$. Therefore, (a, b) is a UCCFP of Γ and Λ.

Finally, we will demonstrate $a = b$.

$$
\begin{aligned}
\psi_\star\left(d(a, b)\right) &= \psi_\star\left(d(\Gamma(a, b), \Gamma(b, a))\right) \\[2mm]
&\leq \Delta\left(\psi_\star\left(M(a, b, b, a)\right), \phi_\star\left(M(a, b, b, a)\right)\right) \\[2mm]
&\leq \psi_\star\left(\ell \max\left\{ d\left(\Lambda a, \Lambda b\right), d\left(\Lambda b, \Lambda a\right) \right\}\right) \\[2mm]
&\leq \psi_\star\left(\ell \max\left\{ d\left(a, b\right), d\left(b, a\right) \right\}\right)
\end{aligned}
$$

by the property of Def. $(1.3.3)$ (ψ_0), we have

$$d(a,b) \leq \ell \max \left\{ d\left(a,b\right), d\left(b,a\right) \right\}.$$

Therefore, we have

$$\max \left\{ d\left(a,b\right), d\left(b,a\right) \right\} \leq \ell \max \left\{ d\left(a,b\right), d\left(b,a\right) \right\}$$

hence, we get $a = b$. Which means that Γ and Λ have a UCFP of the form (a,a). $\square$

Corollary 3.1.2. Let $(\mathcal{S}, \mathcal{T}, d)$ be a CBMS. Suppose that $\Gamma : (\mathcal{S}^2, \mathcal{T}^2) \rightrightarrows (\mathcal{S}, \mathcal{T})$ be a covariant mapping satisfy

$$\psi_\star \left(d(\Gamma(u,v), \Gamma(p,q)) \right)$$

$$\leq \Delta \left(\psi_\star \left(\ell \max \left\{ \begin{array}{c} d\left(u,p\right), \\ d\left(v,q\right) \end{array} \right\} \right), \phi_\star \left(\ell \max \left\{ \begin{array}{c} d\left(u,p\right), \\ d\left(v,q\right) \end{array} \right\} \right) \right)$$

for all $u, v \in \mathcal{S}$ and $p, q \in \mathcal{T}$ and $\Delta \in C$, $\psi_\star \in \mathfrak{F}$, $\phi_\star \in \mathfrak{G}$ with $\ell \in (0,1)$ Then there is a UCFP of Γ in $\mathcal{S} \cup \mathcal{T}$.

Proof. Let us take $\Lambda = I_{\mathcal{S} \cup \mathcal{T}}$ (identity mapping on $\mathcal{S} \cup \mathcal{T}$), from Theorem $(3.1.1)$ we see that Γ has a UCFP. $\square$

Corollary 3.1.3. Let $(\mathcal{S}, \mathcal{T}, d)$ be a CBMS and $\Gamma : (\mathcal{S} \times \mathcal{T}, \mathcal{T} \times \mathcal{S}) \rightrightarrows (\mathcal{S}, \mathcal{T})$ be a covariant mapping satisfy

$$\psi_\star \left(d(\Gamma(u,p), \Gamma(q,v)) \right)$$

$$\leq \Delta\left(\psi_\star\left(\ell\max\left\{\begin{array}{c}d\left(u,q\right),\\d\left(v,p\right)\end{array}\right\}\right),\phi_\star\left(\ell\max\left\{\begin{array}{c}d\left(u,q\right),\\d\left(v,p\right)\end{array}\right\}\right)\right)$$

for all $u,v \in \mathcal{S}$ and $p,q \in \mathcal{T}$ and $\Delta \in C$, $\psi_\star \in \mathfrak{F}$, $\phi_\star \in \mathfrak{G}$ with $\ell \in (0,1)$. Then there is a UCFP of Γ in $\mathcal{S} \cup \mathcal{T}$.

Proof. If we replace the function Γ domain $(\mathcal{S} \times \mathcal{T}, \mathcal{T} \times \mathcal{S})$ in place of $(\mathcal{S} \times \mathcal{S}, \mathcal{T} \times \mathcal{T})$, the rest of proof follows from Corollary 3.1.2. $\square$

Example 3.1. The set of all $n \times n$ upper and lower triangular matrices over $\mathbb{R}$ is denoted by $\mathcal{S} = \mathfrak{U}_n(\mathbb{R})$ and $\mathcal{T} = \mathfrak{L}_n(\mathbb{R})$.

$d(X,Y) = \sum_{i,j=1}^{\kappa} |\alpha_{ij} - \beta_{ij}|$ is the definition of $d : \mathcal{S} \times \mathcal{T} \to [0,\infty)$, assuming that $X = (\alpha_{ij})_{n \times n} \in \mathfrak{U}_n(\mathbb{R})$ and $Y = (\beta_{ij})_{n \times n} \in \mathfrak{L}_n(\mathbb{R})$. Then obviously $(\mathcal{S}, \mathcal{T}, d)$ is a BMS. And define $\Gamma : \mathcal{S}^2 \cup \mathcal{T}^2 \to \mathcal{S} \cup \mathcal{T}$ as

$\Gamma(A,B) = (\frac{a_{ij} - b_{ij}}{16})_{n \times n}$ where $(A = (a_{ij})_{n \times n}, B = (b_{ij})_{n \times n}) \in \mathfrak{U}_n(\mathbb{R})^2 \cup \mathfrak{L}_n(\mathbb{R})^2$ and define $\Lambda : \mathcal{S} \cup \mathcal{T} \to \mathcal{S} \cup \mathcal{T}$ as $\Lambda(A) = (\frac{a_{ij}}{2})_{n \times n}$ and let $\Delta : [0,+\infty) \times [0.+\infty) \to R$ as $\Delta(s^*,t^*) = s^* - t^*$, also define $\psi_\star : [0,\infty) \to [0,\infty)$, $\phi_\star : [0,\infty) \to [0,\infty)$ as $\psi_\star(t^*) = t^*$ and $\phi_\star(t^*) = \frac{t^*}{2}$ respectively. Then obviously, $\Gamma(\mathcal{S}^2 \cup \mathcal{T}^2) \subseteq \Lambda(\mathcal{S} \cup \mathcal{T})$ and the pairs (Γ,Λ) is ω-compatible.

In fact, we have

$$\psi_\star\left(d(\Gamma(A,B),\Gamma(X,Y))\right) = d(\Gamma(A,B),\Gamma(X,Y))$$

$$= \sum_{i,j=1}^{\kappa} |\frac{a_{ij} - b_{ij}}{16} - \frac{x_{ij} - y_{ij}}{16}|$$

$$\leq \frac{1}{8}\left(\sum_{i,j=1}^{\kappa} |\frac{a_{ij}}{2} - \frac{x_{ij}}{2}| + \sum_{i,j=1}^{\kappa} |\frac{b_{ij}}{2} - \frac{y_{ij}}{2}|\right)$$

$$\leq \frac{1}{8}\left(d(\Lambda A, \Lambda X) + d(\Lambda B, \Lambda Y)\right)$$

$$\leq \frac{1}{2}\left(\frac{1}{2}\max\{d(\Lambda A, \Lambda X), d(\Lambda B, \Lambda Y)\}\right)$$

$$\leq \Delta \left(\psi_\star \left(\ell \max \left\{ \begin{array}{c} d(\Lambda A, \Lambda X), \\ d(\Lambda B, \Lambda Y) \end{array} \right\} \right), \phi_\star \left(\ell \max \left\{ \begin{array}{c} d(\Lambda A, \Lambda X), \\ d(\Lambda B, \Lambda Y) \end{array} \right\} \right) \right).$$

Thus all the conditions of the theorem $(3.1.1)$ are satisfied and $(O_{n \times n}, O_{n \times n})$ is unique coupled fixed point.

3.2   Application to Integral Equations

Let $\mathcal{S} = C\left(L^\infty(E_1)\right), \mathcal{T} = C\left(L^\infty(E_2)\right)$ be the set of essential bounded measurable continuous functions on E_1 and E_2 where E_1, E_2 are two Lebesgue measurable sets with $m(E_1 \cup E_2) < \infty$. Define $d : \mathcal{S} \times \mathcal{T} \to R^+$ as $d(\ell, \sigma) = ||\ell - \sigma||$ for all $\ell \in \mathcal{S}, \sigma \in \mathcal{T}$. Therefore, $(\mathcal{S}, \mathcal{T}, d)$ is a complete bipolar metric space.

In this section, we apply our Theorem $(3.1.1)$ to establish the existence and uniqueness solution of nonlinear integral equation defined by:

$$x(t) = f(t) + \kappa \int_{E_1 \cup E_2} \Omega(t, \ell, x(\ell), x(\ell)) d\ell, \tag{3.2.1}$$

where $x \in C\left(L^\infty(E_1) \cup L^\infty(E_2)\right)$, $\kappa \in R$ and $t, \ell \in E_1 \cup E_2$,

$\Omega : E_1^2 \cup E_2^2 \times L^\infty(E_1)^2 \cup L^\infty(E_2)^2 \to R$ and $f : E_1 \cup E_2 \to R$ are given continuous functions

Theorem 3.2.1. Assume that the following conditions are fulfilled

(i) Define, $\Delta : [0, +\infty) \times [0. +\infty) \to R$ as $\Delta(s^*, t^*) = \theta s^*$ where $\theta \in (0, 1)$, let $\psi_\star : [0, \infty) \to [0, \infty)$ as $\psi_\star(t^*) = t^*$. Let $\Lambda : \mathcal{S} \cup \mathcal{T} \to \mathcal{S} \cup \mathcal{T}$ as $\Lambda(x) = x$ and $\Gamma : \mathcal{S}^2 \cup \mathcal{T}^2 \to \mathcal{S} \cup \mathcal{T}$ by

$\Gamma(x, y)(t) = f(t) + \kappa \int_{E_1 \cup E_2} \Omega(t, \ell, x(\ell), y(\ell)) d\ell$

(ii) There exists a continuous function $\chi : E_1^2 \cup E_2^2 \to R^+$ such that for all $x, y \in \mathcal{S}, p, q \in \mathcal{T}$, $\kappa \in R$ and $t, \ell \in E_1 \cup E_2$, we get that

$$||\Omega(t, \ell, x(\ell), y(\ell)) - \Omega(t, \ell, p(\ell), q(\ell))|| \leq \chi(t, \ell) M(x, y, p, q) \text{ where,}$$

$$M(x, y, p, q) = \lambda \max\{d(\Lambda x, \Lambda p), d(\Lambda y, \Lambda q)\} \text{ where } \lambda \in (0, 1)$$

(iii) $||\kappa|| \int\limits_{E_1 \cup E_2} \chi(t, \ell) d\ell \leq \theta$

(iv) $\Gamma\left(\mathcal{S}^2 \cup \mathcal{T}^2\right) \subseteq \Lambda(\mathcal{S} \cup \mathcal{T})$, $\Lambda(\mathcal{S} \cup \mathcal{T})$ is closed and the pair (Γ, Λ) is weakly compatible.

Then there exists unique solution for the Eq.3.2.1 in $C\left(L^\infty(E_1) \cup L^\infty(E_2)\right)$.

Proof. The existence of a solution of Eq.(3.2.1) is equivalent to the existence of a common fixed point of Γ and Λ. Obviously, $\Gamma\left(\mathcal{S}^2 \cup \mathcal{T}^2\right) \subseteq \Lambda(\mathcal{S} \cup \mathcal{T})$, $\Lambda(\mathcal{S} \cup \mathcal{T})$ is closed and the pair (Γ, Λ) is weakly compatible. Using the inequalities, (i), (ii) and (iii), we have

$$\psi_\star\left(d(\Gamma(x, y), \Gamma(p, q))\right)$$

$$= d(\Gamma(x, y), \Gamma(p, q))$$

$$= ||\kappa \int\limits_{E_1 \cup E_2} (\Omega(t, \ell, x(\ell), y(\ell))) d\ell - \kappa \int\limits_{E_1 \cup E_2} (\Omega(t, \ell, p(\ell), q(\ell))) d\ell||$$

$$\leq ||\kappa|| \int\limits_{E_1 \cup E_2} ||\Omega(t, \ell, x(\ell), y(\ell)) - \Omega(t, \ell, p(\ell), q(\ell))|| d\ell$$

$$\leq ||\kappa|| \int\limits_{E_1 \cup E_2} \chi(t, \ell) M(x, y, p, q) d\ell$$

$$\leq ||\kappa|| \left(\int\limits_{E_1 \cup E_2} \chi(t, \ell) d\ell\right) M(x, y, p, q)$$

$$\leq \theta M(x, y, p, q)$$

$$\leq \Delta\left(\psi_\star\left(\lambda \max\left\{\begin{array}{l} d(\Lambda x, \Lambda p), \\ d(\Lambda y, \Lambda q) \end{array}\right\}\right), \phi_\star\left(\lambda \max\left\{\begin{array}{l} d(\Lambda x, \Lambda p), \\ d(\Lambda y, \Lambda q) \end{array}\right\}\right)\right).$$

Hence, all the conditions of Theorem (3.1.1) hold, we conclude that Γ and Λ have a unique solution in $\mathcal{S} \cup \mathcal{T}$ to the integral equation (3.2.1). $\qquad\square$

3.3 Application to Homotopy

We examine the possibility of a unique solution to homotopy in this section.

Theorem 3.3.1. Let $(\mathcal{S}, \mathcal{T}, d)$ be a CBMS, $(\mathcal{P}, \mathcal{Q})$ and $(\overline{\mathcal{P}}, \overline{\mathcal{Q}})$ be an open and closed subset of $(\mathcal{S}, \mathcal{T})$ such that $(\mathcal{P}, \mathcal{Q}) \subseteq (\overline{\mathcal{P}}, \overline{\mathcal{Q}})$. Suppose
$\mathcal{H} : (\overline{\mathcal{P}} \times \overline{\mathcal{Q}}) \cup (\overline{\mathcal{Q}} \times \overline{\mathcal{P}}) \times [0, 1] \to \mathcal{S} \cup \mathcal{T}$ be an operator with following conditions are satisfying,
$\ell_0)$ $\wp \neq \mathcal{H}(\wp, \varpi, s)$, $\varpi \neq \mathcal{H}(\varpi, \wp, s)$, for each $\wp \in \partial\mathcal{P}, \varpi \in \partial\mathcal{Q}$ and $s \in [0, 1]$ (Here $\partial\mathcal{P} \cup \partial\mathcal{Q}$ is boundary of $\mathcal{P} \cup \mathcal{Q}$ in $\mathcal{S} \cup \mathcal{T}$);
$\ell_1)$ for all $\wp, \varpi \in \overline{\mathcal{P}}, \imath, \jmath \in \overline{\mathcal{Q}}, s \in [0, 1]$ and $\psi_\star \in \mathfrak{F}, \phi_\star \in \mathfrak{G}$ $\Delta \in C$ and $\ell \in (0, 1)$ such that

$$\psi_\star \left(d \left(\mathcal{H}(\wp, \imath, s), \mathcal{H}(\jmath, \varpi, s) \right) \right)$$
$$\leq \Delta \left(\psi_\star \left(\ell \max \left\{ \begin{array}{c} d(\wp, \jmath), \\ d(\varpi, \imath) \end{array} \right\} \right), \phi_\star \left(\ell \max \left\{ \begin{array}{c} d(\wp, \jmath), \\ d(\varpi, \imath) \end{array} \right\} \right) \right)$$

$\ell_2)$ $\exists\, M \geq 0 \ni d(\mathcal{H}(\wp, \imath, s), \mathcal{H}(\jmath, \varpi, t)) \preceq M|s - t|$
for every $\wp, \varpi \in \overline{\mathcal{P}}, \imath, \jmath \in \overline{\mathcal{Q}}$ and $s, t \in [0, 1]$.
Then $\mathcal{H}(., 0)$ has a CFP $\iff \mathcal{H}(., 1)$ has a CFP.

Theorem 3.3.2. Let $(\mathcal{S}, \mathcal{T}, d)$ be a CBMS, $(\mathcal{P}, \mathcal{Q})$ and $(\overline{\mathcal{P}}, \overline{\mathcal{Q}})$ be an open and closed subset of $(\mathcal{S}, \mathcal{T})$ such that $(\mathcal{P}, \mathcal{Q}) \subseteq (\overline{\mathcal{P}}, \overline{\mathcal{Q}})$. Suppose

$\mathcal{H} : \left(\overline{\mathcal{P}}^2 \cup \overline{\mathcal{Q}}^2\right) \times [0,1] \to \mathcal{S} \cup \mathcal{T}$ be an operator with following conditions are satisfying,

ℓ_0) $\wp \neq \mathcal{H}(\wp, \varpi, s)$, $\varpi \neq \mathcal{H}(\varpi, \wp, s)$, for each $\wp, \varpi \in \partial \mathcal{P} \cup \partial \mathcal{Q}$ and $s \in [0,1]$ (Here $\partial \mathcal{P} \cup \partial \mathcal{Q}$ is boundary of $\mathcal{P} \cup \mathcal{Q}$ in $\mathcal{S} \cup \mathcal{T}$);

ℓ_1) for all $\wp, \varpi \in \overline{\mathcal{P}}, \imath, \jmath \in \overline{\mathcal{Q}}$, $s \in [0,1]$ and $\psi_\star \in \mathfrak{F}, \phi_\star \in \mathfrak{G}$ $\Delta \in C$ and $\ell \in (0,1)$ such that

$$\psi_\star \left(d\left(\mathcal{H}(\wp, \varpi, s), \mathcal{H}(\imath, \jmath, s)\right)\right)$$
$$\leq \Delta \left(\psi_\star \left(\ell \max \left\{ \begin{array}{c} d(\wp, \imath), \\ d(\varpi, \jmath) \end{array} \right\}\right), \phi_\star \left(\ell \max \left\{ \begin{array}{c} d(\wp, \imath), \\ d(\varpi, \jmath) \end{array} \right\}\right)\right)$$

ℓ_2) $\exists\, M \geq 0 \ni d(\mathcal{H}(\wp, \varpi, s), \mathcal{H}(\imath, \jmath, t)) \preceq M|s - t|$

for every $\wp, \varpi \in \overline{\mathcal{P}}$, $\imath, \jmath \in \overline{\mathcal{Q}}$ and $s, t \in [0,1]$.

Then $\mathcal{H}(., 0)$ has a CFP $\iff$ $\mathcal{H}(., 1)$ has a CFP.

Proof. If we replace the homotopy operator $\mathcal{H}$ domain $\left(\overline{\mathcal{P}}^2 \cup \overline{\mathcal{Q}}^2\right) \times [0,1]$ in place of $\left(\overline{\mathcal{P}} \times \overline{\mathcal{Q}}\right) \cup \left(\overline{\mathcal{Q}} \times \overline{\mathcal{P}}\right) \times [0,1]$, the rest of proof follows from Theorem 3.3.1.

$\square$

3.4   Conclusion

We ensured the existence and uniqueness of a common coupled fixed point for two covariant mappings in the class of complete bipolar metric spaces with example via C-class functions. Two illustrated applications have been provided.

<u>CHAPTER 4</u>

Coupled Fixed Point Results in $C^\star$-Algebra Valued Fuzzy Soft Metric Spaces with Applications

Coupled Fixed Point Results in $C^\star$-Algebra Valued Fuzzy Soft Metric Spaces with Applications

The aim of this chapter is to prove UCCFP theorems via $C_\star$-class functions associated with altering distance function in $C^\star$-AVFSMS and applications to integral equations and homotopy are also provided.

4.1 On certain CFP theorems via $C_\star$-class functions in $C^\star$-AVFSMS

In this section, the concept of $C_\star$-class functions in the setup of $C^\star$-AVFSMS spaces is introduced and CCFP theorems for these mappings in complete $C^\star$-AVFSMS which involve altering distance function is established. A few instances are given to support our major findings.

Definition 4.1.1. Let $\tilde{C}$ is a unital C^*-algebra, then a continuous function $\Gamma : \tilde{C}_+ \times \tilde{C}_+ \to \tilde{C}_+$ is called a $C_\star$-class function if for all $A, B \in \tilde{C}_+$,

   (a) $\Gamma(\tilde{A}, \tilde{B}) \preceq \tilde{A}$;

   (b) $\Gamma(\tilde{A}, \tilde{B}) = \tilde{A} \Rightarrow \tilde{A} = \tilde{0}_{\tilde{C}}$ or $\tilde{B} = \tilde{0}_{\tilde{C}}$.

We denote $C_\star$ as the family of all $C_\star$-class functions.

Definition 4.1.2. A function $\eta : \tilde{C}_+ \to \tilde{C}_+$ is called an altering distance function if the following properties are satisfied:

(a) η is nondecreasing and continuous;

(b) $\eta(\tilde{A}) = \tilde{0}_{\tilde{C}}$ if and only if $\tilde{A} = \tilde{0}_{\tilde{C}}$.

The family of all altering distance functions is denoted by Ω.

Theorem 4.1.1. Assume that C^*-AVFSMS $(\tilde{\Theta}, \tilde{C}, \tilde{d}_{c*})$ and suppose two mappings $S : \tilde{\Theta} \times \tilde{\Theta} \to \tilde{\Theta}$ and $f : \tilde{\Theta} \to \tilde{\Theta}$ be satisfying

$$\eta\left(\tilde{d}_{c*}\left(S(\psi_{\alpha_1}, \phi_{\alpha_1}), S(\psi_{\alpha_2}, \phi_{\alpha_2})\right)\right)$$
$$\preceq \Gamma\left(\eta\left(\tilde{\kappa}^\star \tilde{d}_{c*}(f\psi_{\alpha_1}, f\psi_{\alpha_2})\tilde{\kappa}\right), \theta\left(\tilde{\kappa}^\star \tilde{d}_{c*}(f\phi_{\alpha_1}, f\phi_{\alpha_2})\tilde{\kappa}\right)\right)$$

$$(4.1.1)$$

for all $\psi_{\alpha_1}, \psi_{\alpha_2}, \phi_{\alpha_1}, \phi_{\alpha_2} \in \tilde{\Theta}$, where $\tilde{\kappa} \in \tilde{C}$ with $||\tilde{\kappa}|| < 1$ and $\eta, \theta \in \Omega$ and $\Gamma \in C_\star$.

(4.1.1.1) $S(\tilde{\Theta} \times \tilde{\Theta}) \subseteq f(\tilde{\Theta})$

(4.1.1.2) $\{S, f\}$ is ω-compatible pairs.

(4.1.1.3) $f(\tilde{\Theta})$ is complete subspace of $(\tilde{\Theta}, \tilde{C}, \tilde{d}_{c*})$.

Then, in $\tilde{\Theta}$, S and f have a UCCFP.

Proof. Let $\psi_{\alpha_0}, \phi_{\alpha_0} \in \tilde{\Theta}$. From (4.1.1.1) we can construct the sequences $\{\psi_{\alpha_z}\}_{z=1}^{\infty}$, $\{\varphi_{\alpha_z}\}_{z=1}^{\infty}$, $\{\xi_{\alpha_z}\}_{z=1}^{\infty}$, $\{\zeta_{\alpha_z}\}_{z=1}^{\infty}$ such that

$$S(\psi_{\alpha_z}, \phi_{\alpha_z}) = f\psi_{\alpha_{z+1}} = \xi_{\alpha_z} \quad S(\phi_{\alpha_z}, \psi_{\alpha_z}) = f\phi_{\alpha_{z+1}} = \zeta_{\alpha_z} \text{ for } z = 0, 1, 2, \ldots$$

Observes that in C^*-algebra, if $\tilde{\kappa}, \tilde{b} \in \tilde{C}_+$ and $\tilde{\kappa} \preceq \tilde{b}$, then for any $\tilde{x} \in \tilde{C}_+$ both $\tilde{x}^\star \tilde{\kappa} \tilde{x}$ and $\tilde{x}^\star \tilde{b} \tilde{x}$ are positive We conveniently refer to the element $\tilde{d}_{c^*}(\xi_{\alpha_0}, \xi_{\alpha_1})$ in $\tilde{C}$ as Q.

From Eq. $(4.1.1$), we get

$$
\begin{aligned}
\eta\left(\tilde{d}_{c^*}\left(\xi_{\alpha_z}, \xi_{\alpha_{z+1}}\right)\right) &= \eta\left(\tilde{d}_{c^*}\left(S(\psi_{\alpha_z}, \phi_{\alpha_z}), S(\psi_{\alpha_{z+1}}, \phi_{\alpha_{z+1}})\right)\right) \\
&\preceq \Gamma\left(\eta\left(\tilde{\kappa}^\star \tilde{d}_{c^*}(f\psi_{\alpha_z}, f\psi_{\alpha_{z+1}})\tilde{\kappa}\right), \theta\left(\tilde{\kappa}^\star \tilde{d}_{c^*}(f\phi_{\alpha_z}, f\phi_{\alpha_{z+1}})\tilde{\kappa}\right)\right) \\
&\preceq \eta\left(\tilde{\kappa}^\star \tilde{d}_{c^*}(f\psi_{\alpha_z}, f\psi_{\alpha_{z+1}})\tilde{\kappa}\right) \\
&\preceq \eta\left(\tilde{\kappa}^\star \tilde{d}_{c^*}(\xi_{\alpha_{z-1}}, \xi_{\alpha_z})\tilde{\kappa}\right).
\end{aligned}
$$

By the definition of η, we have

$$
\begin{aligned}
\tilde{d}_{c^*}\left(\xi_{\alpha_z}, \xi_{\alpha_{z+1}}\right) &\preceq \tilde{\kappa}^\star \tilde{d}_{c^*}(\xi_{\alpha_{z-1}}, \xi_{\alpha_z})\tilde{\kappa} \\
&\preceq (\tilde{\kappa}^\star)^2 \tilde{d}_{c^*}(\xi_{\alpha_{z-2}}, \xi_{\alpha_{z-1}})\tilde{\kappa}^2 \\
&\preceq \cdots \\
&\preceq (\tilde{\kappa}^\star)^z \tilde{d}_{c^*}(\xi_{\alpha_0}, \xi_{\alpha_1})\tilde{\kappa}^z \preceq (\tilde{\kappa}^\star)^z Q \tilde{\kappa}^z.
\end{aligned}
$$

So for $z+1 > w$

$$
\begin{aligned}
\tilde{d}_{c^*}\left(\xi_{\alpha_{z+1}}, \xi_{\alpha_w}\right) &\preceq \tilde{d}_{c^*}\left(\xi_{\alpha_{z+1}}, \xi_{\alpha_z}\right) + \tilde{d}_{c^*}\left(\xi_{\alpha_z}, \xi_{\alpha_{z-1}}\right) + \cdots + \tilde{d}_{c^*}\left(\xi_{\alpha_{w+1}}, \xi_{\alpha_w}\right) \\
&\preceq (\tilde{\kappa}^\star)^z Q \tilde{\kappa}^z + (\tilde{\kappa}^\star)^{z-1} Q \tilde{\kappa}^{z-1} + \cdots + (\tilde{\kappa}^\star)^w Q \tilde{\kappa}^w \\
&\preceq \sum_{k=w}^{z} (\tilde{\kappa}^\star)^k Q \tilde{\kappa}^k = \sum_{k=w}^{z} (\tilde{\kappa}^\star)^k Q^{\frac{1}{2}} Q^{\frac{1}{2}} \tilde{\kappa}^k \\
&\preceq \sum_{k=w}^{z} (\tilde{\kappa}^k Q^{\frac{1}{2}})^\star (Q^{\frac{1}{2}} \tilde{\kappa}^k) = \sum_{k=w}^{z} |Q^{\frac{1}{2}} \tilde{\kappa}^k|^2 \\
&\preceq \|\sum_{k=w}^{z} |Q^{\frac{1}{2}} \tilde{\kappa}^k|^2 \| \tilde{I}_{\tilde{C}} \preceq \sum_{k=w}^{z} \|Q^{\frac{1}{2}}\|^2 \|\tilde{\kappa}\|^{2k} \tilde{I}_{\tilde{C}}
\end{aligned}
$$

$$\preceq \; \|Q^{\frac{1}{2}}\|^2 \sum_{k=w}^{z} \|\tilde{\kappa}\|^{2k} \tilde{I}_{\tilde{C}} \preceq \|Q\| \frac{\|\tilde{\kappa}\|^{2w}}{1 - \|\tilde{\kappa}\|} \tilde{I}_{\tilde{C}} \to \tilde{0}_{\tilde{C}} \text{ as } w \to \infty.$$

As a result, $\{\xi_{\alpha_z}\}$ is a CS in $\tilde{\Theta}$ with regard to $\tilde{C}$. We can also demonstrate that $\{\zeta_{\alpha_z}\}$ is a CS with regard to $\tilde{C}$. Let's say $f(\tilde{\Theta})$ the complete subspace of $(\tilde{\Theta}, \tilde{C}, \tilde{d}_{c*})$. Then the sequences $\{\xi_{\alpha_z}\}$ and $\{\zeta_{\alpha_z}\}$ are converge to $\xi_{\alpha'}, \zeta_{\alpha'}$ respectively in $f(\tilde{\Theta})$. Thus there exist $\psi_{\alpha'}, \phi_{\alpha'}$ in $f(\tilde{\Theta})$ Such that

$$\lim_{z \to \infty} \xi_{\alpha_z} = \xi_{\alpha'} = f\psi_{\alpha'} \text{ and } \lim_{z \to \infty} \zeta_{\alpha_z} = \zeta_{\alpha'} = f\phi_{\alpha'}. \tag{4.1.2}$$

Now we claim that $S(\psi_{\alpha'}, \phi_{\alpha'}) = \xi_{\alpha'}$ and $S(\phi_{\alpha'}, \xi_{\alpha'}) = \zeta_{\alpha'}$.

From Eq. (4.1.1) and using the triangular inequality

$$\tilde{0}_{\tilde{C}} \preceq \tilde{d}_{c*}(S(\psi_{\alpha'}, \phi_{\alpha'}), \xi_{\alpha'}) \; \preceq \tilde{d}_{c*}(S(\psi_{\alpha'}, \phi_{\alpha'}), \xi_{\alpha_{z+1}}) + \tilde{d}_{c*}(\xi_{\alpha_{z+1}}, \xi_{\alpha'})$$
$$\preceq \tilde{d}_{c*}(S(\psi_{\alpha'}, \phi_{\alpha'}), S(\psi_{\alpha_{z+1}}, \phi_{\alpha_{z+1}})) + \tilde{d}_{c*}(\xi_{\alpha_{z+1}}, \xi_{\alpha'}).$$

If we assume that the relation's limit is $z \to \infty$, we get

$$\tilde{0}_{\tilde{C}} \preceq \tilde{d}_{c*}(S(\psi_{\alpha'}, \phi_{\alpha'}), \xi_{\alpha'}) \preceq \lim_{z \to \infty} \tilde{d}_{c*}(S(\psi_{\alpha'}, \phi_{\alpha'}), S(\psi_{\alpha_{z+1}}, \phi_{\alpha_{z+1}})).$$

By the definition of η, we have

$$\eta\left(\tilde{d}_{c*}(S(\psi_{\alpha'}, \phi_{\alpha'}), \xi_{\alpha'})\right) \preceq \lim_{z \to \infty} \eta\left(\tilde{d}_{c*}(S(\psi_{\alpha'}, \phi_{\alpha'}), S(\psi_{\alpha_{z+1}}, \phi_{\alpha_{z+1}}))\right)$$
$$\preceq \lim_{z \to \infty} \Gamma\left(\eta\left(\tilde{\kappa}^{\star}\tilde{d}_{c*}(f\psi_{\alpha'}, f\psi_{\alpha_{z+1}})\tilde{\kappa}\right), \theta\left(\tilde{\kappa}^{\star}\tilde{d}_{c*}(f\phi_{\alpha'}, f\phi_{\alpha_{z+1}})\tilde{\kappa}\right)\right)$$
$$\preceq \lim_{z \to \infty} \eta\left(\tilde{\kappa}^{\star}\tilde{d}_{c*}(f\psi_{\alpha'}, f\psi_{\alpha_{z+1}})\tilde{\kappa}\right)$$
$$\preceq \lim_{z \to \infty} \eta\left(\tilde{\kappa}^{\star}\tilde{d}_{c*}(f\psi_{\alpha'}, \xi_{\alpha_z})\tilde{\kappa}\right)$$
$$= \tilde{0}_{\tilde{C}}.$$

Therefore, we have $\tilde{d}_{c^*}(S(\psi_{\alpha'}, \phi_{\alpha'}), \xi_{\alpha'}) = \tilde{0}_{\tilde{C}}$ implies that $S(\psi_{\alpha'}, \phi_{\alpha'}) = \xi_{\alpha'}$.

Similarly, we demonstrate $S(\phi_{\alpha'}, \xi_{\alpha'}) = \zeta_{\alpha'}$.

Therefore, it follows $S(\psi_{\alpha'}, \phi_{\alpha'}) = \xi_{\alpha'} = f\psi_{\alpha'}$ and $S(\phi_{\alpha'}, \psi_{\alpha'}) = \zeta_{\alpha'} = f\phi_{\alpha'}$.

Since $\{S, f\}$ is ω-compatible pair, we have

$S(\xi_{\alpha'}, \zeta_{\alpha'}) = f\xi_{\alpha'}$ and $S(\zeta_{\alpha'}, \xi_{\alpha'}) = f\zeta_{\alpha'}$.

Now, to demonstrate this, $f\xi_{\alpha'} = \xi_{\alpha'}$ and $f\zeta_{\alpha'} = \zeta_{\alpha'}$.

$$
\begin{aligned}
\tilde{0}_{\tilde{C}} \preceq \eta\left(\tilde{d}_{c^*}(f\xi_{\alpha'}, \xi_{\alpha_{z+1}})\right) \ &\preceq \eta\left(\tilde{d}_{c^*}(S(\xi_{\alpha'}, \zeta_{\alpha'}), S(\psi_{\alpha_{z+1}}, \phi_{\alpha_{z+1}}))\right) \\
&\preceq \Gamma\left(\eta\left(\tilde{\kappa}^\star \tilde{d}_{c^*}(f\xi_{\alpha'}, f\psi_{\alpha_{z+1}})\tilde{\kappa}\right), \theta\left(\tilde{\kappa}^\star \tilde{d}_{c^*}(f\zeta_{\alpha'}, f\phi_{\alpha_{z+1}})\tilde{\kappa}\right)\right) \\
&\preceq \eta\left(\tilde{\kappa}^\star \tilde{d}_{c^*}(f\xi_{\alpha'}, f\psi_{\alpha_{z+1}})\tilde{\kappa}\right) \\
&\preceq \eta\left(\tilde{\kappa}^\star \tilde{d}_{c^*}(f\xi_{\alpha'}, \xi_{\alpha_z})\tilde{\kappa}\right).
\end{aligned}
$$

Using the concept of η and the limit as $z \to \infty$ in the preceding relation, we obtain

$$
\tilde{0}_{\tilde{C}} \preceq \tilde{d}_{c^*}(f\xi_{\alpha'}, \xi_{\alpha'}) \preceq \tilde{\kappa}^\star \tilde{d}_{c^*}(f\xi_{\alpha'}, \xi_{\alpha'})\tilde{\kappa}
$$

we have

$$
\begin{aligned}
0 \leq \|\tilde{d}_{c^*}(f\xi_{\alpha'}, \xi_{\alpha'})\| \ &\leq \|\tilde{\kappa}^\star \tilde{d}_{c^*}(f\xi_{\alpha'}, \xi_{\alpha'})\tilde{\kappa}\| \\
&\leq \|\tilde{\kappa}^\star\| \|\tilde{d}_{c^*}(f\xi_{\alpha'}, \xi_{\alpha'})\| \|\tilde{\kappa}\| \\
&\leq \|\tilde{\kappa}\|^2 \|\tilde{d}_{c^*}(f\xi_{\alpha'}, \xi_{\alpha'})\| < \|\tilde{d}_{c^*}(f\xi_{\alpha'}, \xi_{\alpha'})\|.
\end{aligned}
$$

It is impossible. So $\tilde{d}_{c^*}(f\xi_{\alpha'}, \xi_{\alpha'}) = 0$ implies that $f\xi_{\alpha'} = \xi_{\alpha'}$. Likewise, we demonstrate that $f\zeta_{\alpha'} = \zeta_{\alpha'}$. Therefore, $S(\xi_{\alpha'}, \zeta_{\alpha'}) = f\xi_{\alpha'} = \xi_{\alpha'}$ and

$S(\zeta_{\alpha'}, \xi_{\alpha'}) = f\zeta_{\alpha'} = \zeta_{\alpha'}$.

Thus $(\xi_{\alpha'}, \zeta_{\alpha'})$ is CCFP of S and f. The following will demonstrate the distinctness of the CCFP in $\tilde{\Theta}$. Take into account that there is a second CFP $(\xi_{\alpha''}, \zeta_{\alpha''})$ for S and f. Then

$$
\begin{aligned}
\eta\left(\tilde{d}_{c^*}(\xi_{\alpha'}, \xi_{\alpha''})\right) &= \eta\left(\tilde{d}_{c^*}(S(\xi_{\alpha'}, \zeta_{\alpha'}), S(\xi_{\alpha''}, \zeta_{\alpha''}))\right) \\
&\preceq \Gamma\left(\eta\left(\tilde{\kappa}^\star \tilde{d}_{c^*}(f\xi_{\alpha'}, f\xi_{\alpha''})\tilde{\kappa}\right), \theta\left(\tilde{\kappa}^\star \tilde{d}_{c^*}(f\zeta_{\alpha'}, f\zeta_{\alpha''})\tilde{\kappa}\right)\right) \\
&\preceq \eta\left(\tilde{\kappa}^\star \tilde{d}_{c^*}(f\xi_{\alpha'}, f\xi_{\alpha''})\tilde{\kappa}\right) \\
&\preceq \eta\left(\tilde{\kappa}^\star \tilde{d}_{c^*}(\xi_{\alpha'}, \xi_{\alpha''})\tilde{\kappa}\right).
\end{aligned}
$$

By the definition of η, which further induces that

$$
||\tilde{d}_{c^*}(\xi_{\alpha'}, \xi_{\alpha''})|| \leq ||\tilde{\kappa}^\star \tilde{d}_{c^*}(\xi_{\alpha'}, \xi_{\alpha''})\tilde{\kappa}|| \leq ||\tilde{\kappa}||^2 ||\tilde{d}_{c^*}(\xi_{\alpha'}, \xi_{\alpha''})|| < ||\tilde{d}_{c^*}(\xi_{\alpha'}, \xi_{\alpha''})||.
$$

It is impossible. So $\tilde{d}_{c^*}(\xi_{\alpha'}, \xi_{\alpha''}) = 0$ implies $\xi_{\alpha'} = \xi_{\alpha''}$. In the same way, we demonstrate that $\zeta_{\alpha'} = \zeta_{\alpha''}$ and, consequently, $(\xi_{\alpha'}, \zeta_{\alpha'}) = (\xi_{\alpha''}, \zeta_{\alpha''})$, indicating the uniqueness of the coupled fixed point. All that is needed to establish the unique fixed point of S and f is to show that $\xi_{\alpha'} = \zeta_{\alpha'}$. we have

$$
\begin{aligned}
\eta\left(\tilde{d}_{c^*}(\xi_{\alpha'}, \zeta_{\alpha'})\right) &= \eta\left(\tilde{d}_{c^*}(S(\xi_{\alpha'}, \zeta_{\alpha'}), S(\zeta_{\alpha'}, \xi_{\alpha'}))\right) \\
&\preceq \Gamma\left(\eta\left(\tilde{\kappa}^\star \tilde{d}_{c^*}(f\xi_{\alpha'}, f\zeta_{\alpha'})\tilde{\kappa}\right), \theta\left(\tilde{\kappa}^\star \tilde{d}_{c^*}(f\zeta_{\alpha'}, f\xi_{\alpha'})\tilde{\kappa}\right)\right) \\
&\preceq \eta\left(\tilde{\kappa}^\star \tilde{d}_{c^*}(f\xi_{\alpha'}, f\zeta_{\alpha'})\tilde{\kappa}\right) \\
&\preceq \eta\left(\tilde{\kappa}^\star \tilde{d}_{c^*}(\xi_{\alpha'}, \zeta_{\alpha'})\tilde{\kappa}\right).
\end{aligned}
$$

By the definition of η, which further induces that

$$
||\tilde{d}_{c^*}(\xi_{\alpha'}, \zeta_{\alpha'})|| \leq ||\tilde{\kappa}^\star \tilde{d}_{c^*}(\xi_{\alpha'}, \zeta_{\alpha'})\tilde{\kappa}|| \leq ||\tilde{\kappa}||^2 ||\tilde{d}_{c^*}(\xi_{\alpha'}, \zeta_{\alpha'})||.
$$

It follows from the fact $||\tilde{\kappa}|| < 1$ that $||\tilde{d}_{c^*}(\xi_{\alpha'}, \zeta_{\alpha'})|| = 0$, thus $\xi_{\alpha'} = \zeta_{\alpha'}$. This indicates that a UFP for S and f exists in $\tilde{\Theta}$.

$$\square$$

Corollary 4.1.2. Let $(\tilde{\Theta}, \tilde{C}, \tilde{d}_{c^*})$ be a complete C^*-AVFSMS. Suppose $S \colon \tilde{\Theta} \times \tilde{\Theta} \to \tilde{\Theta}$ satisfies

$$\eta\left(\tilde{d}_{c^*}\left(S(\psi_{\alpha_1}, \phi_{\alpha_1}), S(\psi_{\alpha_2}, \phi_{\alpha_2}))\right)\right) \preceq \Gamma\left(\eta\left(\tilde{\kappa}^\star \tilde{d}_{c^*}(\psi_{\alpha_1}, \psi_{\alpha_2})\tilde{\kappa}\right), \theta\left(\tilde{\kappa}^\star \tilde{d}_{c^*}(\phi_{\alpha_1}, \phi_{\alpha_2})\tilde{\kappa}\right)\right)$$

for all $\psi_{\alpha_1}, \psi_{\alpha_2}, \phi_{\alpha_1}, \phi_{\alpha_2} \in \tilde{\Theta}$, where $\tilde{\kappa} \in \tilde{C}$ with $||\tilde{\kappa}|| < 1$ and $\eta, \theta \in \Omega$ and $\Gamma \in C_\star$. Then S has a UFP in $\tilde{\Theta}$.

Proof. Let us take $f = I_{\tilde{\Theta}}$ (identity mapping on $\tilde{\Theta}$), from Theorem 4.1.1, we see that S has a UFP. $\square$

Corollary 4.1.3. Let $(\tilde{\Theta}, \tilde{C}, \tilde{d}_{c^*})$ be a complete C^*-AVFSMS. Suppose $S \colon \tilde{\Theta} \times \tilde{\Theta} \to \tilde{\Theta}$ satisfies

$$\tilde{d}_{c^*}\left(S(\psi_{\alpha_1}, \phi_{\alpha_1}), S(\psi_{\alpha_2}, \phi_{\alpha_2})\right) \preceq \Gamma\left(\tilde{\kappa}^\star \tilde{d}_{c^*}(\psi_{\alpha_1}, \psi_{\alpha_2})\tilde{\kappa}, \tilde{\kappa}^\star \tilde{d}_{c^*}(\phi_{\alpha_1}, \phi_{\alpha_2})\tilde{\kappa}\right)$$

for all $\psi_{\alpha_1}, \psi_{\alpha_2}, \phi_{\alpha_1}, \phi_{\alpha_2} \in \tilde{\Theta}$, where $\tilde{\kappa} \in \tilde{C}$ with $||\tilde{\kappa}|| < 1$ and $\Gamma \in C_\star$. Then S has a UFP in $\tilde{\Theta}$.

Proof. The proof follows from Theorems (4.1.1) and Corollary (4.1.2) by taking $\eta(t) = t$ and $\theta(t) = t$. $\square$

Example 4.1. Let $\Theta = \{\alpha_1, \alpha_2, \alpha_3\}, U = \{x, y, z, w\}$ and $C = \{\alpha_1, \alpha_2, \alpha_3\}$,

$D = \{\alpha_1, \alpha_2, \}$ be two subset of Θ. Define fuzzy soft set as,

$$(\psi_\Theta, C) = \left\{ \begin{array}{c} \alpha_1 = \{x_{0.7}, y_{0.6}, z_{0.6}, w_{0.5}\}, \alpha_2 = \{x_{0.8}, y_{0.7}, z_{0.8}, w_{0.6}\}, \\ \alpha_3 = \{x_{0.9}, y_{0.7}, z_{0.9}, w_{0.8}\} \end{array} \right\}$$

$$(\phi_\Theta, D) = \{\alpha_1 = \{x_{0.5}, y_{0.6}, z_{0.5}, w_{0.3}\}, \alpha_2 = \{x_{0.7}, y_{0.7}, z_{0.8}, w_{0.5}\}\}$$

$$\psi_{\alpha_1} = \mu_{\psi_{\alpha_1}} = \{x_{0.7}, y_{0.6}, z_{0.6}, w_{0.5}\}, \psi_{\alpha_2} = \mu_{\psi_{\alpha_2}} = \{x_{0.8}, y_{0.7}, z_{0.8}, w_{0.6}\}$$

$$\psi_{\alpha_3} = \mu_{\psi_{\alpha_3}} = \{x_{0.9}, y_{0.7}, z_{0.9}, w_{0.8}\}$$

$$\phi_{\alpha_1} = \mu_{\phi_{\alpha_1}} = \{x_{0.5}, y_{0.6}, z_{0.5}, w_{0.3}\}, \phi_{\alpha_2} = \mu_{\phi_{\alpha_2}} = \{x_{0.7}, y_{0.7}, z_{0.8}, w_{0.5}\}$$

and $FSC(F_\Theta) = \{\psi_{\alpha_1}, \psi_{\alpha_2}, \psi_{\alpha_3}, \phi_{\alpha_1}, \phi_{\alpha_2}\}$, let $\tilde{\Theta}$ be absolute fuzzy soft set, that is $\tilde{\Theta}(\alpha) = \tilde{1}$ for

all $\alpha \in \Theta$, and $\tilde{C} = M_2(\mathcal{R}(C)^*)$, be the C^*-algebra. Define $\tilde{d}_{c^*} \colon \tilde{\Theta} \times \tilde{\Theta} \to \tilde{C}$ by $\tilde{d}_{c^*}(\psi_{\alpha_1}, \psi_{\alpha_2}) =$

$\left(\begin{array}{cc} \inf\{|\psi_{\alpha_1}(x) - \psi_{\alpha_2}(x)|/x \in U\} & 0 \end{array} \right)$ then obviously $(\tilde{\Theta}, \tilde{C}, \tilde{d}_{c^*})$ is a complete C^*-AVFSMS. We

define $S \colon \tilde{\Theta} \times \tilde{\Theta} \to \tilde{\Theta}$ by $S(\psi_{\alpha_1}, \phi_{\alpha_1})(x) = \frac{\psi_{\alpha_1} + 2\phi_{\alpha_1} + 3}{12}$, $f \colon \tilde{\Theta} \to \tilde{\Theta}$ by $f\psi_{\alpha_1} = \frac{2\psi_{\alpha_1} + 1}{5}$ for all $x \in U$ and

$\psi_{\alpha_1}, \phi_{\alpha_1} \in \tilde{\Theta}$. Let two continuous functions $\eta, \theta \colon \tilde{C}_+ \to \tilde{C}_+$ $\eta(\tilde{\kappa}) = \tilde{\kappa}$ and $\theta(\tilde{\kappa}) = \frac{\tilde{\kappa}}{5}$ for all $\tilde{\kappa} \in \tilde{C}_+$

and $\Gamma \colon \tilde{C}_+ \times \tilde{C}_+ \to \tilde{C}_+$ by $\Gamma(\tilde{\kappa}, \tilde{b}) = \tilde{\kappa} - \theta(\tilde{\kappa})$ for all $\tilde{\kappa}, \tilde{b} \in \tilde{C}_+$. Then obviously, $S(\tilde{\Theta} \times \tilde{\Theta}) \subseteq f(\tilde{\Theta})$

and $\{S, f\}$ is ω-compatible pair. Observe that $f\psi_{\alpha_1} = \frac{2\psi_{\alpha_1} + 1}{5} = \{0.48, 0.44, 0.44, 0.4\}$ and

$f\psi_{\alpha_2} = \frac{2\psi_{\alpha_2} + 1}{5} = \{0.52, 0.48, 0.52, 0.44\}$.

Thus, $\inf\{|\mu^x_{f\psi_{\alpha_1}}(s) - \mu^x_{f\psi_{\alpha_2}}(s)|/s \in C\} = \inf\{0.04, 0.04, 0.08, 0.04\} = 0.04.$

Therefore, $\tilde{d}_{c^*}(f\psi_{\alpha_1}, f\psi_{\alpha_2}) = \begin{bmatrix} 0.04 & 0 \\ 0 & 0.04 \end{bmatrix}$

also, $f\phi_{\alpha_1} = \frac{2\phi_{\alpha_1} + 1}{5} = \{0.4, 0.44, 0.4, 0.32\}$ and $f\phi_{\alpha_2} = \frac{2\phi_{\alpha_2} + 1}{5} = \{0.48, 0.48, 0.52, 0.4\}$. Thus,

$\inf\{|\mu^x_{f\phi_{\alpha_1}}(s) - \mu^x_{f\phi_{\alpha_2}}(s)|/s \in C\} = \inf\{0.08, 0.04, 0.12, 0.08\} = 0.04$ and

$$\tilde{d}_{c^*}(f\phi_{\alpha_1}, f\phi_{\alpha_2}) = \begin{bmatrix} 0.04 & 0 \\ 0 & 0.04 \end{bmatrix}.$$

Moreover, $S(\psi_{\alpha_1}, \phi_{\alpha_1})(x) = \frac{\psi_{\alpha_1} + 2\phi_{\alpha_1} + 3}{12} = \{0.391, 0.4, 0.383, 0.341\}$

and $S(\psi_{\alpha_2}, \phi_{\alpha_2})(x) = \frac{\psi_{\alpha_2} + 2\phi_{\alpha_2} + 3}{12} = \{0.433, 0.425, 0.45, 0.383\}.$

Then

$$\eta\left(\tilde{d}_{c^*}(S(\psi_{\alpha_1}, \phi_{\alpha_1}), S(\psi_{\alpha_2}, \phi_{\alpha_2}))\right) = \begin{bmatrix} 0.025 & 0 \\ 0 & 0.025 \end{bmatrix}$$

$$\preceq \frac{4}{5}\left(\begin{bmatrix} \frac{2}{\sqrt{5}} & 0 \\ 0 & \frac{2}{\sqrt{5}} \end{bmatrix}\begin{bmatrix} 0.04 & 0 \\ 0 & 0.04 \end{bmatrix}\begin{bmatrix} \frac{2}{\sqrt{5}} & 0 \\ 0 & \frac{2}{\sqrt{5}} \end{bmatrix}\right)$$

$$\preceq \left(\begin{bmatrix} \frac{2}{\sqrt{5}} & 0 \\ 0 & \frac{2}{\sqrt{5}} \end{bmatrix}\begin{bmatrix} 0.04 & 0 \\ 0 & 0.04 \end{bmatrix}\begin{bmatrix} \frac{2}{\sqrt{5}} & 0 \\ 0 & \frac{2}{\sqrt{5}} \end{bmatrix}\right)$$

$$- \frac{1}{5}\left(\begin{bmatrix} \frac{2}{\sqrt{5}} & 0 \\ 0 & \frac{2}{\sqrt{5}} \end{bmatrix}\begin{bmatrix} 0.04 & 0 \\ 0 & 0.04 \end{bmatrix}\begin{bmatrix} \frac{2}{\sqrt{5}} & 0 \\ 0 & \frac{2}{\sqrt{5}} \end{bmatrix}\right)$$

$$\preceq \Gamma\left(\eta\left(\tilde{\kappa}^\star \tilde{d}_{c^*}(f\psi_{\alpha_1}, f\psi_{\alpha_2})\tilde{\kappa}\right), \theta\left(\tilde{\kappa}^\star \tilde{d}_{c^*}(f\phi_{\alpha_1}, f\phi_{\alpha_2})\tilde{\kappa}\right)\right).$$

Here $\tilde{\kappa} = \begin{bmatrix} \frac{2}{\sqrt{5}} & 0 \\ 0 & \frac{2}{\sqrt{5}} \end{bmatrix}$ with $||\tilde{\kappa}|| = \frac{2}{\sqrt{5}} < 1.$

Therefore, all the conditions of Theorem 4.1.1 satisfied and $(\frac{1}{3}, \frac{1}{3})$ is coupled fixed point of S and

f.

4.2 Applications To Integral Equations

Existence and uniqueness theorems for a class of integral equation and operator equation are provided as applications of contractive mapping theorem on complete C^*-AVFSMS.

The example that follows demonstrates C^*-AVFSMS.

Example 4.2. Given $\Theta = C = [0,1]$, $\mathcal{W} = L^2(C)$, and the absolute fuzzy soft set $\tilde{\Theta} = L^\infty(C)$ where C is a Lebesgue measurable set. The set of bounded linear operators on Hilbert space $\mathcal{W}$ is denoted by $L(\mathcal{W})$. $L(\mathcal{W})$ is undoubtedly a C^*-algebra with the standard operator norm. Define $\tilde{d}_{c^*} : \tilde{\Theta} \times \tilde{\Theta} \to L(\mathcal{W})$ by $\tilde{d}_{c^*}(\psi_{\alpha_1}, \psi_{\alpha_2}) = \mathbb{M}_{\inf\{|\mu^a_{\psi_{\alpha_1}}(s) - \mu^a_{\psi_{\alpha_2}}(s)|/s \in C\}}$ for all $\psi_{\alpha_1}, \psi_{\alpha_2} \in \tilde{\Theta}$, where $\mathbb{M}_u : \mathcal{W} \to \mathcal{W}$ is the multiplication operator defined by $\mathbb{M}_u(\eta) = u.\eta$ for $\eta \in \mathcal{W}$. Then $\tilde{d}_{c^*}$ is a C^*- AVFSMS and $(\tilde{\Theta}, L(\mathcal{W}), \tilde{d}_{c^*})$ is a complete C^*-AVFSMS.

Yes, it is sufficient to confirm the accuracy. Given $L(\mathcal{W})$, let $\{\psi_{\alpha_z}\} \in \tilde{\Theta}$ be a CS, there exists a natural number $N(\epsilon)$ such that, for a given $\epsilon > 0$, for any $z, w \geq N(\epsilon)$,

$$\tilde{d}_{c^*}(\psi_{\alpha_z}, \psi_{\alpha_w}) = \mathbb{M}_{\inf\{|\mu^a_{\psi_{\alpha_z}}(s) - \mu^a_{\psi_{\alpha_w}}(s)|/s \in C\}}$$

$$||\tilde{d}_{c^*}(\psi_{\alpha_z}, \psi_{\alpha_w})|| = ||\mathbb{M}_{\inf\{|\mu^a_{\psi_{\alpha_z}}(s) - \mu^a_{\psi_{\alpha_w}}(s)|/s \in C\}}||$$

$$= ||\inf\{|\mu^a_{\psi_{\alpha_z}}(s) - \mu^a_{\psi_{\alpha_w}}(s)|/s \in C\}||_\infty < \epsilon$$

then $\{\psi_{\alpha_z}\}$ is a CS in the space $\tilde{\Theta}$. Thus, there is a $\psi_{\alpha'} \in \tilde{\Theta}$ and natural number $N_1(\epsilon)$ such that

$||\inf\{|\mu^a_{\psi_{\alpha z}}(s) - \mu^a_{\psi_{\alpha'}}(s)|/s \in C\}||_\infty < \epsilon$ if $z > N_1$. Its follows,

$$||\tilde{d}_{c^*}(\psi_{\alpha z}, \psi_{\alpha'})|| = ||\mathbb{M}_{\inf\{|\mu^a_{\psi_{\alpha z}}(s) - \mu^a_{\psi_{\alpha'}}(s)|/s \in C\}}||$$

$$= ||\inf\{|\mu^a_{\psi_{\alpha z}}(s) - \mu^a_{\psi_{\alpha'}}(s)|/s \in C\}||_\infty < \epsilon.$$

Accordingly, with respect to $L(\mathcal{W})$, the sequence $\{\psi_{\alpha z}\}$ converges to the function $\psi_{\alpha'} \in \tilde{\Theta}$; that is, $(\tilde{\Theta}, L(\mathcal{W}), \tilde{d}_{c^*})$ is complete with regard to $L(\mathcal{W})$.

Theorem 4.2.1. Consider the integral equation

$$\psi_\alpha(t) = \int_C \mathcal{G}(t, \psi_\alpha(s), \psi_\alpha(s))ds + \mathfrak{f}(t), \quad t \in \Theta, \tag{4.2.1}$$

where a Lebesgue measurable set C is defined. Suppose

(i) $\mathcal{G} : \Theta \times \mathbb{R}(C)^* \times \mathbb{R}(C)^* \to \mathbb{R}(C)^*$ and $\mathfrak{f} \in L^\infty(C)$.

(ii) there exist a continuous function $\eta : C \to \mathbb{R}(C)^*_+$ and $r \in (0,1)$ such that

$$\inf\{|\mathcal{G}(t, \mathbb{A}_\alpha(s), \mathbb{B}_\alpha(s)) - \mathcal{G}(t, \mathbb{C}_\alpha(s), \mathbb{D}_\alpha(s))|\}$$

$$\leq \tfrac{r}{2}\inf\{|\eta(t)|\} . \min \left\{ \begin{array}{c} \inf\{|\mathbb{A}_\alpha(s) - \mathbb{C}_\alpha(s)|\}, \\ \inf\{|\mathbb{B}_\alpha(s) - \mathbb{D}_\alpha(s)|\} \end{array} \right\},$$

for $t, s \in C$ and $\mathbb{A}_\alpha(s), \mathbb{B}_\alpha(s), \mathbb{C}_\alpha(s), \mathbb{D}_\alpha(s) \in \mathbb{R}(C)^*$

(iii) $\sup\limits_{t \in C} \int_C \inf\{|\eta(t)|\}ds \leq 1$.

Hence there is only one solution to the integral equation in $L^\infty(C)$.

Proof. Let $\tilde{\Theta} = L^\infty(C)$ and $\mathcal{W} = L^2(C)$. Set $\tilde{d}_{c^*}$ as a above example, then $\tilde{d}_{c^*}$ is a C^*-AVFSM and $(\tilde{\Theta}, L(\mathcal{W}), \tilde{d}_{c^*})$ is a complete C^*- AVFSMS with respect to $L(\mathcal{W})$ and define $\Gamma : L(\mathcal{W}) \times L(\mathcal{W}) \to L(\mathcal{W})$ by $\Gamma(\tilde{a}, \tilde{b}) = \tilde{a} - \tilde{b}$ for all $\tilde{a}, \tilde{b} \in L(\mathcal{W})$.

Let $\mathbf{T} : L^\infty(C) \times L^\infty(C) \to L^\infty(C)$ be such that

$$\mathbf{T}(\mathbb{A}_\alpha(t), \mathbb{B}_\alpha(t)) = \int_C \mathcal{G}(t, \mathbb{A}_\alpha(t), \mathbb{B}_\alpha(s)) ds + \mathfrak{f}(t), t \in \Theta.$$

Let $\tilde{C} = r\tilde{I}_{\tilde{C}}$ then $\tilde{C} \in L(\mathcal{W})_+$ and $||\tilde{C}|| = r < 1$. For any $u \in \mathcal{W}$,

$$\tilde{d}_{c^*}(\mathbf{T}(\psi_{\alpha_1}, \varpi_{\alpha_1}), \mathbf{T}(\psi_{\alpha_2}, \varpi_{\alpha_2})) = \mathbb{M}_{\inf\{|\mu^a_{\mathbf{T}(\psi_{\alpha_1},\varpi_{\alpha_1})}(s) - \mu^a_{\mathbf{T}(\psi_{\alpha_2},\varpi_{\alpha_2})}(s)|/s \in C\}}$$

$$||\tilde{d}_{c^*}(\mathbf{T}(\psi_{\alpha_1}, \varpi_{\alpha_1}), \mathbf{T}(\psi_{\alpha_2}, \varpi_{\alpha_2}))|| = \sup_{||h||=1} (\mathbb{M}_{\inf\{|\mu^a_{\mathbf{T}(\psi_{\alpha_1},\varpi_{\alpha_1})}(s) - \mu^a_{\mathbf{T}(\psi_{\alpha_2},\varpi_{\alpha_2})}(s)|/s \in C\}} u, u)$$

$$= \sup_{||u||=1} \int_C \left[\inf\{| \int_C (\mathcal{G}(t, \psi_{\alpha_1}(s), \varpi_{\alpha_1}(s)) - \mathcal{G}(t, \psi_{\alpha_2}(s), \varpi_{\alpha_2}(s)))|\} ds \right] u(t)\overline{u(t)} dt$$

$$\leq \sup_{||u||=1} \int_C \left[\int_C \inf\{|\mathcal{G}(t, \psi_{\alpha_1}(s), \varpi_{\alpha_1}(s)) - \mathcal{G}(t, \psi_{\alpha_2}(s), \varpi_{\alpha_2}(s))|\} ds \right] |u(t)|^2 dt$$

$$\leq \sup_{||u||=1} \int_C \left[\int_C \frac{r}{2} \inf\{|\eta(t)| \left(\min \left\{ \begin{array}{l} \inf\{\psi_{\alpha_1}(s) - \psi_{\alpha_2}(s)\}, \\ \inf\{\varpi_{\alpha_1}(s) - \varpi_{\alpha_2}(s)\} \end{array} \right\} \right) |\} ds \right] |u(t)|^2 dt$$

$$\leq \frac{r}{2} \sup_{||u||=1} \int_C \left[\int_C \inf\{|\eta(t)|\} \min \left\{ \begin{array}{l} \inf\{|\psi_{\alpha_1}(s) - \psi_{\alpha_2}(s)|\}, \\ \inf\{|\varpi_{\alpha_1}(s) - \varpi_{\alpha_2}(s)|\} \end{array} \right\} ds \right] |u(t)|^2 dt$$

$$\leq \frac{r}{2}\sup_{||u||=1}\int_C\left[\int_C\inf\{|\eta(t)|\}ds\right]|u(t)|^2dt.||\min\left\{\begin{array}{l}\inf\{|\psi_{\alpha_1}(s)-\psi_{\alpha_2}(s)|\},\\[2mm]\inf\{|\varpi_{\alpha_1}(s)-\varpi_{\alpha_2}(s)|\}\end{array}\right\}||_\infty$$

$$\leq \frac{r}{2}\sup_{||u||=1}\int_C\inf\{|\eta(t)|\}ds.\sup_{||u||=1}\int_C|u(t)|^2dt.||\min\left\{\begin{array}{l}\inf\{|\psi_{\alpha_1}(s)-\psi_{\alpha_2}(s)|\},\\[2mm]\inf\{|\varpi_{\alpha_1}(s)-\varpi_{\alpha_2}(s)|\}\end{array}\right\}||_\infty$$

$$\leq r.||\inf\{|\psi_{\alpha_1}(s)-\psi_{\alpha_2}(s)|\}-\inf\{|\varpi_{\alpha_1}(s)-\varpi_{\alpha_2}(s)|\}||_\infty$$

$$\leq r||\tilde{d}_{c^*}(\psi_{\alpha_1},\psi_{\alpha_2})-\tilde{d}_{c^*}(\varpi_{\alpha_1},\varpi_{\alpha_2})||$$

$$\leq ||\tilde{a}||||\tilde{d}_{c^*}(\psi_{\alpha_1},\psi_{\alpha_2})-\tilde{d}_{c^*}(\varpi_{\alpha_1},\varpi_{\alpha_2})||.$$

Thus,

$$\tilde{d}_{c^*}(\mathbf{T}(\psi_{\alpha_1},\varpi_{\alpha_1}),\mathbf{T}(\psi_{\alpha_2},\varpi_{\alpha_2}))\preceq\Gamma\left(\tilde{a}^\star\tilde{d}_{c^*}(\psi_{\alpha_1},\psi_{\alpha_2})\tilde{a},\tilde{a}^\star\tilde{d}_{c^*}(\varpi_{\alpha_1},\varpi_{\alpha_2})\tilde{a}\right).$$

Since $||\tilde{a}||<1$, It follows from Corollary $(4.1.3)$, we conclude that the equation $(4.2.1)$ has a unique solution in $L^\infty(C)$. $\qquad\square$

4.3   Application to Homotopy

We now provide the primary result in terms of application to homotopy.

Theorem 4.3.1. Let $(\tilde{\Theta},\tilde{C},\tilde{d}_{c^*})$ be complete C^*-AVFSMS, Δ and $\overline{\Delta}$ be an open and closed subset of $\tilde{\Theta}$ such that $\Delta\subseteq\overline{\Delta}$. Assume the operator $\mathcal{H}:\overline{\Delta}^2\times[0,1]\to\tilde{\Theta}$ satisfies the following requirements.

$i_0)$ $\wp_\alpha\neq\mathcal{H}(\wp_\alpha,\varpi_\alpha,s)$, $\varpi_\alpha\neq\mathcal{H}(\varpi_\alpha,\wp_\alpha,s)$, for each $\wp_\alpha,\varpi_\alpha\in\partial\Delta$ and $s\in[0,1]$ (Here $\partial\Delta$ is boundary of Δ in Θ);

ii_1) for all $\wp_\alpha, \varpi_\alpha, \imath_\alpha, \jmath_\alpha \in \overline{\Delta}$, $s \in [0,1]$ and $\eta, \theta \in \Omega$, $\Gamma \in C_\star$ and $\tilde{\kappa} \in \tilde{C}$ with $||\tilde{\kappa}|| < 1$such that

$$\eta\left(\tilde{d}_{c^*}\left(\mathcal{H}(\wp_\alpha, \varpi_\alpha, s), \mathcal{H}(\imath_\alpha, \jmath_\alpha, s)\right)\right) \preceq \Gamma\left(\eta\left(\tilde{\kappa}\tilde{d}_{c^*}(\wp_\alpha, \imath_\alpha)\tilde{\kappa}^*\right), \theta\left(\tilde{\kappa}\tilde{d}_{c^*}(\varpi_\alpha, \jmath_\alpha)\tilde{\kappa}^*\right)\right).$$

iii_2) $\exists\, \tilde{M} \in \tilde{C}_+ \ni \tilde{d}_{c^*}(\mathcal{H}(\wp_\alpha, \varpi_\alpha, s), \mathcal{H}(\wp_\alpha, \varpi_\alpha, t)) \preceq ||\tilde{M}|||s - t|$

for every $\wp_\alpha, \varpi_\alpha \in \overline{\Delta}$and $s, t \in [0,1]$.

Then $\mathcal{H}(., 0)$ has a CFP $\iff$ $\mathcal{H}(., 1)$ has a CFP.

Proof. Let the set

$$\Theta = \left\{ s \in [0,1] : \mathcal{H}(\wp_\alpha, \varpi_\alpha, s) = \wp_\alpha, \mathcal{H}(\varpi_\alpha, \wp_\alpha, s) = \varpi_\alpha \text{ for some } \wp_\alpha, \varpi_\alpha \in \Delta \right\}.$$

Suppose that $\mathcal{H}(., 0)$ has a CFP in Δ^2, we have that $(0, 0) \in \Theta^2$ for Θ to be a non-empty set.

Using the connectedness $\Theta = [0, 1]$, we now demonstrate that Θ is both closed and open in $[0, 1]$. Consequently, there is a CFP for $\mathcal{H}(., 1)$ in Δ^2. Initially, we demonstrate that Θ is closed in $[0, 1]$. To see this, Let $\{s_{\alpha_p}\}_{p=1}^\infty \subseteq \Theta$ with $s_{\alpha_p} \to s_{\alpha'} \in [0, 1]$ as $p \to \infty$. We have to demonstrate that $s_{\alpha'} \in \Theta$. Since $s_{\alpha_p} \in \Theta$ for $p = 0, 1, 2, 3, \cdots$, there exists sequences $\{\wp_{\alpha_p}\}, \{\varpi_{\alpha_p}\} \subseteq \Delta$ with $\wp_{\alpha_p} = \mathcal{H}(\wp_{\alpha_p}, \varpi_{\alpha_p}, s_{\alpha_p}), \varpi_{\alpha_p} = \mathcal{H}(\varpi_{\alpha_p}, \wp_{\alpha_p}, s_{\alpha_p})$.

Consider

$$\tilde{d}_{c^*}(\wp_{\alpha_p}, \wp_{\alpha_{p+1}}) = \tilde{d}_{c^*}\left(\mathcal{H}(\wp_{\alpha_p}, \varpi_{\alpha_p}, s_{\alpha_p}), \mathcal{H}(\wp_{\alpha_{p+1}}, \varpi_{\alpha_{p+1}}, s_{\alpha_{p+1}})\right)$$

$$\preceq \begin{aligned}&\tilde{d}_{c^*}\left(\mathcal{H}(\wp_{\alpha_p}, \varpi_{\alpha_p}, s_{\alpha_p}), \mathcal{H}(\wp_{\alpha_{p+1}}, \varpi_{\alpha_{p+1}}, s_{\alpha_p})\right)\\ &+\tilde{d}_{c^*}\left(\mathcal{H}(\wp_{\alpha_{p+1}}, \varpi_{\alpha_{p+1}}, s_{\alpha_p}), \mathcal{H}(\wp_{\alpha_{p+1}}, \varpi_{\alpha_{p+1}}, s_{\alpha_{p+1}})\right)\end{aligned}$$

$$\preceq \tilde{d}_{c^*}\left(\mathcal{H}(\wp_{\alpha_p}, \varpi_{\alpha_p}, s_{\alpha_p}), \mathcal{H}(\wp_{\alpha_{p+1}}, \varpi_{\alpha_{p+1}}, s_{\alpha_p})\right) + ||\tilde{M}|||s_{\alpha_p} - s_{\alpha_{p+1}}|.$$

Letting $p \to \infty$, we get

$$\lim_{p \to \infty} \tilde{d}_{c^*}(\wp_{\alpha_p}, \wp_{\alpha_{p+1}}) \preceq \lim_{p \to \infty} \tilde{d}_{c^*}\left(\mathcal{H}(\wp_{\alpha_p}, \varpi_{\alpha_p}, s_{\alpha_p}), \mathcal{H}(\wp_{\alpha_{p+1}}, \varpi_{\alpha_{p+1}}, s_{\alpha_p})\right) + 0.$$

Since η, θ are continuous and non-decreasing, we obtain

$$\lim_{p \to \infty} \eta\left(\tilde{d}_{c^*}(\wp_{\alpha_p}, \wp_{\alpha_{p+1}})\right) \preceq \lim_{p \to \infty} \eta\left(\tilde{d}_{c^*}\left(\mathcal{H}(\wp_{\alpha_p}, \varpi_{\alpha_p}, s_{\alpha_p}), \mathcal{H}(\wp_{\alpha_{p+1}}, \varpi_{\alpha_{p+1}}, s_{\alpha_p})\right)\right)$$
$$\preceq \lim_{p \to \infty} \Gamma\left(\eta\left(\tilde{\kappa}\tilde{d}_{c^*}(\wp_{\alpha_p}, \wp_{\alpha_{p+1}})\tilde{\kappa}^*\right), \theta\left(\tilde{\kappa}\tilde{d}_{c^*}(\varpi_{\alpha_p}, \varpi_{\alpha_{p+1}})\tilde{\kappa}^*\right)\right)$$
$$\preceq \lim_{p \to \infty} \eta\left(\tilde{\kappa}\tilde{d}_{c^*}(\wp_{\alpha_p}, \wp_{\alpha_{p+1}})\tilde{\kappa}^*\right).$$

By the definition of η, and $||\tilde{\kappa}|| < 1$ it follows that

$$\lim_{p \to \infty} ||\tilde{d}_{c^*}(\wp_{\alpha_p}, \wp_{\alpha_{p+1}})|| \leq \lim_{p \to \infty} ||\tilde{\kappa}\tilde{d}_{c^*}(\wp_{\alpha_p}, \wp_{\alpha_{p+1}})\tilde{\kappa}^*|| \leq ||\tilde{\kappa}||^2 \lim_{p \to \infty} ||\tilde{d}_{c^*}(\wp_{\alpha_p}, \wp_{\alpha_{p+1}})||.$$

So that

$$\lim_{p \to \infty} \tilde{d}_{c^*}(\wp_{\alpha_p}, \wp_{\alpha_{p+1}}) = \tilde{0}_{\tilde{C}}.$$

Now for $q > p$, by use of triangular inequalilty , we have

$$\tilde{d}_{c^*}\left(\wp_{\alpha_p}, \wp_{\alpha_q}\right) \preceq \tilde{d}_{c^*}\left(\wp_{\alpha_p}, \wp_{\alpha_{p+1}}\right) + \tilde{d}_{c^*}\left(\wp_{\alpha_{p+1}}, \wp_{\alpha_{p+2}}\right) + \tilde{d}_{c^*}\left(\wp_{\alpha_{p+2}}, \wp_{\alpha_{p+3}}\right)$$
$$+ \ldots + \tilde{d}_{c^*}\left(\wp_{\alpha_{q-2}}, \wp_{\alpha_{q-1}}\right) + \tilde{d}_{c^*}\left(\wp_{\alpha_{q-1}}, \wp_{\alpha_q}\right) \to 0 \text{ as } p, q \to \infty.$$

Hence $\{\wp_{\alpha_p}\}$ is a CS in C^*-AVFSMS $(\tilde{\Theta}, \tilde{C}, \tilde{d}_{c^*})$. In a similar way, we can demonstrate that $\{\varpi_{\alpha_p}\}$ is CS in $(\tilde{\Theta}, \tilde{C}, \tilde{d}_{c^*})$ and by the completeness of $(\tilde{\Theta}, \tilde{C}, \tilde{d}_{c^*})$, there exist $\tilde{u}', \tilde{v}' \in \Theta$ with

$$\lim_{p \to \infty} \wp_{\alpha_{p+1}} = u_{\alpha'} = \lim_{p \to \infty} \wp_{\alpha_p} \qquad \lim_{p \to \infty} \varpi_{\alpha_{p+1}} = v_{\alpha'} = \lim_{p \to \infty} \varpi_{\alpha_p}$$

we have

$$
\begin{aligned}
\eta\left(\tilde{d}_{c^*}\left(u_{\alpha'}, \mathcal{H}(u_{\alpha'}, v_{\alpha'}, s_{\alpha'})\right)\right) &= \lim_{p\to\infty} \eta\left(\tilde{d}_{c^*}\left(\mathcal{H}(\wp_{\alpha_p}, \varpi_{\alpha_p}, s_{\alpha'}), \mathcal{H}(u_{\alpha'}, v_{\alpha'}, s_{\alpha'})\right)\right) \\
&\preceq \lim_{p\to\infty} \Gamma\left(\eta\left(\tilde{\kappa}\tilde{d}_{c^*}(\wp_{\alpha_p}, u_{\alpha'})\tilde{\kappa}^\star\right), \theta\left(\tilde{\kappa}\tilde{d}_{c^*}(\varpi_{\alpha_p}, v_{\alpha'})\tilde{\kappa}^\star\right)\right) \\
&\preceq \lim_{p\to\infty} \eta\left(\tilde{\kappa}\tilde{d}_{c^*}(\wp_{\alpha_p}, u_{\alpha'})\tilde{\kappa}^\star\right) = 0.
\end{aligned}
$$

It follows that $\mathcal{H}(u_{\alpha'}, v_{\alpha'}, s_{\alpha'}) = u_{\alpha'}$. Similarly, we can prove $\mathcal{H}(v_{\alpha'}, u_{\alpha'}, s_{\alpha'}) = v_{\alpha'}$. Thus $s_{\alpha'} \in \Theta$.

Hence Θ is closed in $[0, 1]$. Let $s_{\alpha_0} \in \Theta$, then there exist

$\wp_{\alpha_0}, \varpi_{\alpha_0} \in \Delta$ with $\wp_{\alpha_0} = \mathcal{H}(\wp_{\alpha_0}, \varpi_{\alpha_0}, s_{\alpha_0})$, $\varpi_{\alpha_0} = \mathcal{H}(\varpi_{\alpha_0}, \wp_{\alpha_0}, s_{\alpha_0})$. Since Δ is open, then there

exist $\tilde{r} > 0$ such that $B_{d_{c^*}}(\wp_{\alpha_0}, \tilde{r}) \subseteq \Delta$.

Choose $s_{\alpha'} \in (s_{\alpha_0} - \epsilon, s_{\alpha_0} + \epsilon)$ such that $|s_{\alpha'} - s_{\alpha_0}| \leq \frac{1}{\|\tilde{M}^p\|} < \frac{\epsilon}{2}$, then for

$\wp_{\alpha'} \in \overline{B_{\tilde{d}_{c^*}}(\wp_{\alpha_0}, \tilde{r})} = \left\{\wp_{\alpha'} \in \Theta / \tilde{d}_{c^*}(\wp_{\alpha'}, \wp_{\alpha_0}) \leq \tilde{r} + \tilde{d}_{c^*}(\wp_{\alpha_0}, \wp_{\alpha_0})\right\}$. Now we have

$$
\begin{aligned}
&\tilde{d}_{c^*}\left(\mathcal{H}(\wp_{\alpha'}, \varpi_{\alpha'}, s_{\alpha'}), \wp_{\alpha_0}\right) = \tilde{d}_{c^*}\left(\mathcal{H}(\wp_{\alpha'}, \varpi_{\alpha'}, s_{\alpha'}), \mathcal{H}_b(\wp_{\alpha_0}, \varpi_{\alpha_0}, s_{\alpha_0})\right) \\
&\preceq \tilde{d}_{c^*}\left(\mathcal{H}(\wp_{\alpha'}, \varpi_{\alpha'}, s_{\alpha'}), \mathcal{H}(\wp_{\alpha'}, \varpi_{\alpha'}, s_{\alpha_0})\right) \\
&\quad + \tilde{d}_{c^*}\left(\mathcal{H}(\wp_{\alpha'}, \varpi_{\alpha'}, s_{\alpha_0}), \mathcal{H}(\wp_{\alpha_0}, \varpi_{\alpha_0}, s_{\alpha_0})\right) \\
&\preceq \|\tilde{M}\|\,|s_{\alpha'} - s_{\alpha_0}| + \tilde{d}_{c^*}\left(\mathcal{H}(\wp_{\alpha'}, \varpi_{\alpha'}, s_{\alpha_0}), \mathcal{H}(\wp_{\alpha_0}, \varpi_{\alpha_0}, s_{\alpha_0})\right) \\
&\preceq \frac{1}{\|\tilde{M}^{p-1}\|} + \tilde{d}_{c^*}\left(\mathcal{H}(\wp_{\alpha'}, \varpi_{\alpha'}, s_{\alpha_0}), \mathcal{H}(\wp_{\alpha_0}, \varpi_{\alpha_0}, s_{\alpha_0})\right).
\end{aligned}
$$

Letting $p \to \infty$, we obtain

$$
\tilde{d}_{c^*}\left(\mathcal{H}(\wp_{\alpha'}, \varpi_{\alpha'}, s_{\alpha'}), \wp_{\alpha_0}\right) \preceq \tilde{d}_{c^*}\left(\mathcal{H}(\wp_{\alpha'}, \varpi_{\alpha'}, s_{\alpha_0}), \mathcal{H}(\wp_{\alpha_0}, \varpi_{\alpha_0}, s_{\alpha_0})\right).
$$

Since η, θ are continuous and non-decreasing, we obtain

$$
\begin{aligned}
\eta\left(\tilde{d}_{c^*}\left(\mathcal{H}(\wp_{\alpha'}, \varpi_{\alpha'}, s_{\alpha'}), \wp_{\alpha_0}\right)\right) &\preceq \eta\left(\tilde{d}_{c^*}\left(\mathcal{H}(\wp_{\alpha'}, \varpi_{\alpha'}, s_{\alpha_0}), \mathcal{H}(\wp_{\alpha_0}, \varpi_{\alpha_0}, s_{\alpha_0})\right)\right) \\
&\preceq \Gamma\left(\eta(\tilde{\kappa}\tilde{d}_{c^*}(\wp_{\alpha'}, \wp_{\alpha_0})\tilde{\kappa}^*), \theta(\tilde{\kappa}\tilde{d}_{c^*}(\varpi_{\alpha'}, \varpi_{\alpha_0})\tilde{\kappa}^*)\right) \\
&\preceq \eta\left(\tilde{\kappa}\tilde{d}_{c^*}(\wp_{\alpha'}, \wp_{\alpha_0}))\tilde{\kappa}^*\right).
\end{aligned}
$$

Since η is non-decreasing, we have

$$
\begin{aligned}
||\tilde{d}_{c^*}\left(\mathcal{H}(\wp_{\alpha'}, \varpi_{\alpha'}, s_{\alpha'}), \wp_{\alpha_0}\right)|| &\leq ||\tilde{\kappa}\tilde{d}_{c^*}(\wp_{\alpha'}, \wp_{\alpha_0}))\tilde{\kappa}^*|| \leq ||\tilde{\kappa}||^2||\tilde{d}_{c^*}(\wp_{\alpha'}, \wp_{\alpha_0}))|| \\
&\leq r + ||\tilde{d}_{c^*}(\wp_{\alpha_0}, \wp_{\alpha_0})||.
\end{aligned}
$$

Similarly, we can prove,

$$
||\tilde{d}_{c^*}\left(\mathcal{H}(\varpi_{\alpha'}, \wp_{\alpha'}, s_{\alpha'}), \varpi_{\alpha_0}\right)|| \leq r + ||\tilde{d}_{c^*}(\varpi_{\alpha_0}, \varpi_{\alpha_0})||.
$$

Thus for each fixed $s_{\alpha'} \in (s_{\alpha_0} - \epsilon, s_{\alpha_0} + \epsilon)$, $\mathcal{H}(., s_{\alpha'}) : \overline{B_{\tilde{d}_{c^*}}(\wp_{\alpha_0}, \tilde{r})} \to \overline{B_{\tilde{d}_{c^*}}(\wp_{\alpha_0}, \tilde{r})}$,

$\mathcal{H}(., s_{\alpha'}) : \overline{B_{\tilde{d}_{c^*}}(\varpi_{\alpha_0}, \tilde{r})} \to \overline{B_{\tilde{d}_{c^*}}(\varpi_{\alpha_0}, \tilde{r})}$.

Then, Theorem 3.3.2 is satisfied in all its conditions. Thus, we deduce that there is a CFP for $\mathcal{H}(., s_{\alpha'})$ in $\overline{\Delta}^2$. But Δ^2 must be used for this. Because (i_0) is true. For each $s_{\alpha'} \in (s_{\alpha_0} - \epsilon, s_{\alpha_0} + \epsilon)$, $s_{\alpha'} \in \Theta$. Thus $(s_{\alpha_0} - \epsilon, s_{\alpha_0} + \epsilon) \subseteq \Theta$, as a result. Θ is obviously open in $[0, 1]$.

We employ the identical method for the opposite inference. $\qquad\square$

4.4 Conclusion

In this chapter, we conclude some applications to homotopy theory and integral equations and via $C_\star$-class functions coupled fixed point theorem proved with example in the set up of $C^\star$-algebra valued fuzzy soft metric spaces .

Tripled Fixed Point Theorem in Partial b-Metric Spaces with Applications

Tripled Fixed Point Theorem in Partial b- Metric Spaces with Applications

This chapter's goal is to demonstrate popular several common tripled fixed point solutions for $(\alpha, \varphi) - K$-type contractive mappings in partial-b-metric space. We also look at a few applications of integral equations and homotopy. In order to support our conclusion, we also provided an example.

5.1 On Certian Tripled fixed point Theorems via $(\alpha, \varphi) - K$-type Contraction mappings in PbMS

We prove the existence and uniqueness of CTFP outcomes for $(\alpha, \varphi) - K$-type contraction in complete PbMS. Furthermore, we provide an instance demonstrating the applicability of the obtained results.

Let Δ be a family of functions $\varphi : [0, \infty) \to [0, \infty)$ satisfying the following conditions:

(a) φ is nondecreasing;

(b) $\varphi(s) < s$ for $s \in [0, \infty)$

Definition 5.1.1. Let $(\Im, P_b)$ be a P*b*MS with the coefficient $\kappa \geq 1$ and $\alpha : \Im^3 \to R^+$, two mappings $\mathcal{T} : \Im^3 \to \Im$, $\int : \Im \to \Im$ has $(\alpha, \varphi) - K$ type-contraction if it satisfies for all $\ell_1, \ell_2, \ell_3, \wp_1, \wp_2, \wp_3 \in \Im$;

$$\alpha\left(\int \ell_1, \int \ell_2, \int \ell_3\right) P_b\left(\mathcal{T}(\ell_1, \ell_2, \ell_3), \mathcal{T}(\wp_1, \wp_2, \wp_3)\right) \leq \varphi\left(\lambda K(\ell_1, \ell_2, \ell_3, \wp_1, \wp_2, \wp_3)\right)$$

$$(5.1.1)$$

where, $\varphi \in \Delta$, $\lambda \in [0, \frac{1}{2\kappa^2})$ and

$$K(\ell_1, \ell_2, \ell_3, \wp_1, \wp_2, \wp_3) = \max \left\{ \begin{array}{c} P_b(\int \ell_1, \int \wp_1), P_b(\int \ell_2, \int \wp_2), P_b(\int \ell_3, \int \wp_3), \\[6pt] P_b(\int \ell_1, \mathcal{T}(\ell_1, \ell_2, \ell_3)), P_b(\int \ell_2, \mathcal{T}(\ell_2, \ell_3, \ell_1)), \\[6pt] P_b(\int \ell_3, \mathcal{T}(\ell_3, \ell_1, \ell_2)), P_b(\int \wp_1, \mathcal{T}(\wp_1, \wp_2, \wp_3)), \\[6pt] P_b(\int \wp_2, \mathcal{T}(\wp_2, \wp_3, \wp_1)), P_b(\int \wp_3, \mathcal{T}(\wp_3, \wp_1, \wp_2)), \\[6pt] \frac{P_b(\int \ell_1, \mathcal{T}(\ell_1, \ell_2, \ell_3)) P_b(\int \wp_1, \mathcal{T}(\wp_1, \wp_2, \wp_3))}{2\kappa^2 [1 + P_b(\int \ell_1, \int \wp_1)]}, \\[6pt] \frac{P_b(\int \ell_2, \mathcal{T}(\ell_2, \ell_3, \ell_1)) P_b(\int \wp_2, \mathcal{T}(\wp_2, \wp_3, \wp_1))}{2\kappa^2 [1 + P_b(\int \ell_2, \int \wp_2)]}, \\[6pt] \frac{P_b(\int \ell_3, \mathcal{T}(\ell_3, \ell_1, \ell_2)) P_b(\int \wp_3, \mathcal{T}(\wp_3, \wp_1, \wp_2))}{2\kappa^2 [1 + P_b(\int \ell_3, \int \wp_3)]}, \end{array} \right\}.$$

Theorem 5.1.1. Let $(\Im, P_b)$ be a P*b*MS with the coefficient $\kappa \geq 1$ and $\mathcal{T} : \Im^3 \to \Im$ and $\int : \Im \to \Im$ be two mappings satisfying $(\alpha, \varphi) - K$ type-contraction and assume that

(5.1.1.1) $\mathcal{T}(\Im^3) \subseteq \int(\Im)$ and $\int(\Im)$ is complete subspace of $\Im$

(5.1.1.2) $\mathcal{T}$ and $\int$ are α-admissible,

(5.1.1.3) $\exists \, \ell_0, \wp_0, \aleph_0 \in \Im \ni \alpha(\mathcal{T}(\ell_0, \wp_0, \aleph_0), \mathcal{T}(\wp_0, \aleph_0, \ell_0), \mathcal{T}(\int \aleph_0, \int \ell_0, \int \wp_0) \geq 1,$

(5.1.1.4) $(\mathcal{T}, \int)$ is ω-compatible pair.

Then $\mathcal{T}$ and $\int$ have a UCTFP in $\Im$.

Proof. Let $\ell_0, \wp_0, \aleph_0$ be arbitrary points in $\Im$. From condition $(5.1.1.1)$, There exist sequences $\{\ell_z\}$, $\{\wp_z\},\{\aleph_z\}, \{\xi_z\}, \{\varkappa_z\}$and $\{\varpi_z\}$ in $\Im$ such that, for all $z \geq 0$

$$\mathcal{T}(\ell_z, \wp_z, \aleph_z) = \int \ell_{z+1} = \xi_z \qquad \mathcal{T}(\wp_z, \aleph_z, \ell_z) = \int \wp_{z+1} = \varkappa_z$$

$$\mathcal{T}(\aleph_z, \ell_z, \wp_z) = \int \aleph_{z+1} = \varpi_z.$$

For simplification we denote $\Omega_z = \max \left\{ \begin{array}{c} P_b(\xi_z, \xi_{z+1}), \\ P_b(\varkappa_z, \varkappa_{z+1}), \\ P_b(\varpi_z, \varpi_{z+1}) \end{array} \right\}.$

Case(i): If for some ϖ_0, we have

$$\xi_{\varpi_0} = \xi_{\varpi_0+1} = \mathcal{T}(\ell_{\varpi_0}, \wp_{\varpi_0}, \aleph_{\varpi_0}) = \int \ell_{\varpi_0+1}$$

$$\varkappa_{\varpi_0} = \varkappa_{\varpi_0+1} = \mathcal{T}(\wp_{\varpi_0}, \aleph_{\varpi_0}, \ell_{\varpi_0}) = \int \wp_{\varpi_0+1}$$

$$\varpi_{\varpi_0} = \varpi_{\varpi_0+1} = \mathcal{T}(\aleph_{\varpi_0}, \ell_{\varpi_0}, \wp_{\varpi_0}) = \int \aleph_{\varpi_0+1},$$

then $(\xi_{\varpi_0}, \varkappa_{\varpi_0}, \varpi_{\varpi_0})$ is common tripled fixed point of $\mathcal{T}$ and $\int$.

Case (ii): Suppose that $\xi_z \neq \xi_{z+1}$, $\varkappa_z \neq \varkappa_{z+1}$ and $\varpi_z \neq \varpi_{z+1}$ for all $z \geq 0$. Since $\mathcal{T}$ and $\int$ are α-admissible, we have

$$\alpha(\int \ell_0, \int \wp_0, \int \aleph_1) = \alpha(\int \ell_0 \int \wp_0, \mathcal{T}(\aleph_0, \ell_0, \wp_0)) \geq 1$$

$$\Rightarrow \alpha(\mathcal{T}(\ell_0, \wp_0, \aleph_0)\mathcal{T}(\wp_0, \aleph_0, \ell_0), \mathcal{T}(\aleph_1, \ell_1, \wp_1)) \geq 1$$

$$\alpha(\int \ell_1, \int \wp_1, \int \aleph_2) \geq 1.$$

Recursively, we find that $\alpha(\int \ell_z, \int \wp_z, \int \aleph_{z+1}) \geq 1$, for all $z = 0, 1, ...$

From Eq. (5.1.1), condition (5.1.1.2) and (5.1.1.3), we have that

$$
\begin{aligned}
P_b\left(\xi_z, \xi_{z+1}\right) &= P_b\left(\mathcal{T}(\ell_z, \wp_z, \aleph_z), \mathcal{T}(\ell_{z+1}, \wp_{z+1}, \aleph_{z+1})\right) \\[4pt]
&\leq \alpha\left(\int \ell_z, \int \wp_z, \int \aleph_z\right) P_b\left(\mathcal{T}(\ell_z, \wp_z, \aleph_z), \mathcal{T}(\ell_{z+1}, \wp_{z+1}, \aleph_{z+1})\right) \\[4pt]
&\leq \varphi\left(\lambda K(\ell_z, \wp_z, \aleph_z, \ell_{z+1}, \wp_{z+1}, \aleph_{z+1})\right)
\end{aligned}
\tag{5.1.2}
$$

where,

$$
K(\ell_z, \wp_z, \aleph_z, \ell_{z+1}, \wp_{z+1}, \aleph_{z+1})
$$

$$
= \max \left\{
\begin{array}{c}
P_b(\int \ell_z, \int \ell_{z+1}), P_b(\int \wp_z, \int \wp_{z+1}), P_b(\int \aleph_z, \int \aleph_{z+1}), \\[4pt]
P_b(\int \ell_z, \mathcal{T}(\ell_z, \wp_z, \aleph_z)), P_b(\int \wp_z, \mathcal{T}(\wp_z, \aleph_z, \ell_z)), \\[4pt]
P_b(\int \aleph_z, \mathcal{T}(\aleph_z, \ell_z, \wp_z)), \\[4pt]
P_b(\int \ell_{z+1}, \mathcal{T}(\ell_{z+1}, \wp_{z+1}, \aleph_{z+1})), P_b(\int \wp_{z+1}, \mathcal{T}(\wp_{z+1}, \aleph_{z+1}, \ell_{z+1})), \\[4pt]
P_b(\int \aleph_{z+1}, \mathcal{T}(\aleph_{z+1}, \ell_{z+1}, \wp_{z+1})), \\[4pt]
\dfrac{P_b(\int \ell_z, \mathcal{T}(\ell_z, \wp_z, \aleph_z)) P_b(\int \ell_{z+1}, \mathcal{T}(\ell_{z+1}, \wp_{z+1}, \aleph_{z+1}))}{2\kappa^2[1 + P_b(\int \ell_z, \int \ell_{z+1})]}, \\[8pt]
\dfrac{P_b(\int \wp_z, \mathcal{T}(\wp_z, \aleph_z, \ell_z)) P_b(\int \wp_{z+1}, \mathcal{T}(\wp_{z+1}, \aleph_{z+1}, \ell_{z+1}))}{2\kappa^2[1 + P_b(\int \wp_z, \int \wp_{z+1})]}, \\[8pt]
\dfrac{P_b(\int \aleph_z, \mathcal{T}(\aleph_z, \ell_z, \wp_z)) P_b(\int \aleph_{z+1}, \mathcal{T}(\aleph_{z+1}, \ell_{z+1}, \wp_{z+1}))}{2\kappa^2[1 + P_b(\int \aleph_z, \int \aleph_{z+1})]},
\end{array}
\right\}
$$

$$
= \max \left\{
\begin{array}{c}
P_b(\xi_{z-1}, \xi_z), P_b(\varkappa_{z-1}, \varkappa_z), P_b(\varpi_{z-1}, \varpi_z), \\[4pt]
P_b(\xi_{z-1}, \xi_z), P_b(\varkappa_{z-1}, \varkappa_z), P_b(\varpi_{z-1}, \varpi_z), \\[4pt]
P_b(\xi_z, \xi_{z+1}), P_b(\varkappa_z, \varkappa_{z+1}), P_b(\varpi_z, \varpi_{z+1}) \\[4pt]
\dfrac{P_b(\xi_{z-1}, \xi_z) P_b(\xi_z, \xi_{z+1})}{2\kappa^2[1 + P_b(\xi_{z-1}, \xi_z)]}, \; \dfrac{P_b(\varkappa_{z-1}, \varkappa_z) P_b(\varkappa_z, \varkappa_{z+1})}{2\kappa^2[1 + P_b(\varkappa_{z-1}, \varkappa_z)]}, \\[8pt]
\dfrac{P_b(\varpi_{z-1}, \varpi_z) P_b(\varpi_z, \varpi_{z+1})}{2\kappa^2[1 + P_b(\varpi_{z-1}, \varpi_z)]},
\end{array}
\right\}
$$

$$
\leq \max \left\{
\begin{array}{c}
P_b(\xi_{z-1}, \xi_z), P_b(\varkappa_{z-1}, \varkappa_z), P_b(\varpi_{z-1}, \varpi_z), \\[4pt]
P_b(\xi_z, \xi_{z+1}), P_b(\varkappa_z, \varkappa_{z+1}), P_b(\varpi_z, \varpi_{z+1})
\end{array}
\right\}.
$$

From Eq. (5.1.2), we have

$$P_b\left(\xi_z, \xi_{z+1}\right) \le \varphi\left(\lambda \max\left\{ \begin{array}{l} P_b(\xi_{z-1}, \xi_z), P_b(\varkappa_{z-1}, \varkappa_z), P_b(\varpi_{z-1}, \varpi_z), \\ P_b(\xi_z, \xi_{z+1}), P_b(\varkappa_z, \varkappa_{z+1}), P_b(\varpi_z, \varpi_{z+1}) \end{array} \right\}\right).$$

$$(5.1.3)$$

Similarly, we can prove that

$$P_b\left(\varkappa_z, \varkappa_{z+1}\right) \le \varphi\left(\lambda \max\left\{ \begin{array}{l} P_b(\xi_{z-1}, \xi_z), P_b(\varkappa_{z-1}, \varkappa_z), P_b(\varpi_{z-1}, \varpi_z), \\ P_b(\xi_z, \xi_{z+1}), P_b(\varkappa_z, \varkappa_{z+1}), P_b(\varpi_z, \varpi_{z+1}) \end{array} \right\}\right)$$

$$(5.1.4)$$

and

$$P_b\left(\varpi_z, \varpi_{z+1}\right) \le \varphi\left(\lambda \max\left\{ \begin{array}{l} P_b(\xi_{z-1}, \xi_z), P_b(\varkappa_{z-1}, \varkappa_z), P_b(\varpi_{z-1}, \varpi_z), \\ P_b(\xi_z, \xi_{z+1}), P_b(\varkappa_z, \varkappa_{z+1}), P_b(\varpi_z, \varpi_{z+1}) \end{array} \right\}\right).$$

$$(5.1.5)$$

Combining Eq. (5.1.3), Eq. (5.1.4) and Eq. (5.1.5), we get

$$\max\left\{ \begin{array}{l} P_b(\xi_z, \xi_{z+1}), \\ P_b(\varkappa_z, \varkappa_{z+1}), \\ P_b(\varpi_z, \varpi_{z+1}) \end{array} \right\} \le \varphi\left(\lambda \max\left\{ \begin{array}{l} P_b(\xi_{z-1}, \xi_z), P_b(\varkappa_{z-1}, \varkappa_z), P_b(\varpi_{z-1}, \varpi_z), \\ P_b(\xi_z, \xi_{z+1}), P_b(\varkappa_z, \varkappa_{z+1}), P_b(\varpi_z, \varpi_{z+1}) \end{array} \right\}\right).$$

If $P_b(\xi_{z-1}, \xi_z) < P_b(\xi_z, \xi_{z+1})$, $P_b(\varkappa_{z-1}, \varkappa_z) < P_b(\varkappa_z, \varkappa_{z+1})$ and

$P_b(\varpi_{z-1}, \varpi_z) < P_b(\varpi_z, \varpi_{z+1})$, then we have

$$\max \left\{ \begin{array}{l} P_b(\xi_z, \xi_{z+1}), \\ P_b(\varkappa_z, \varkappa_{z+1}), \\ P_b(\varpi_z, \varpi_{z+1}) \end{array} \right\} \leq \varphi \left(\lambda \max \left\{ \begin{array}{c} P_b(\xi_z, \xi_{z+1}), P_b(\varkappa_z, \varkappa_{z+1}), \\ P_b(\varpi_z, \varpi_{z+1}) \end{array} \right\} \right)$$

$$< \lambda \max \left\{ \begin{array}{c} P_b(\xi_z, \xi_{z+1}), P_b(\varkappa_z, \varkappa_{z+1}), \\ P_b(\varpi_z, \varpi_{z+1}) \end{array} \right\}$$

a contradiction. Accordingly, we conclude that

$$\max \left\{ \begin{array}{l} P_b(\xi_z, \xi_{z+1}), \\ P_b(\varkappa_z, \varkappa_{z+1}), \\ P_b(\varpi_z, \varpi_{z+1}) \end{array} \right\} \leq \varphi \left(\lambda \max \left\{ \begin{array}{c} P_b(\xi_{z-1}, \xi_z), P_b(\varkappa_{z-1}, \varkappa_z), \\ P_b(\varpi_{z-1}, \varpi_z) \end{array} \right\} \right)$$

$$< \lambda \max \left\{ \begin{array}{c} P_b(\xi_{z-1}, \xi_z), P_b(\varkappa_{z-1}, \varkappa_z), \\ P_b(\varpi_{z-1}, \varpi_z) \end{array} \right\} \forall \ z \geq 1.$$

Thus

$$\Omega_z < \lambda \Omega_{z-1} \quad \forall \ z \geq 1. \tag{5.1.6}$$

Therefore, $\{\Omega_z\}$ is decreasing sequence and converges to $\delta \geq 0$. Suppose $\delta > 0$ and letting $z \to \infty$ in Eq. (5.1.6), we have that $\delta \leq \lambda.\delta < \delta$, is a contradiction . Hence $\delta = 0$. Thus $\lim_{z \to \infty} \Omega_z = 0$. It follows that

$$\lim_{z \to \infty} P_b(\xi_z, \xi_{z+1}) = \lim_{z \to \infty} P_b(\varkappa_z, \varkappa_{z+1}) = \lim_{z \to \infty} P_b(\varpi_z, \varpi_{z+1}) = 0. \tag{5.1.7}$$

From Eq. (5.1.7) and def. (1.5.1) of (P_b2), we have that

$$\lim_{z \to \infty} P_b(\xi_z, \xi_z) = \lim_{z \to \infty} P_b(\varkappa_z, \varkappa_z) = \lim_{z \to \infty} P_b(\varpi_z, \varpi_z) = 0. \tag{5.1.8}$$

From definition (1.5.3) of d_{P_b}, Eq. (5.1.7) and Eq. (5.1.8), we have that

$$\lim_{z \to \infty} d_b(\xi_z, \xi_{z+1}) = \lim_{z \to \infty} d_b(\varkappa_z, \varkappa_{z+1}) = \lim_{z \to \infty} d_b(\varpi_z, \varpi_{z+1}) = 0. \tag{5.1.9}$$

We now demonstrate that the sequences $\{\xi_z\}$, $\{\varkappa_z\}$ and $\{\varpi_z\}$ in PbMS $(\Im, P_b)$ are CS. If sufficient to demonstrate that the sequences $\{\xi_z\}$, $\{\varkappa_z\}$ and $\{\varpi_z\}$ in b-metric space are CS $(\Im, d_{P_b})$. Assume, however, that $\{\xi_z\}$, $\{\varkappa_z\}$ and $\{\varpi_z\}$ are not Cauchy sequences. This results in z, w for $d_{P_b}(\xi_z, \xi_w) \nrightarrow 0$, $d_{P_b}(\varkappa_z, \varkappa_w) \nrightarrow 0$ and $d_{P_b}(\varpi_z, \varpi_w) \nrightarrow 0$ as $z, w \to \infty$.

Consequently, $\max\{d_{P_b}(\xi_z, \xi_w), d_{P_b}(\varkappa_z, \varkappa_w), d_{P_b}(\varpi_z, \varpi_w)\} \nrightarrow 0$ as $z, w \to \infty$.

Then there exist an $\epsilon > 0$ and monotonically increases sequences of natural numbers $\{w_k\}$, $\{z_k\}$ such that $z_k > w_k > k$,

$$\max\{d_{P_b}(\xi_{z_k}, \xi_{w_k}), d_{P_b}(\varkappa_{z_k}, \varkappa_{w_k}), d_{P_b}(\varpi_{z_k}, \varpi_{w_k})\} \geq \epsilon \tag{5.1.10}$$

and

$$\max\{d_{P_b}(\xi_{z_k-1}, \xi_{w_k}), d_{P_b}(\varkappa_{z_k-1}, \varkappa_{w_k}), d_{P_b}(\varpi_{z_k-1}, \varpi_{w_k})\} < \epsilon. \tag{5.1.11}$$

From Eq. (5.1.10) and Eq. (5.1.11), we have that

$$\begin{aligned}
\epsilon &\leq \max\{d_{P_b}(\xi_{z_k}, \xi_{w_k}), d_{P_b}(\varkappa_{z_k}, \varkappa_{w_k}), d_{P_b}(\varpi_{z_k}, \varpi_{w_k})\} \\
&\leq \kappa. \max\{d_{P_b}(\xi_{w_k}, \xi_{z_k-1}), d_{P_b}(\varkappa_{w_k}, \varkappa_{z_k-1}), d_{P_b}(\varpi_{w_k}, \varpi_{z_k-1})\}
\end{aligned}$$

$$+\kappa.\max\left\{d_{P_b}(\xi_{z_k-1},\xi_{z_k}),d_{P_b}(\varkappa_{z_k-1},\varkappa_{z_k}),d_{P_b}(\varpi_{z_k-1},\varpi_{z_k})\right\}$$

$$<\ \kappa.\epsilon+\kappa.\max\left\{d_{P_b}(\xi_{z_k-1},\xi_{z_k}),d_{P_b}(\varkappa_{z_k-1},\varkappa_{z_k}),d_{P_b}(\varpi_{z_k-1},\varpi_{z_k})\right\}.$$

Using $k\to\infty$ as the upper limit and Eq. (5.1.9), we may deduce that

$$\epsilon\leq\limsup_{k\to\infty}\max\left\{d_{P_b}(\xi_{z_k},\xi_{w_k}),d_{P_b}(\varkappa_{z_k},\varkappa_{w_k}),d_{P_b}(\varpi_{z_k},\varpi_{w_k})\right\}\leq\kappa.\epsilon. \tag{5.1.12}$$

Also

$$\epsilon\ \leq\ \max\left\{d_{P_b}(\xi_{z_k},\xi_{w_k}),d_{P_b}(\varkappa_{z_k},\varkappa_{w_k}),d_{P_b}(\varpi_{z_k},\varpi_{w_k})\right\}$$

$$\leq\ \kappa.\max\left\{d_{P_b}(\xi_{w_k},\xi_{z_k+1}),d_{P_b}(\varkappa_{w_k},\varkappa_{z_k+1}),d_{P_b}(\varpi_{w_k},\varpi_{z_k+1})\right\}$$

$$+\kappa.\max\left\{d_{P_b}(\xi_{z_k+1},\xi_{z_k}),d_{P_b}(\varkappa_{z_k+1},\varkappa_{z_k}),d_{P_b}(\varpi_{z_k+1},\varpi_{z_k})\right\}.$$

Using $k\to\infty$ as the upper limit and Eq. (5.1.9), we may deduce that

$$\frac{\epsilon}{\kappa}\leq\limsup_{k\to\infty}\max\left\{d_{P_b}(\xi_{w_k},\xi_{z_k+1}),d_{P_b}(\varkappa_{w_k},\varkappa_{z_k+1}),d_{P_b}(\varpi_{w_k},\varpi_{z_k+1})\right\}. \tag{5.1.13}$$

On other hand

$$\max\left\{d_{P_b}(\xi_{w_k},\xi_{z_k+1}),d_{P_b}(\varkappa_{w_k},\varkappa_{z_k+1})\right\}$$

$$\leq\ \kappa.\max\left\{d_{P_b}(\xi_{w_k},\xi_{z_k}),d_{P_b}(\varkappa_{w_k+1},\varkappa_{z_k})\right\}+\kappa.\max\left\{d_{P_b}(\xi_{z_k},\xi_{z_k+1}),d_{P_b}(\varkappa_{z_k},\varkappa_{z_k+1})\right\}.$$

Using $k\to\infty$ as the upper limit and Eq. (5.1.9), we may deduce that

$$\limsup_{k\to\infty}\max\left\{d_{P_b}(\xi_{w_k},\xi_{z_k+1}),d_{P_b}(\varkappa_{w_k},\varkappa_{z_k+1})\right\}\leq\epsilon\kappa^2 \tag{5.1.14}$$

also, from Eq. (5.1.10), we have that

$$
\begin{aligned}
\epsilon \;\leq\; & \max\left\{d_{P_b}(\xi_{z_k},\xi_{w_k}),d_{P_b}(\varkappa_{z_k},\varkappa_{w_k}),d_{P_b}(\varpi_{z_k},\varpi_{w_k})\right\} \\[2mm]
\leq\; & \kappa.\max\left\{d_{P_b}(\xi_{w_k},\xi_{w_k+1}),d_{P_b}(\varkappa_{w_k},\varkappa_{w_k+1}),d_{P_b}(\varpi_{w_k},\varpi_{w_k+1})\right\} \\[1mm]
& +\kappa.\max\left\{d_{P_b}(\xi_{w_k+1},\xi_{z_k}),d_{P_b}(\varkappa_{w_k+1},\varkappa_{z_k}),d_{P_b}(\varpi_{w_k+1},\varpi_{z_k})\right\} \\[2mm]
\leq\; & \left\{
\begin{array}{l}
\kappa.\max\left\{d_{P_b}(\xi_{w_k},\xi_{w_k+1}),d_{P_b}(\varkappa_{w_k},\varkappa_{w_k+1}),d_{P_b}(\varpi_{w_k},\varpi_{w_k+1})\right\} \\[1mm]
+\kappa^2.\max\left\{d_{P_b}(\xi_{w_k+1},\xi_{z_k+2}),d_{P_b}(\varkappa_{w_k+1},\varkappa_{z_k+2}),d_{P_b}(\varpi_{w_k+1},\varpi_{z_k+2})\right\} \\[1mm]
+\kappa^2.\max\left\{d_{P_b}(\xi_{z_k+2},\xi_{z_k}),d_{P_b}(\varkappa_{z_k+2},\varkappa_{z_k}),d_{P_b}(\varpi_{z_k+2},\varpi_{z_k})\right\}
\end{array}
\right\} \\[3mm]
\leq\; & \left\{
\begin{array}{l}
\kappa.\max\left\{d_{P_b}(\xi_{w_k},\xi_{w_k+1}),d_{P_b}(\varkappa_{w_k},\varkappa_{w_k+1}),d_{P_b}(\varpi_{w_k},\varpi_{w_k+1})\right\} \\[1mm]
+\kappa^2.\max\left\{d_{P_b}(\xi_{w_k+1},\xi_{z_k+2}),d_{P_b}(\varkappa_{w_k+1},\varkappa_{z_k+2}),d_{P_b}(\varpi_{w_k+1},\varpi_{z_k+2})\right\} \\[1mm]
+\kappa^3.\max\left\{d_{P_b}(\xi_{z_k+2},\xi_{z_k+1}),d_{P_b}(\varkappa_{z_k+2},\varkappa_{z_k+1}),d_{P_b}(\varpi_{z_k+2},\varpi_{z_k+1})\right\} \\[1mm]
+\kappa^3.\max\left\{d_{P_b}(\xi_{z_k+1},\xi_{z_k}),d_{P_b}(\varkappa_{z_k+1},\varkappa_{z_k}),d_{P_b}(\varpi_{z_k+1},\varpi_{z_k})\right\}
\end{array}
\right\}.
\end{aligned}
$$

Using $k \to \infty$ as the upper limit and Eq. (5.1.9), we may deduce that

$$
\frac{\epsilon}{\kappa^2} \leq \limsup_{k\to\infty} \max\left\{d_{P_b}(\xi_{w_k+1},\xi_{z_k+2}),d_{P_b}(\varkappa_{w_k+1},\varkappa_{z_k+2}),d_{P_b}(\varpi_{w_k+1},\varpi_{z_k+2})\right\}.
$$

On other hand

$$
\begin{aligned}
& \max\left\{d_{P_b}(\xi_{w_k+1},\xi_{z_k+2}),d_{P_b}(\varkappa_{w_k+1},\varkappa_{z_k+2}),d_{P_b}(\varpi_{w_k+1},\varpi_{z_k+2})\right\} \\[2mm]
\leq\; & \kappa.\max\left\{d_{P_b}(\xi_{w_k+1},\xi_{w_k}),d_{P_b}(\varkappa_{w_k+1},\varkappa_{w_k}),d_{P_b}(\varpi_{w_k+1},\varpi_{w_k})\right\} \\[1mm]
& +\kappa.\max\left\{d_{P_b}(\xi_{w_k},\xi_{z_k+2}),d_{P_b}(\varkappa_{w_k},\varkappa_{z_k+2}),d_{P_b}(\varpi_{w_k},\varpi_{z_k+2})\right\}
\end{aligned}
$$

$$\leq \left\{ \begin{array}{l} \kappa.\max\left\{d_{P_b}(\xi_{w_k+1},\xi_{w_k}), d_{P_b}(\varkappa_{w_k+1},\varkappa_{w_k}), d_{P_b}(\varpi_{w_k+1},\varpi_{w_k})\right\} \\[2mm] +\kappa^2.\max\left\{d_{P_b}(\xi_{w_k},\xi_{z_k}), d_{P_b}(\varkappa_{w_k},\varkappa_{z_k}), d_{P_b}(\varpi_{w_k},\varpi_{z_k})\right\} \\[2mm] +\kappa^3.\max\left\{d_{P_b}(\xi_{z_k},\xi_{z_k+1}), d_{P_b}(\varkappa_{z_k},\varkappa_{z_k+1}), d_{P_b}(\varpi_{z_k},\varpi_{z_k+1})\right\} \\[2mm] +\kappa^3.\max\left\{d_{P_b}(\xi_{z_k+1},\xi_{z_k+2}), d_{P_b}(\varkappa_{z_k+1},\varkappa_{z_k+2}), d_{P_b}(\varpi_{z_k+1},\varpi_{z_k+2})\right\} \end{array} \right\}.$$

Taking upper limit as $k \to \infty$ and from Eq. (5.1.9), Eq. (5.1.12), we have that

$$\limsup_{k\to\infty}\max\left\{d_{P_b}(\xi_{w_k+1},\xi_{z_k+2}), d_{P_b}(\varkappa_{w_k+1},\varkappa_{z_k+2}), d_{P_b}(\varpi_{w_k+1},\varpi_{z_k+2})\right\} \leq \epsilon.\kappa^3.$$

$$(5.1.15)$$

Now

$$P_b\left(\xi_{w_k+1},\xi_{z_k+2}\right)$$

$$= P_b\left(\mathcal{T}(\ell_{w_k+1},\wp_{w_k+1},\aleph_{w_k+1}),\mathcal{T}(\ell_{z_k+2},\wp_{z_k+2},\aleph_{z_k+2})\right)$$

$$\leq \alpha\left(\int\ell_{w_k+1},\int\wp_{w_k+1},\int\aleph_{w_k+1}\right) P_b\left(\mathcal{T}(\ell_{w_k+1},\wp_{w_k+1},\aleph_{w_k+1}),\mathcal{T}(\ell_{z_k+2},\wp_{z_k+2},\aleph_{z_k+2})\right)$$

$$\leq \varphi\left(\lambda K(\ell_{w_k+1},\wp_{w_k+1},\aleph_{w_k+1},\ell_{z_k+2},\wp_{z_k+2},\aleph_{z_k+2})\right) \qquad (5.1.16)$$

where,

$$K(\ell_{w_k+1},\wp_{w_k+1},\aleph_{w_k+1},\ell_{z_k+2},\wp_{z_k+2},\aleph_{z_k+2})$$

$$= \max \left\{ \begin{array}{c} P_b(\int \ell_{w_k+1}, \int \ell_{z_k+2}),\ P_b(\int \wp_{w_k+1}, \int \wp_{z_k+2}), \\[2mm] P_b(\int \aleph_{w_k+1}, \int \aleph_{z_k+2}), \\[2mm] P_b(\int \ell_{w_k+1}, \mathcal{T}(\ell_{w_k+1}, \wp_{w_k+1}, \aleph_{w_k+1})), \\[2mm] P_b(\int \wp_{w_k+1}, \mathcal{T}(\wp_{w_k+1}, \aleph_{w_k+1}, \ell_{w_k+1})), \\[2mm] P_b(\int \aleph_{w_k+1}, \mathcal{T}(\aleph_{w_k+1}, \ell_{w_k+1}, \wp_{w_k+1})), \\[2mm] P_b(\int \ell_{z_k+2}, \mathcal{T}(\ell_{z_k+2}, \wp_{z_k+2}, \aleph_{z_k+2})), \\[2mm] P_b(\int \wp_{z_k+2}, \mathcal{T}(\wp_{z_k+2}, \aleph_{z_k+2}, \ell_{z_k+2})), \\[2mm] P_b(\int \aleph_{z_k+2}, \mathcal{T}(\aleph_{z_k+2}, \ell_{z_k+2}, \wp_{z_k+2})), \\[2mm] \frac{P_b(\int \ell_{w_k+1}, \mathcal{T}(\ell_{w_k+1}, \wp_{w_k+1}, \aleph_{w_k+1})) P_b(\int \ell_{z_k+2}, \mathcal{T}(\ell_{z_k+2}, \wp_{z_k+2}, \aleph_{z_k+2}))}{2\kappa^2 [1 + P_b(\int \ell_{w_k+1}, \int \ell_{z_k+2})]}, \\[3mm] \frac{P_b(\int \wp_{w_k+1}, \mathcal{T}(\wp_{w_k+1}, \aleph_{w_k+1}, \ell_{w_k+1})) P_b(\int \wp_{z_k+2}, \mathcal{T}(\wp_{z_k+2}, \aleph_{z_k+2}, \ell_{z_k+2}))}{2\kappa^2 [1 + P_b(\int \wp_{w_k+1}, \int \wp_{z_k+2})]}, \\[3mm] \frac{P_b(\int \aleph_{w_k+1}, \mathcal{T}(\aleph_{w_k+1}, \ell_{w_k+1}, \wp_{w_k+1})) P_b(\int \aleph_{z_k+2}, \mathcal{T}(\aleph_{z_k+2}, \ell_{z_k+2}, \wp_{z_k+2}))}{2\kappa^2 [1 + P_b(\int \aleph_{w_k+1}, \int \aleph_{z_k+2})]}, \end{array} \right\}$$

$$\leq \max \left\{ \begin{array}{c} P_b(\xi_{w_k}, \xi_{z_k+1}),\ P_b(\varkappa_{w_k}, \varkappa_{z_k+1}),\ P_b(\varpi_{w_k}, \varpi_{z_k+1}) \\[2mm] P_b(\xi_{w_k}, \xi_{w_k+1}),\ P_b(\varkappa_{w_k}, \varkappa_{w_k+1}),\ P_b(\varpi_{w_k}, \varpi_{w_k+1}) \\[2mm] P_b(\xi_{z_k+1}, \xi_{z_k+2}),\ P_b(\varkappa_{z_k+1}, \varkappa_{z_k+2}),\ P_b(\varpi_{z_k+1}, \varpi_{z_k+2}) \\[2mm] \frac{P_b(\xi_{w_k}, \xi_{w_k+1}) \cdot P_b(\xi_{z_k+1}, \xi_{z_k+2})}{2\kappa^2 [1 + P_b(\xi_{w_k}, \xi_{z_k+1})]},\ \frac{P_b(\varkappa_{w_k}, \varkappa_{w_k+1}) \cdot P_b(\varkappa_{z_k+1}, \varkappa_{z_k+2})}{2\kappa^2 [1 + P_b(\varkappa_{w_k}, \varkappa_{z_k+1})]} \\[3mm] \frac{P_b(\varpi_{w_k}, \varpi_{w_k+1}) \cdot P_b(\varpi_{z_k+1}, \varpi_{z_k+2})}{2\kappa^2 [1 + P_b(\varpi_{w_k}, \varpi_{z_k+1})]} \end{array} \right\}.$$

Therefore, from Eq. (5.1.16), we have

$$P_b\left(\xi_{w_k+1}, \xi_{z_k+2}\right)$$

$$\leq \varphi\left(\lambda\max\left\{\begin{array}{c} P_b(\xi_{w_k},\xi_{z_k+1}), P_b(\varkappa_{w_k},\varkappa_{z_k+1}), P_b(\varpi_{w_k},\varpi_{z_k+1}) \\[4pt] P_b(\xi_{w_k},\xi_{w_k+1}), P_b(\varkappa_{w_k},\varkappa_{w_k+1}), P_b(\varpi_{w_k},\varpi_{w_k+1}) \\[4pt] P_b(\xi_{z_k+1},\xi_{z_k+2}), P_b(\varkappa_{z_k+1},\varkappa_{z_k+2}), P_b(\varpi_{z_k+1},\varpi_{z_k+2}) \\[4pt] \dfrac{P_b\big(\xi_{w_k},\xi_{w_k+1}\big).P_b\big(\xi_{z_k+1},\xi_{z_k+2}\big)}{2\kappa^2\big[1+P_b(\xi_{w_k},\xi_{z_k+1})\big]},\ \dfrac{P_b\big(\varkappa_{w_k},\varkappa_{w_k+1}\big).P_b\big(\varkappa_{z_k+1},\varkappa_{z_k+2}\big)}{2\kappa^2\big[1+P_b(\varkappa_{w_k},\varkappa_{z_k+1})\big]} \\[10pt] \dfrac{P_b\big(\varpi_{w_k},\varpi_{w_k+1}\big).P_b\big(\varpi_{z_k+1},\varpi_{z_k+2}\big)}{2\kappa^2\big[1+P_b(\varpi_{w_k},\varpi_{z_k+1})\big]} \end{array}\right\}\right)$$

$$< \lambda\max\left\{\begin{array}{c} P_b(\xi_{w_k},\xi_{z_k+1}), P_b(\varkappa_{w_k},\varkappa_{z_k+1}), P_b(\varpi_{w_k},\varpi_{z_k+1}) \\[4pt] P_b(\xi_{w_k},\xi_{w_k+1}), P_b(\varkappa_{w_k},\varkappa_{w_k+1}), P_b(\varpi_{w_k},\varpi_{w_k+1}) \\[4pt] P_b(\xi_{z_k+1},\xi_{z_k+2}), P_b(\varkappa_{z_k+1},\varkappa_{z_k+2}), P_b(\varpi_{z_k+1},\varpi_{z_k+2}) \\[4pt] \dfrac{P_b\big(\xi_{w_k},\xi_{w_k+1}\big).P_b\big(\xi_{z_k+1},\xi_{z_k+2}\big)}{2\kappa^2\big[1+P_b(\xi_{w_k},\xi_{z_k+1})\big]},\ \dfrac{P_b\big(\varkappa_{w_k},\varkappa_{w_k+1}\big).P_b\big(\varkappa_{z_k+1},\varkappa_{z_k+2}\big)}{2\kappa^2\big[1+P_b(\varkappa_{w_k},\varkappa_{z_k+1})\big]} \\[10pt] \dfrac{P_b\big(\varpi_{w_k},\varpi_{w_k+1}\big).P_b\big(\varpi_{z_k+1},\varpi_{z_k+2}\big)}{2\kappa^2\big[1+P_b(\varpi_{w_k},\varpi_{z_k+1})\big]} \end{array}\right\}.$$

Thus

$$\max\left\{\begin{array}{c} P_b\big(\xi_{w_k+1},\xi_{z_k+2}\big), \\[4pt] P_b\big(\varkappa_{w_k+1},\varkappa_{z_k+2}\big) \\[4pt] P_b\big(\varpi_{w_k+1},\varpi_{z_k+2}\big) \end{array}\right\} < \lambda\max\left\{\begin{array}{c} P_b(\xi_{w_k},\xi_{z_k+1}), P_b(\varkappa_{w_k},\varkappa_{z_k+1}), \\[4pt] P_b(\varpi_{w_k},\varpi_{z_k+1}), P_b(\xi_{w_k},\xi_{w_k+1}), \\[4pt] P_b(\varkappa_{w_k},\varkappa_{w_k+1}), P_b(\varpi_{w_k},\varpi_{w_k+1}) \\[4pt] P_b(\xi_{z_k+1},\xi_{z_k+2}), P_b(\varkappa_{z_k+1},\varkappa_{z_k+2}), \\[4pt] P_b(\varpi_{z_k+1},\varpi_{z_k+2}), \\[4pt] \dfrac{P_b\big(\xi_{w_k},\xi_{w_k+1}\big).P_b\big(\xi_{z_k+1},\xi_{z_k+2}\big)}{2\kappa^2\big[1+P_b(\xi_{w_k},\xi_{z_k+1})\big]}, \\[10pt] \dfrac{P_b\big(\varkappa_{w_k},\varkappa_{w_k+1}\big).P_b\big(\varkappa_{z_k+1},\varkappa_{z_k+2}\big)}{2\kappa^2\big[1+P_b(\varkappa_{w_k},\varkappa_{z_k+1})\big]}, \\[10pt] \dfrac{P_b\big(\varpi_{w_k},\varpi_{w_k+1}\big).P_b\big(\varpi_{z_k+1},\varpi_{z_k+2}\big)}{2\kappa^2\big[1+P_b(\varpi_{w_k},\varpi_{z_k+1})\big]} \end{array}\right\}.$$

Taking upper limit as $k \to \infty$ and from Eq. (5.1.7), Eq. (5.1.14) and Eq. (5.1.15) we have that

$$\epsilon.\kappa^3 \leq \lambda\epsilon\kappa^2$$

Sub Case (i): If $\kappa = 1$

$$\epsilon \leq \lambda.\epsilon < \epsilon,$$

is contradiction.

Sub Case (ii): If $\kappa > 1$

$$\epsilon.\kappa^3 \leq \lambda\epsilon\kappa^2.$$

It follows that $\kappa \leq \lambda < 1$, is contradiction. Hence, $\{\xi_z\}$, $\{\varkappa_z\}$ and $\{\varpi_z\}$ are Cauchy sequence in $(\Im, d_{P_b})$. Suppose $\int(\Im)$ is complete subspace of $\Im$, then $\{\int\ell_{z+1}\}$, $\{\int\wp_{z+1}\}$ and $\{\int\aleph_{z+1}\}$ are converges to ∂, $\mho$, $\eth$ in $(\int(\Im), d_{P_b})$,

thus $d_{P_b}(\int\ell_{z+1}, \partial) = 0, d_{P_b}(\int\wp_{z+1}, \mho) = 0, d_{P_b}(\int\aleph_{z+1}, \eth) = 0$ for some $\partial = \int\ell$, $\mho = \int\wp$ and $\eth = \int\aleph$.

we have that

$$P_b(\partial, \partial) = \lim_{z,w\to\infty} P_b(\int\ell_z, \int\ell_w) = \lim_{z\to\infty} P_b(\int\ell_z, \partial) = \lim_{z\to\infty} P_b(\int\ell_{z+1}, \partial) = 0.$$

$$(5.1.17)$$

and

$$P_b(\mho, \mho) = \lim_{z,w\to\infty} P_b(\int\wp_z, \int\wp_w) = \lim_{z\to\infty} P_b(\int\wp_z, \mho) = \lim_{z\to\infty} P_b(\int\wp_{z+1}, \mho) = 0.$$

$$(5.1.18)$$

also

$$P_b(\eth, \eth) = \lim_{z,w\to\infty} P_b(\int\aleph_z, \int\aleph_w) = \lim_{z\to\infty} P_b(\int\aleph_z, \eth) = \lim_{z\to\infty} P_b(\int\aleph_{z+1}, \eth) = 0.$$

$$(5.1.19)$$

Now, assume that $(\mathcal{T}, \int)$ is α-admissible mappings. Therefore, there is a sub sequence $\{\xi_{z_k}\}$, $\{\varkappa_{z_k}\}$ and $\{\varpi_{z_k}\}$ of $\{\xi_z\}$, $\{\varkappa_z\}$ and $\{\varpi_z\}$ respectively such that $\alpha\left(\ell_{z_k}, \wp_{z_k}, \aleph_{z_k+1}\right) \geq 1$ for all $k \in N$ and $\alpha(\int\ell, \int\wp, \int\aleph) \geq 1$.

Now we claim that $\mathcal{T}(\ell, \wp, \aleph) = \eth$, $\mathcal{T}(\wp, \aleph, \ell) = \mho$ and $\mathcal{T}(\aleph, \ell, \wp) = \eth$.

From Eq. (5.1.1), we have

$$P_b\left(\mathcal{T}(\ell, \wp, \aleph), \mathcal{T}(\ell_z, \wp_z, \aleph_z)\right) \leq \alpha\left(\int\ell, \int\wp, \int\aleph\right) P_b\left(\mathcal{T}(\ell, \wp, \aleph), \mathcal{T}(\ell_z, \wp_z, \aleph_z)\right)$$

$$\leq \varphi\left(\lambda K(\ell, \wp, \aleph, \ell_z, \wp_z, \aleph_z)\right)$$

$$< \lambda \max \left\{ \begin{array}{c} P_b(\int\ell, \int\ell_z), P_b(\int\wp, \int\wp_z), P_b(\int\aleph, \int\aleph_z), \\[2mm] P_b(\int\ell, \mathcal{T}(\ell, \wp, \aleph)), P_b(\int\wp, \mathcal{T}(\wp, \aleph, \ell)), \\[2mm] P_b(\int\aleph, \mathcal{T}(\aleph, \ell, \wp)), \\[2mm] P_b(\int\ell_z, \mathcal{T}(\ell_z, \wp_z, \aleph_z)), P_b(\int\wp_z, \mathcal{T}(\wp_z, \aleph_z, \ell_z)), \\[2mm] P_b(\int\aleph_z, \mathcal{T}(\aleph_z, \ell_z, \wp_z)), \\[2mm] \frac{P_b(\int\ell, \mathcal{T}(\ell, \wp, \aleph)) P_b(\int\ell_z, \mathcal{T}(\ell_z, \wp_z, \aleph_z))}{2\kappa^2 [1 + P_b(\int\ell, \int\ell_z)]}, \\[2mm] \frac{P_b(\int\wp, \mathcal{T}(\wp, \aleph, \ell)) P_b(\int\wp_z, \mathcal{T}(\wp_z, \aleph_z, \ell_z))}{2\kappa^2 [1 + P_b(\int\wp, \int\wp_z)]}, \\[2mm] \frac{P_b(\int\aleph, \mathcal{T}(\aleph, \ell, \wp)) P_b(\int\aleph_z, \mathcal{T}(\aleph_z, \ell_z, \wp_z))}{2\kappa^2 [1 + P_b(\int\aleph, \int\aleph_z)]}, \end{array} \right\}$$

$$< \lambda \max \left\{ \begin{array}{c} P_b(\eth, \int \ell_z), P_b(\mho, \int \wp_z), P_b(\eth, \int \aleph_z), \\[4pt] P_b(\eth, \mathcal{T}(\ell, \wp, \aleph)), P_b(\mho, \mathcal{T}(\wp, \aleph, \ell)), P_b(\eth, \mathcal{T}(\aleph, \ell, \wp)), \\[4pt] P_b(\int \ell_z, \mathcal{T}(\ell_z, \wp_z, \aleph_z)), P_b(\int \wp_z, \mathcal{T}(\wp_z, \aleph_z, \ell_z)), \\[4pt] P_b(\int \aleph_z, \mathcal{T}(\aleph_z, \ell_z, \wp_z)), \\[4pt] \frac{P_b(\eth, \mathcal{T}(\ell, \wp, \aleph)) P_b(\int \ell_z, \mathcal{T}(\ell_z, \wp_z, \aleph_z))}{2\kappa^2 [1 + P_b(\eth, \int \ell_z)]}, \\[4pt] \frac{P_b(\mho, \mathcal{T}(\wp, \aleph, \ell)) P_b(\int \wp_z, \mathcal{T}(\wp_z, \aleph_z, \ell_z))}{2\kappa^2 [1 + P_b(\mho, \int \wp_z)]}, \\[4pt] \frac{P_b(\eth, \mathcal{T}(\aleph, \ell, \wp)) P_b(\int \aleph_z, \mathcal{T}(\aleph_z, \ell_z, \wp_z))}{2\kappa^2 [1 + P_b(\eth, \int \aleph_z)]}, \end{array} \right\}.$$

Letting $z \to \infty$ in the above inequality, then we obtain that

$$P_b\left(\mathcal{T}(\ell, \wp, \aleph), \eth\right) < \lambda \max \left\{ \begin{array}{c} P_b(\eth, \mathcal{T}(\ell, \wp, \aleph)), P_b(\mho, \mathcal{T}(\wp, \aleph, \ell)), \\[4pt] P_b(\eth, \mathcal{T}(\aleph, \ell, \wp)) \end{array} \right\}.$$

Similarly, we can prove

$$P_b\left(\mathcal{T}(\wp, \aleph, \ell), \mho\right) < \lambda \max \left\{ \begin{array}{c} P_b(\eth, \mathcal{T}(\ell, \wp, \aleph)), P_b(\mho, \mathcal{T}(\wp, \aleph, \ell)), \\[4pt] P_b(\eth, \mathcal{T}(\aleph, \ell, \wp)) \end{array} \right\}$$

and

$$P_b\left(\mathcal{T}(\aleph, \ell, \wp), \eth\right) < \lambda \max \left\{ \begin{array}{c} P_b(\eth, \mathcal{T}(\ell, \wp, \aleph)), P_b(\mho, \mathcal{T}(\wp, \aleph, \ell)), \\[4pt] P_b(\eth, \mathcal{T}(\aleph, \ell, \wp)) \end{array} \right\}.$$

Therefore,

$$\max \left\{ \begin{array}{c} P_b(\mathcal{T}(\ell, \wp, \aleph), \partial), \\ P_b(\mathcal{T}(\wp, \aleph, \ell), \mho), \\ P_b(\mathcal{T}(\aleph, \ell, \wp), \eth) \end{array} \right\} < \lambda \max \left\{ \begin{array}{c} P_b(\partial, \mathcal{T}(\ell, \wp, \aleph)), \\ P_b(\mho, \mathcal{T}(\wp, \aleph, \ell)), \\ P_b(\eth, \mathcal{T}(\aleph, \ell, \wp)) \end{array} \right\}.$$

It follows that $\mathcal{T}(\ell, \wp, \aleph) = \partial = f\ell$, $\mathcal{T}(\wp, \aleph, \ell) = \mho = f\wp$ and $\mathcal{T}(\aleph, \ell, \wp) = \eth = f\aleph$.

Since $(\mathcal{T}, f)$ is weakly compatible pair, We have $\mathcal{T}(\partial, \mho, \eth) = f\partial$, $\mathcal{T}(\mho, \eth, \partial) = f\mho$ and $\mathcal{T}(\eth, \partial, \mho) = f\eth$.

From Eq. (5.1.1), we have that

$$P_b\left(\mathcal{T}(\partial, \mho, \eth), \mathcal{T}(\ell_z, \wp_z, \aleph_z)\right) \le \alpha\left(f\partial, f\mho, f\eth\right) P_b\left(\mathcal{T}(\partial, \mho, \eth), R(\ell_z, \wp_z, \aleph_z)\right)$$

$$\le \varphi\left(\lambda K(\partial, \mho, \eth, \ell_z, \wp_z, \aleph_z)\right)$$

$$< \lambda \max \left\{ \begin{array}{c} P_b(f\partial, f\ell_z), P_b(f\mho, f\wp_z), P_b(f\eth, f\aleph_z), \\[4pt] P_b(f\partial, \mathcal{T}(\partial, \mho, \eth)), P_b(f\mho, \mathcal{T}(\mho, \eth, \partial)), P_b(f\eth, \mathcal{T}(\eth, \partial, \mho)), \\[4pt] P_b(f\ell_z, \mathcal{T}(\ell_z, \wp_z, \aleph_z)), P_b(f\wp_z, \mathcal{T}(\wp_z, \aleph_z, \ell_z)), \\[4pt] P_b(f\aleph_z, \mathcal{T}(\aleph_z, \ell_z, \wp_z)), \\[4pt] \frac{P_b(f\partial, \mathcal{T}(\partial, \mho, \eth)) P_b(f\ell_z, \mathcal{T}(\ell_z, \wp_z, \aleph_z))}{2\kappa^2[1 + P_b(f\partial, f\ell_z)]}, \\[4pt] \frac{P_b(f\mho, \mathcal{T}(\mho, \eth, \partial)) P_b(f\wp_z, \mathcal{T}(\wp_z, \aleph_z, \ell_z))}{2\kappa^2[1 + P_b(f\mho, f\wp_z)]}, \\[4pt] \frac{P_b(f\eth, \mathcal{T}(\eth, \partial, \mho)) P_b(f\aleph_z, \mathcal{T}(\aleph_z, \ell_z, \wp_z))}{2\kappa^2[1 + P_b(f\eth, f\aleph_z)]}, \end{array} \right\}.$$

Letting $z \to \infty$, in the above inequality, we have that

$$P_b\left(\mathcal{T}(\partial, \mho, \eth), \partial\right) < \lambda \max \left\{ \begin{array}{c} P_b(\mathcal{T}(\partial, \mho, \eth), \partial), P_b(\mathcal{T}(\mho, \eth, \partial), \mho), \\[4pt] P_b(\mathcal{T}(\eth, \partial, \mho), \eth) \end{array} \right\}.$$

similarly, we can prove the remaining two conditions,

Therefore,

$$\max\left\{\begin{array}{c} P_b(\mathcal{T}(\eth,\mho,ð),\eth),\\[4pt] P_b(\mathcal{T}(\mho,ð,\eth),\mho),\\[4pt] P_b(\mathcal{T}(ð,\eth,\mho),ð) \end{array}\right\} < \lambda\max\left\{\begin{array}{c} P_b(\mathcal{T}(\eth,\mho,ð),\eth),\\[4pt] P_b(\mathcal{T}(\mho,ð,\eth),\mho),\\[4pt] P_b(\mathcal{T}(ð,\eth,\mho),ð) \end{array}\right\}.$$

It follows $\mathcal{T}(\eth,\mho,ð) = \eth = \int\eth$, $\mathcal{T}(\mho,ð,\eth) = \mho = \int\mho$ and $\mathcal{T}(ð,\eth,\mho) = ð = \int ð$. Therefore $(\eth,\mho,ð)$ is CTFP of $\mathcal{T}$ and $\int$ for uniqueness let us suppose $(\eth^*,\mho^*,ð^*)$ be another CTFP of $\mathcal{T}$ and $\int$ such that $\eth \neq \eth^*$, $\mho \neq \mho^*$ and $ð \neq ð^*$.

Now from Eq. (5.1.1), we have that

$$
\begin{aligned}
P_b(\eth,\eth^*) &= P_b\left(\mathcal{T}(\eth,\mho,ð),\mathcal{T}(\eth^*,\mho^*,ð^*)\right)\\[6pt]
&\leq \alpha\left(\int\eth,\int\mho,\int ð\right) P_b\left(\mathcal{T}(\eth,\mho,ð),\mathcal{T}(\eth^*,\mho^*,ð^*)\right)\\[6pt]
&\leq \varphi\left(\lambda K(\eth,\mho,ð,\eth^*,\mho^*,ð^*)\right)
\end{aligned}
$$

$$
< \lambda\max\left\{\begin{array}{c}
P_b(\int\eth,\int\eth^*), P_b(\int\mho,\int\mho^*), P_b(\int ð,\int ð^*),\\[6pt]
P_b(\int\eth,\mathcal{T}(\eth,\mho,ð)), P_b(\int\mho,\mathcal{T}(\mho,ð,\eth)),\\[6pt]
P_b(\int ð,\mathcal{T}(ð,\eth,\mho)),\\[6pt]
P_b(\int\eth^*,\mathcal{T}(\eth^*,\mho^*,ð^*)), P_b(\int\mho^*,\mathcal{T}(\mho^*,ð^*,\eth^*)),\\[6pt]
P_b(\int ð^*,\mathcal{T}(ð^*,\eth^*,\mho^*)),\\[6pt]
\dfrac{P_b(\int\eth,\mathcal{T}(\eth,\mho,ð))\,P_b(\int\eth^*,\mathcal{T}(\eth^*,\mho^*,ð^*))}{2\kappa^2[1+P_b(\int\eth,\int\eth^*)]},\\[6pt]
\dfrac{P_b(\int\mho,\mathcal{T}(\mho,ð,\eth))\,P_b(\int\mho^*,\mathcal{T}(\mho^*,ð^*,\eth^*))}{2\kappa^2[1+P_b(\int\mho,\int\mho^*)]},\\[6pt]
\dfrac{P_b(\int ð,\mathcal{T}(ð,\eth,\mho))\,P_b(\int ð^*,\mathcal{T}(ð^*,\eth^*,\mho^*))}{2\kappa^2[1+P_b(\int ð,\int ð^*)]},
\end{array}\right\}
$$

$$
< \lambda\max\left\{ P_b(\eth,\eth^*), P_b(\mho,\mho^*), P_b(ð,ð^*), \right\}.
$$

Therefore,

$$\max\left\{P_b(\partial,\partial^*),P_b(\mho,\mho^*),P_b(\eth,\eth^*)\right\} \;<\; \lambda\max\left\{\begin{array}{l} P_b(\partial,\partial^*),\\[4pt] P_b(\mho,\mho^*),\\[4pt] P_b(\eth,\eth^*) \end{array}\right\}.$$

It is a contradiction.

Hence $(\partial,\mho,\eth)$ is UCTFP of $\mathcal{T}$ and $\smallint$. $\qquad\square$

Example 5.1. Let $\Im = [0,1]$ and $\mathcal{T} : \Im^3 \to \Im$ be as $\mathcal{T}(\ell,\wp,\aleph) = \frac{\ell^2+\wp^2+\aleph^2}{16(\ell+\wp+\aleph+1)}$ and $\smallint : \Im \to \Im$ by $\smallint(\ell) = \frac{\ell}{4}$, define $\varphi : [0,\infty) \to [0,\infty)$ as $\varphi(t) = \frac{2t}{5}$ and

$$\alpha : \Im^3 \to R^+ \text{ as } \alpha(\ell,\wp,\aleph) = \left\{\begin{array}{ll} 1 & \text{for} \quad (\ell,\wp,\aleph) \in [0,1]\\[6pt] 0 & \text{for} \quad \text{otherwise} \end{array}\right.,$$

$P_b : \Im^2 \to [0,\infty)$ such that $P_b(\ell;\wp) = [\max\{\ell,\wp\}]^2 + |\ell-\wp|^2$, for all $\ell,\wp \in \Im$ is a complete PbMS on $\Im$. We show that $\mathcal{T},\smallint$ are α-admissible mappings.

Let for $\ell,\wp,\aleph \in \Im$, $\alpha\left(\smallint\ell,\smallint\wp,\smallint\aleph\right) \geq 1$. On the other hand, for all $\ell,\wp,\aleph \in [0,1]$ then $\mathcal{T}(\ell,\wp,\aleph) \leq 1$.

It follows that $\alpha\left(\mathcal{T}(\ell,\wp,\aleph),\mathcal{T}(\wp,\aleph,\ell),\mathcal{T}(\aleph,\ell,\wp)\right) \geq 1.$ Therefore, the predication holds. In support of the above argument $\alpha(\smallint 0,\smallint 0,\smallint 0) > 1.$ Now, if $\{\ell_z\}$, $\{\wp_z\}$ and $\{\aleph_z\}$ are a sequence in $\Im$ such that $\alpha(\smallint\ell_z,\smallint\wp_z,\smallint\aleph_z) > 1$ and

$\ell_z \to \ell, \wp_z \to \wp, \aleph_z \to \aleph \in \Im$ for all $z \in N \cup \{0\}$, then $\ell_z,\wp_z,\aleph_z \subseteq [0,1]$ and hence $\ell,\wp,\aleph \in [0,1]$ which implies $\alpha(\smallint\ell,\smallint\wp,\smallint\aleph) \geq 1$. Let $\ell,\wp,\aleph \in [0,1]$. Then

$$\begin{aligned} &P_b(\mathcal{T}(\ell,\wp,\aleph),\mathcal{T}(\partial,\mho,\eth))\\[6pt] &= \left[\max\left\{\frac{\ell^2+\wp^2+\aleph^2}{16(\ell+\wp+\aleph+1)},\frac{\partial^2+\mho^2+\eth^2}{16(\partial+\mho+\eth+1)}\right\}\right]^2\\[6pt] &\quad + \left|\frac{\ell^2+\wp^2+\aleph^2}{16(\ell+\wp+\aleph+1)} - \frac{\partial^2+\mho^2+\eth^2}{16(\partial+\mho+\eth+1)}\right|^2 \end{aligned}$$

$$
= \frac{1}{256}\left\{ \left[\max\left\{ \begin{array}{c} \frac{\ell^2}{\ell+\wp+\aleph+1}, \\ \frac{\partial^2}{\partial+\mho+\eth+1} \end{array} \right\} + \max\left\{ \begin{array}{c} \frac{\wp^2}{\ell+\wp+\aleph+1}, \\ \frac{\mho^2}{\partial+\mho+\eth+1} \end{array} \right\} + \max\left\{ \begin{array}{c} \frac{\aleph^2}{\ell+\wp+\aleph+1}, \\ \frac{\eth^2}{\partial+\mho+\eth+1} \end{array} \right\} \right]^2 \right.
$$

$$
\left. + \left| \frac{\ell^2}{(\ell+\wp+\aleph+1)} - \frac{\partial^2}{(\partial+\mho+\eth+1)} \right|^2 + \left| \frac{\wp^2}{(\ell+\wp+\aleph+1)} - \frac{\mho^2}{(\partial+\mho+\eth+1)} \right|^2 \right.
$$

$$
\left. + \left| \frac{\aleph^2}{(\ell+\wp+\aleph+1)} - \frac{\eth^2}{(\partial+\mho+\eth+1)} \right|^2 \right\}
$$

$$
\leq \frac{1}{256}\left\{ \left[\max\left\{ \frac{\ell^2}{\ell+1}, \frac{\partial^2}{\partial+1} \right\} + \max\left\{ \frac{\wp^2}{\wp+1}, \frac{\mho^2}{\mho+1} \right\} + \max\left\{ \frac{\aleph^2}{\aleph+1}, \frac{\eth^2}{\eth+1} \right\} \right]^2 \right.
$$

$$
\left. + \left| \frac{\ell^2}{(\ell+1)} - \frac{\partial^2}{(\partial+1)} \right|^2 + \left| \frac{\wp^2}{(\wp+1)} - \frac{\mho^2}{(\mho+1)} \right|^2 + \left| \frac{\aleph^2}{(\aleph+1)} - \frac{\eth^2}{(\eth+1)} \right|^2 \right\}
$$

$$
\leq \frac{1}{256}\left\{ \begin{array}{c} \left[\max\left\{ \frac{\ell}{\ell+1}, \frac{\partial}{\partial+1} \right\}\right]^2 + \left| \frac{\ell}{(\ell+1)} - \frac{\partial}{(\partial+1)} \right|^2 \\[4pt] + \left[\max\left\{ \frac{\wp}{\wp+1}, \frac{\mho}{\mho+1} \right\}\right]^2 + \left| \frac{\wp}{(\wp+1)} - \frac{\mho}{(\mho+1)} \right|^2 \\[4pt] + \left[\max\left\{ \frac{\aleph}{\aleph+1}, \frac{\eth}{\eth+1} \right\}\right]^2 + \left| \frac{\aleph}{(\aleph+1)} - \frac{\eth}{(\eth+1)} \right|^2 \end{array} \right\}
$$

$$
\leq \frac{1}{16}\left\{ \begin{array}{c} \left[\max\left\{ \frac{\ell}{4}, \frac{\partial}{4} \right\}\right]^2 + \left| \frac{\ell}{4} - \frac{\partial}{4} \right|^2 \\[4pt] + \left[\max\left\{ \frac{\wp}{4}, \frac{\mho}{4} \right\}\right]^2 + \left| \frac{\wp}{4} - \frac{\mho}{4} \right|^2 \\[4pt] + \left[\max\left\{ \frac{\aleph}{4}, \frac{\eth}{4} \right\}\right]^2 + \left| \frac{\aleph}{4} - \frac{\eth}{4} \right|^2 \end{array} \right\}
$$

$$
= \frac{1}{16}\left[P_b(\smallint\ell, \smallint\partial) + P_b(\smallint\wp, \smallint\mho) + P_b(\smallint\aleph, \smallint\eth) \right]
$$

$$
\leq \frac{2}{5}\left(\frac{1}{2}\max\left\{ P_b(\smallint\ell, \smallint\partial), P_b(\smallint\wp, \smallint\mho), P_b(\smallint\aleph, \smallint\eth) \right\} \right)
$$

$$
\leq \varphi\left(\lambda K(\ell, \wp, \aleph, \partial, \mho, \eth) \right).
$$

Hence all conditions of Theorem (5.1.1) are holds and $(0,0,0)$ is UCTFP of $\mathcal{T}$ and $\smallint$.

5.2 Application to Integral Equations

As an application to Theorem 5.1.1, we examine the presence of a unique solution to an IVP in this section.

Theorem 5.2.1. Consider the IVP

$$\ell'(t) = \Gamma(\delta, \ell(\delta), \ell(\delta), \ell(\delta)), \quad \delta \in I = [0,1], \quad \ell(0) = \ell_0 \tag{5.2.1}$$

where $\Gamma : I \times \left[\frac{\ell_0}{2\kappa^2}, \infty\right)^3 \to \left[\frac{\ell_0}{2\kappa^2}, \infty\right)$ and $\ell_0 \in \mathbb{R}$ and

$$\int_0^\delta \Gamma(\tau, \ell(\tau), \wp(\tau), \aleph(\tau))d\tau \leq \max \left\{ \begin{array}{l} \frac{1}{8}\int_0^\delta \Gamma(\tau, \ell(\tau), \ell(\tau), \ell(\tau))d\tau - \frac{7\ell_0}{16\kappa^2}, \\[2mm] \frac{1}{8}\int_0^\delta \Gamma(\tau, \wp(\tau), \wp(\tau), \wp(\tau))d\tau - \frac{7\ell_0}{16\kappa^2}, \\[2mm] \frac{1}{8}\int_0^\delta \Gamma(\tau, \aleph(\tau), \aleph(\tau), \aleph(\tau))d\tau - \frac{7\ell_0}{16\kappa^2}, \end{array} \right\}.$$

Define $\varphi : [0, \infty) \to [0, \infty)$ as $\varphi(t) = \frac{t}{2}$ and consider the following conditions:

(a) If there exist a function $\eta : \left[\frac{\ell_0}{2\kappa^2}, \infty\right)^3 \to R^+$ such that there is an

$\ell_1 \in C\left(I, \left[\frac{\ell_0}{2\kappa^2}, \infty\right)\right)$, for all $\delta \in I$, we have:

$$\eta\left(\ell_1(\delta), \ell_1(\delta), \int_0^\delta \Gamma(\tau, \ell_1(\tau), \ell_1(\tau), \ell_1(\tau))d\tau\right) \geq 0,$$

(b) For all $\delta \in I$ and for all $\ell, \wp, \aleph \in C\left(I, \left[\frac{\ell_0}{2\kappa^2}, \infty\right)\right)$,

$$\eta(\ell(\delta), \wp(\delta), \aleph(\delta)) \geq 0 \Rightarrow \eta(A, B, C) \geq 0$$

where, $A = \frac{\ell_0}{\kappa^2} + \int_0^\delta \Gamma(\tau, \ell(\tau), \ell(\tau), \ell(\tau))d\tau$, $B = \frac{\wp_0}{\kappa^2} + \int_0^\delta \Gamma(\tau, \wp(\tau), \wp(\tau), \wp(\tau))d\tau$

and $C = \frac{\aleph_0}{\kappa^2} + \int_0^\delta \Gamma(\tau, \aleph(\tau), \aleph(\tau), \aleph(\tau))d\tau$;

(c) For any point ℓ of a sequence $\{\ell_z\}$ of points in $C\left(I, \left[\frac{\ell_0}{2\kappa^2}, \infty\right)\right)$ with

$\eta(\ell_z, \ell_z, \ell_{z+1}) \geq 0, \ \lim\inf\limits_{z \to \infty} \eta(\ell_z, \ell_z, \ell) \geq 0.$

Then, equation 5.2.1 has a unique solution in $C\left(I, \left[\frac{\ell_0}{2\kappa^2}, \infty\right)\right)$.

5.3   Application to Homotopy

In this section, we study the existence of a unique solution to Homotopy theory.

Theorem 5.3.1. Let $(\Im, P_b)$ be a complete PbMS, $\overline{U}$ be closed subset of $\Im$ such that $U \subseteq \overline{U}$. Suppose $H : \overline{U}^3 \times [0,1] \to \Im$ be an operator such that the following conditions are satisfying,

(i) $\wp \neq H(\wp, \varkappa, \varpi, \lambda)$ $\varkappa \neq H(\varkappa, \varpi, \wp, \lambda)$, & $\varpi \neq H(\varpi, \wp, \varkappa, \lambda)$ for each $\wp, \varkappa, \varpi \in \partial U$ and $\lambda \in [0,1]$, (here ∂U denotes the boundary of U in $\Im$),

(ii) $\kappa P_b(H(\wp, \varkappa, \varpi, \lambda), H(\imath, \jmath, \eta, \lambda)) \leq \varphi \left(\delta \max \left\{ \ P_b(\wp, \imath), P_b(\varkappa, \jmath), P_b(\varpi, \eta) \ \right\} \right)$

where, $\varphi \in \Delta$, $\delta \in [0, \frac{1}{2\kappa^2})$

(iii) there exists $M \geq 0$ such that

$$P_b(H(\wp, \varkappa, \varpi, \lambda), H(\wp, \varkappa, \varpi, \mu)) \leq M|\lambda - \mu|$$

for every $\wp, \varkappa, \varpi \in \overline{U}$ and $\lambda, \mu \in [0,1]$.

Then $H(.,0)$ has a TFP if and only if $H(.,1)$ has a TFP.

Proof. Consider the set

$$A = \left\{ \begin{array}{l} \lambda \in [0,1] : \wp = H(\wp, \varkappa, \varpi, \lambda), \varkappa = H(\varkappa, \varpi, \wp, \lambda), \text{ and} \\[2mm] \varpi = H(\varpi, \wp, \varkappa, \lambda) \text{ for some } \wp, \varkappa, \varpi \in U \end{array} \right\}.$$

We have that $0 \in A$ since $H(.,0)$ has a TFP in U. so that the set A is not empty. We shall demonstrate that A is open and closed in $[0,1]$. As a result, $A = [0,1]$ according to the connectedness principle. TFP for $H(.,1)$ is thus in U. We first demonstrate the closure of A in $[0,1]$.

To see this let $\{\lambda_z\}_{z=1}^{\infty} \subseteq A$ with $\lambda_z \to \lambda \in [0,1]$ as $z \to \infty$.

To prove that $\lambda \in A$, we must.

Since $\lambda_z \in A$ for $n = 1, 2, 3, \cdots$, there exist $\wp_z, \varkappa_z, \varpi_z \in U$ with

$$\wp_z = H(\wp_z, \varkappa_z, \varpi_z, \lambda_z), \ \varkappa_z = H(\varkappa_z, \varpi_z, \wp_z, \lambda_z) \text{ and } \varpi_z = H(\varpi_z, \wp_z, \varkappa_z, \lambda_z).$$

Consider

$$
\begin{aligned}
P_b(\wp_z, \wp_{z+1}) \ &= P_b(H(\wp_z, \varkappa_z, \varpi_z, \lambda_z), H(\wp_{z+1}, \varkappa_{z+1}, \varpi_{z+1}, \lambda_{z+1})) \\[2mm]
&\leq \kappa \left\{
\begin{array}{l}
P_b(H(\wp_z, \varkappa_z, \varpi_z, \lambda_z), H(\wp_{z+1}, \varkappa_{z+1}, \varpi_{z+1}\lambda_z)) \\[2mm]
+ P_b(H(\wp_{z+1}, \varkappa_{z+1}, \varpi_{z+1}, \lambda_z), H(\wp_{z+1}, \varkappa_{z+1}, \varpi_{z+1}, \lambda_{z+1})) \\[2mm]
- P_b(H(\wp_{z+1}, \varkappa_{z+1}, \varpi_{z+1}, \lambda_z), H(\wp_{z+1}, \varkappa_{z+1}, \varpi_{z+1}, \lambda_z))
\end{array}
\right\} \\[2mm]
&\leq \kappa P_b(H(\wp_z, \varkappa_z, \varpi_z, \lambda_z), H(\wp_{z+1}, \varkappa_{z+1}, \varpi_{z+1}, \lambda_z)) + \kappa M |\lambda_z - \lambda_{z+1}|.
\end{aligned}
$$

Letting $z \to \infty$, we get

$$\lim_{z \to \infty} P_b(\wp_z, \wp_{z+1}) \leq \lim_{z \to \infty} \kappa P_b(H(\wp_z, \varkappa_z, \varpi_z, \lambda_z), H(\wp_{z+1}, \varkappa_{z+1}, \varpi_{z+1}, \lambda_z)) + 0.$$

From condition (ii) we obtain

$$
\begin{aligned}
\lim_{z \to \infty} P_b(\wp_z, \wp_{z+1}) \ &\leq \lim_{z \to \infty} \kappa P_b(H(\wp_z, \varkappa_z, \varpi_z, \lambda_z), H(\wp_{z+1}, \varkappa_{z+1}, \varpi_{z+1}\lambda_z))) \\[2mm]
&\leq \lim_{z \to \infty} \varphi\left(\delta \max\{P_b(\wp_z, \wp_{z+1}), P_b(\varkappa_z, \varkappa_{z+1}), P_b(\varpi_z, \varpi_{z+1})\}\right).
\end{aligned}
$$

Similarly

$$\lim_{z \to \infty} P_b(\varkappa_z, \varkappa_{z+1}) \ \leq \lim_{z \to \infty} \varphi\left(\delta \max\{P_b(\wp_z, \wp_{z+1}), P_b(\varkappa_z, \varkappa_{z+1}), P_b(\varpi_z, \varpi_{z+1})\}\right)$$

and

$$\lim_{z \to \infty} P_b(\varpi_z, z_{z+1}) \ \leq \lim_{z \to \infty} \varphi\left(\delta \max\{P_b(\wp_z, \wp_{z+1}), P_b(\varkappa_z, \varkappa_{z+1}), P_b(\varpi_z, \varpi_{z+1})\}\right).$$

Therefore,

$$\lim_{z\to\infty} \max \left\{ \begin{array}{c} P_b(\wp_z, \wp_{z+1}) \\ P_b(\varkappa_z, \varkappa_{z+1}) \\ P_b(\varpi_z, z_{z+1}) \end{array} \right\} \leq \lim_{z\to\infty} \varphi \left(\delta \max \left\{ \begin{array}{c} P_b(\wp_z, \wp_{z+1}) \\ P_b(\varkappa_z, \varkappa_{z+1}) \\ P_b(\varpi_z, z_{z+1}) \end{array} \right\} \right)$$

$$< \lim_{z\to\infty} \delta \max \left\{ \begin{array}{c} P_b(\wp_z, \wp_{z+1}) \\ P_b(\varkappa_z, \varkappa_{z+1}) \\ P_b(\varpi_z, z_{z+1}) \end{array} \right\}.$$

It follows that

$$\lim_{z\to\infty} P_b(\wp_z, \wp_{z+1}) = 0 = \lim_{z\to\infty} P_b(\varkappa_z, \varkappa_{z+1}) = 0 = \lim_{z\to\infty} P_b(\varpi_z, \varpi_{z+1}). \tag{5.3.1}$$

From def. $(1.5.1)$ of (P_b2),

$$\lim_{z\to\infty} p(\wp_z, \wp_z) = 0 = \lim_{z\to\infty} p(\varkappa_z, \varkappa_z) = 0 = \lim_{z\to\infty} p(\varpi_z, \varpi_z). \tag{5.3.2}$$

By definition $(1.5.3)$ of d_{P_b}, we obtain

$$\lim_{z\to\infty} d_{p_b}(\wp_z, \wp_{z+1}) = 0 = \lim_{z\to\infty} d_{p_b}(\varkappa_z, \varkappa_{z+1}) = 0 = \lim_{z\to\infty} d_{p_b}(\varpi_z, \varpi_{z+1}). \tag{5.3.3}$$

Now we prove that $\{\wp_z\}$, $\{\varkappa_z\}$ and $\{\varpi_z\}$ are CS in $(\Im, d_{p_b})$.

On contrary suppose that $\{\wp_z\}$ or $\{\varkappa_z\}$ or $\{\varpi_z\}$ is not Cauchy.

There exists an $\epsilon > 0$ and monotone increasing sequence of natural numbers $\{w_k\}$ and $\{z_k\}$ such that $z_k > w_k$,

$$\max\{d_{p_b}(\wp_{w_k}, \wp_{z_k}), d_{p_b}(\varkappa_{w_k}, \varkappa_{z_k}), d_{p_b}(\varpi_{w_k}, \varpi_{z_k})\} \geq \epsilon \tag{5.3.4}$$

and

$$\max\{d_{p_b}(\wp_{w_k}, \wp_{z_k-1}), d_{p_b}(\varkappa_{w_k}, \varkappa_{z_k-1}), d_{p_b}(\varpi_{w_k}, \varpi_{z_k-1})\} < \epsilon. \tag{5.3.5}$$

From Eq. (5.3.4) and Eq. (5.3.5), we obtain

$$
\begin{aligned}
\epsilon \ &\leq \max\{d_{p_b}(\wp_{w_k}, \wp_{z_k}), d_{p_b}(\varkappa_{w_k}, \varkappa_{z_k}), d_{p_b}(\varpi_{w_k}, \varpi_{z_k})\} \\
&\leq \kappa \max\{d_{p_b}(\wp_{w_k}, \wp_{z_k-1}), d_{p_b}(\varkappa_{w_k}, \varkappa_{z_k-1}), d_{p_b}(\varpi_{w_k}, \varpi_{z_k-1})\} \\
&\quad +\kappa \max\{d_{p_b}(\wp_{z_k-1}, \wp_{z_k}), d_{p_b}(\varkappa_{z_k-1}, \varkappa_{z_k}), d_{p_b}(\varpi_{z_k-1}, \varpi_{z_k})\} \\
&< \kappa\epsilon + \kappa \max\{d_{p_b}(\wp_{z_k-1}, \wp_{z_k}), d_{p_b}(\varkappa_{z_k-1}, \varkappa_{z_k}), d_{p_b}(\varpi_{z_k-1}, \varpi_{z_k})\}.
\end{aligned}
$$

Taking upper limit as $k \to \infty$ and from Eq. (5.3.1) , we have that

$$\epsilon \leq \limsup_{k \to \infty} \max\{d_{P_b}(\wp_{w_k}, \wp_{z_k}), d_{P_b}(\varkappa_{w_k}, \varkappa_{z_k}), d_{P_b}(\varpi_{w_k}, \varpi_{z_k})\} \leq k\epsilon. \tag{5.3.6}$$

Also

$$
\begin{aligned}
\epsilon \ &\leq \ \max\{d_{P_b}(\wp_{w_k}, \wp_{z_k}), d_{P_b}(\varkappa_{w_k}, \varkappa_{z_k}), d_{P_b}(\varpi_{w_k}, \varpi_{z_k})\} \\
&\leq \ \kappa.\max\{d_{P_b}(\wp_{z_k}, \wp_{w_k+1}), d_{P_b}(\varkappa_{z_k}, \varkappa_{w_k+1}), d_{P_b}(\varpi_{z_k}, \varpi_{w_k+1})\} \\
&\quad +\kappa.\max\{d_{P_b}(\wp_{w_k+1}, \wp_{w_k}), d_{P_b}(\varkappa_{w_k+1}, \varkappa_{w_k}), d_{P_b}(\varpi_{w_k+1}, \varpi_{w_k})\}.
\end{aligned}
$$

Taking upper limit as $k \to \infty$ and from Eq. (5.3.3) , we have that

$$\frac{\epsilon}{\kappa} \leq \limsup_{k \to \infty} \max\{d_{P_b}(\wp_{z_k}, \wp_{w_k+1}), d_{P_b}(\varkappa_{z_k}, \varkappa_{w_k+1}), d_{P_b}(\varpi_{z_k}, \varpi_{w_k+1})\}. \tag{5.3.7}$$

On other hand

$$\max\{d_{P_b}(\wp_{z_k}, \wp_{w_k+1}), d_{P_b}(\varkappa_{z_k}, \varkappa_{w_k+1}), d_{P_b}(\varpi_{z_k}, \varpi_{w_k+1})\}$$

$$\leq \ \kappa.\max\left\{d_{P_b}(\wp_{z_k},\wp_{w_k}),d_{P_b}(\varkappa_{z_k+1},\varkappa_{w_k}),d_{P_b}(\varpi_{z_k+1},\varpi_{w_k})\right\}$$

$$+\kappa.\max\left\{d_{P_b}(\wp_{w_k},\wp_{w_k+1}),d_{P_b}(\varkappa_{w_k},\varkappa_{w_k+1}),d_{P_b}(\varpi_{w_k},\varpi_{w_k+1})\right\}.$$

Taking upper limit as $k \to \infty$ and from Eq. $(5.3.3)$, we have that

$$\limsup_{k\to\infty}\max\left\{d_{P_b}(\wp_{z_k},\wp_{w_k+1}),d_{P_b}(\varkappa_{z_k},\varkappa_{w_k+1}),d_{P_b}(\varpi_{z_k},\varpi_{w_k+1})\right\}\leq \epsilon\kappa^2 \qquad (5.3.8)$$

also, from Eq. $(5.3.4)$, we have that

$$\epsilon \ \leq \ \max\left\{d_{P_b}(\wp_{w_k},\wp_{z_k}),d_{P_b}(\varkappa_{w_k},\varkappa_{z_k}),d_{P_b}(\varpi_{w_k},\varpi_{z_k})\right\}$$

$$\leq \ \kappa.\max\left\{d_{P_b}(\wp_{z_k},\wp_{z_k+1}),d_{P_b}(\varkappa_{z_k},\varkappa_{z_k+1}),d_{P_b}(\varpi_{z_k},\varpi_{z_k+1})\right\}$$

$$+\kappa.\max\left\{d_{P_b}(\wp_{w_k+1},\wp_{w_k}),d_{P_b}(\varkappa_{w_k+1},\varkappa_{w_k}),d_{P_b}(\varpi_{w_k+1},\varpi_{w_k})\right\}$$

$$\leq \left\{\begin{array}{l} \kappa.\max\left\{d_{P_b}(\wp_{z_k},\wp_{z_k+1}),d_{P_b}(\varkappa_{z_k},\varkappa_{z_k+1}),d_{P_b}(\varpi_{z_k},\varpi_{z_k+1})\right\} \\[4pt] +\kappa^2.\max\left\{d_{P_b}(\wp_{z_k+1},\wp_{w_k+2}),d_{P_b}(\varkappa_{z_k+1},\varkappa_{w_k+2}),d_{P_b}(\varpi_{z_k+1},\varpi_{w_k+2})\right\} \\[4pt] +\kappa^2.\max\left\{d_{P_b}(\wp_{w_k+2},\wp_{w_k}),d_{P_b}(\varkappa_{w_k+2},\varkappa_{w_k}),d_{P_b}(\varpi_{w_k+2},\varpi_{w_k})\right\} \end{array}\right\}$$

$$\leq \left\{\begin{array}{l} \kappa.\max\left\{d_{P_b}(\wp_{z_k},\wp_{z_k+1}),d_{P_b}(\varkappa_{z_k},\varkappa_{z_k+1}),d_{P_b}(\varpi_{z_k},\varpi_{z_k+1})\right\} \\[4pt] +\kappa^2.\max\left\{d_{P_b}(\wp_{w_k+1},\wp_{w_k+2}),d_{P_b}(\varkappa_{w_k+1},\varkappa_{w_k+2}),d_{P_b}(\varpi_{w_k+1},\varpi_{w_k+2})\right\} \\[4pt] +\kappa^3.\max\left\{d_{P_b}(\wp_{w_k+2},\wp_{w_k+1}),d_{P_b}(\varkappa_{w_k+2},\varkappa_{w_k+1}),d_{P_b}(\varpi_{w_k+2},\varpi_{w_k+1})\right\} \\[4pt] +\kappa^3.\max\left\{d_{P_b}(\wp_{w_k+1},\wp_{w_k}),d_{P_b}(\varkappa_{w_k+1},\varkappa_{w_k}),d_{P_b}(\varpi_{w_k+1},\varpi_{w_k})\right\} \end{array}\right\}.$$

Taking upper limit as $k \to \infty$ and from Eq. $(5.3.3)$, we have that

$$\frac{\epsilon}{\kappa^3} \leq \limsup_{k\to\infty}\max\left\{d_{P_b}(\wp_{z_k+1},\wp_{w_k+2}),d_{P_b}(\varkappa_{z_k+1},\varkappa_{w_k+2}),d_{P_b}(\varpi_{z_k+1},\varpi_{w_k+2})\right\}.$$

On other hand

$$\max\left\{d_{P_b}(\wp_{z_k+1},\wp_{w_k+2}),d_{P_b}(\varkappa_{z_k+1},\varkappa_{w_k+2}),d_{P_b}(\varpi_{z_k+1},\varpi_{w_k+2})\right\}$$

$$\leq\ \kappa.\max\left\{d_{P_b}(\wp_{z_k+1},\wp_{z_k}),d_{P_b}(\varkappa_{z_k+1},\varkappa_{z_k}),d_{P_b}(\varpi_{z_k+1},\varpi_{z_k})\right\}$$

$$+\kappa.\max\left\{d_{P_b}(\wp_{z_k},\wp_{w_k+2}),d_{P_b}(\varkappa_{z_k},\varkappa_{w_k+2}),d_{P_b}(\varpi_{z_k},\varpi_{w_k+2})\right\}$$

$$\leq\left\{\begin{array}{c}\kappa.\max\left\{d_{P_b}(\wp_{z_k+1},\wp_{z_k}),d_{P_b}(\varkappa_{z_k+1},\varkappa_{z_k}),d_{P_b}(\varpi_{z_k+1},\varpi_{z_k})\right\}\\[4pt]+\kappa^2.\max\left\{d_{P_b}(\wp_{z_k},\wp_{w_k}),d_{P_b}(\varkappa_{z_k},\varkappa_{w_k}),d_{P_b}(\varpi_{z_k},\varpi_{w_k})\right\}\\[4pt]+\kappa^3.\max\left\{d_{P_b}(\wp_{w_k},\wp_{w_k+1}),d_{P_b}(\varkappa_{w_k},\varkappa_{w_k+1}),d_{P_b}(\varpi_{w_k},\varpi_{w_k+1})\right\}\\[4pt]+\kappa^3.\max\left\{d_{P_b}(\wp_{w_k+1},\wp_{w_k+2}),d_{P_b}(\varkappa_{w_k+1},\varkappa_{w_k+2}),d_{P_b}(\varpi_{w_k+1},\varpi_{w_k+2})\right\}\end{array}\right\}.$$

Taking upper limit as $k\to\infty$ and from Eq. (5.3.3), Eq. (5.3.6) we have that

$$\limsup_{k\to\infty}\max\left\{d_{P_b}(\wp_{z_k+1},\wp_{w_k+2}),d_{P_b}(\varkappa_{z_k+1},\varkappa_{w_k+2}),d_{P_b}(\varpi_{z_k+1},\varpi_{w_k+2})\right\}\leq\epsilon.\kappa^3.$$

$$(5.3.9)$$

Now

$$P_b\left(\wp_{z_k+1},\wp_{w_k+2}\right)$$

$$=\ P_b\left(H(\wp_{z_k+1},\varkappa_{z_k+1},\varpi_{z_k+1},\lambda_{z_k+1}),H(\wp_{w_k+2},\varkappa_{w_k+2},\varpi_{w_k+2},\lambda_{w_k+2})\right)$$

$$\leq\ \kappa\left\{\begin{array}{c}P_b(H(\wp_{z_k+1},\varkappa_{z_k+1},\varpi_{z_k+1},\lambda_{z_k+1}),H(\wp_{z_k+1},\varkappa_{z_k+1},\varpi_{z_k+1},\lambda_{w_k+2}))\\[4pt]+P_b(H(\wp_{z_k+1},\varkappa_{z_k+1},\varpi_{z_k+1},\lambda_{w_k+2}),H(\wp_{w_k+2},\varkappa_{w_k+2},z_{w_k+2},\lambda_{w_k+2}))\\[4pt]-P_b(H(\wp_{z_k+1},\varkappa_{z_k+1},\varpi_{z_k+1},\lambda_{w_k+2}),H(\wp_{z_k+1},\varkappa_{z_k+1},\varkappa_{z_k+1},\lambda_{w_k+2})\end{array}\right\}$$

$$\leq\ \kappa M|\lambda_{z_k+1}-\lambda_{w_k+2}|$$

$$+\kappa P_b(H(\wp_{z_k+1},\varkappa_{z_k+1},\varpi_{z_k+1},\lambda_{w_k+2}),H(\wp_{w_k+2},\varkappa_{w_k+2},z_{w_k+2},\lambda_{w_k+2}))$$

$$\leq\ \kappa M|\lambda_{z_k+1}-\lambda_{w_k+2}|$$

$$+\varphi\left(\delta\max\left\{d_{P_b}(\wp_{z_k+1},\wp_{w_k+2}),d_{P_b}(\varkappa_{z_k+1},\varkappa_{w_k+2}),d_{P_b}(\varpi_{z_k+1},z_{w_k+2})\right\}\right).$$

Similarly,

$$P_b\left(\varkappa_{z_k+1},\varkappa_{w_k+2}\right)\ \leq\ \kappa M|\lambda_{z_k+1}-\lambda_{w_k+2}|$$
$$+\varphi\left(\delta\max\left\{\begin{array}{c}d_{P_b}(\wp_{z_k+1},\wp_{w_k+2}),\\[4pt]d_{P_b}(\varkappa_{z_k+1},\varkappa_{w_k+2}),\\[4pt]d_{P_b}(\varpi_{z_k+1},z_{w_k+2})\end{array}\right\}\right).$$

and

$$P_b\left(\varpi_{z_k+1},\varpi_{w_k+2}\right)\ \leq\ \kappa M|\lambda_{z_k+1}-\lambda_{w_k+2}|$$
$$+\varphi\left(\delta\max\left\{\begin{array}{c}d_{P_b}(\wp_{z_k+1},\wp_{w_k+2}),\\[4pt]d_{P_b}(\varkappa_{z_k+1},\varkappa_{w_k+2}),\\[4pt]d_{P_b}(\varpi_{z_k+1},z_{w_k+2})\end{array}\right\}\right).$$

Thus

$$\max\left\{\begin{array}{c}P_b\left(\wp_{z_k+1},\wp_{w_k+2}\right),\\[4pt]P_b\left(\varkappa_{z_k+1},\varkappa_{w_k+2}\right)\\[4pt]P_b\left(\varpi_{z_k+1},\varpi_{w_k+2}\right)\end{array}\right\}\ \leq\ \kappa M|\lambda_{z_k+1}-\lambda_{w_k+2}|$$
$$+\varphi\left(\delta\max\left\{\begin{array}{c}P_b\left(\wp_{z_k+1},\wp_{w_k+2}\right),\\[4pt]P_b\left(\varkappa_{z_k+1},\varkappa_{w_k+2}\right)\\[4pt]P_b\left(\varpi_{z_k+1},\varpi_{w_k+2}\right)\end{array}\right\}\right).$$

Taking upper limit as $k \to \infty$ and from Eq. $(5.3.9)$ we have that

$$\epsilon.\kappa^3 \leq \delta\epsilon\kappa^3.$$

It follows that $\delta \geq 1$, is contradiction to $\delta \in (0,1)$. Hence $\{\wp_z\}$, $\{\varkappa_z\}$ and $\{\varpi_z\}$ are CS in $(\Im, d_{p_b})$

and

$$\lim_{z,w\to\infty} d_{p_b}(\wp_z, \wp_w) = 0 = \lim_{z,w\to\infty} d_{p_b}(\varkappa_z, \varkappa_w) = 0 = \lim_{z,w\to\infty} d_{p_b}(\varpi_z, \varpi_w).$$

By definition $(1.5.3)$ of d_{p_b} and Eq. $(5.1.11)$, we get

$$\lim_{z,w\to\infty} p(\wp_z, \wp_w) = 0 = \lim_{z,w\to\infty} p(\varkappa_z, \varkappa_w) = 0 = \lim_{z,w\to\infty} p(\varpi_z, \varpi_w).$$

From Lemma $1.5.2$, $\{\wp_z\}$, $\{\varkappa_z\}$ and $\{\varpi_z\}$ are Cauchy sequences in $(\Im, P_b)$.

Since $(\Im, P_b)$ is complete, there exists $\imath, \jmath, \eta \in U$ with

$$P_b(\imath, \imath) = \lim_{z\to\infty} P_b(\wp_z, \imath) = \lim_{z\to\infty} P_b(\wp_{z+1}, \imath) = \lim_{z,\ w\to\infty} P_b(\wp_z, \wp_w) = 0.$$

$$P_b(\jmath, \jmath) = \lim_{z\to\infty} P_b(\varkappa_z, \jmath) = \lim_{z\to\infty} P_b(\varkappa_{z+1}, \jmath) = \lim_{z,\ w\to\infty} P_b(\varkappa_z, \varkappa_w) = 0.$$

and

$$P_b(\eta, \eta) = \lim_{z\to\infty} P_b(\varpi_z, \eta) = \lim_{z\to\infty} P_b(\varpi_{z+1}, \eta) = \lim_{z,\ w\to\infty} P_b(\varpi_z, \varpi_w) = 0.$$

From Lemma $1.5.2$, we get $\lim\limits_{z\to\infty} P_b(\wp_z, H(\imath, \jmath, \eta, \lambda)) = P_b(\imath, H(\imath, \jmath, \eta, \lambda))$.

Now,

$$
\begin{aligned}
P_b(\wp_z, H(\imath, \jmath, \eta, \lambda)) \ &= P_b(H(\wp_z, \varkappa_z, \varpi_z, \lambda_z), H(\imath, \jmath, \eta, \lambda)) \\
&\leq s \left\{
\begin{array}{l}
P_b(H(\wp_z, \varkappa_z, \varpi_z, \lambda_z), H(\wp_z, \varkappa_z, \varpi_z, \lambda)) \\[4pt]
+ P_b(H(\wp_z, \varkappa_z, \varpi_z, \lambda), H(\imath, \jmath, \eta, \lambda)) \\[4pt]
- P_b(H(\wp_z, \varkappa_z, \varpi_z, \lambda), H(\wp_z, \varkappa_z, \varpi_z, \lambda))
\end{array}
\right\} \\[4pt]
&\leq \kappa M |\lambda_z - \lambda| + \kappa P_b(H(\wp_z, \varkappa_z, \varpi_z, \lambda), H(\imath, \jmath, \eta, \lambda)).
\end{aligned}
$$

Letting $z \to \infty$, we obtain

$$
\begin{aligned}
P\left(\imath, H(\imath, \jmath, \eta, \lambda)\right) &\leq \lim_{z \to \infty} \kappa P_b(H(\wp_z, \varkappa_z, \varpi_z, \lambda), H(\imath, \jmath, \eta, \lambda)) \\
&\leq \lim_{z \to \infty} \varphi\left(\delta \max\left\{P_b(\wp_z, \imath), P_b(\varkappa_z, \jmath), P_b(\varpi_z, \eta)\right\}\right) = 0.
\end{aligned}
$$

It follows that $P(\imath, H(\imath, \jmath, \eta, \lambda)) = 0$. So that $\imath = H(\imath, \jmath, \eta, \lambda)$.

Similarly $\jmath = H(\jmath, \eta, \imath, \lambda)$ and $\eta = H(\eta, \imath, \jmath, \lambda)$. Thus $\lambda \in A$. Hence A is closed in $[0, 1]$.

Let $\lambda_0 \in A$. Then there exists $\wp_0, \varkappa_0, \varpi_0 \in U$ with $\wp_0 = H(\wp_0, \varkappa_0, \varpi_0, \lambda_0)$,

$\varkappa_0 = H(\varkappa_0, \varpi_0, \wp_0, \lambda_0)$ and $\varpi_0 = H(\varpi_0, \wp_0, \varkappa_0, \lambda_0)$

Since U is open, then there exists $r > 0$ such that $B_{P_b}(\wp_0, r) \subseteq U$, $B_{P_b}(\varkappa_0, r) \subseteq U$ and $B_{P_b}(\varpi_0, r) \subseteq U$.

Choose $\lambda \in (\lambda_0 - \epsilon, \lambda_0 + \epsilon)$ such that $|\lambda - \lambda_0| \leq \frac{1}{M^z} < \epsilon$.

Then for $\wp \in \overline{B_{P_b}(\wp_0, r)} = \{\wp \in \Im / P_b(\wp, \wp_0) \leq r + P_b(\wp_0, \wp_0)\}$,

$\varkappa \in \overline{B_{P_b}(\varkappa_0, r)} = \{\varkappa \in \Im / P_b(\varkappa, \varkappa_0) \leq r + P_b(\varkappa_0, \varkappa_0)\}$ and

$\varpi \in \overline{B_{P_b}(\varpi_0, r)} = \{\varpi \in \Im / P_b(\varpi, \varpi_0) \leq r + P_b(\varpi_0, \varpi_0)\}$.

Now

$$
\begin{aligned}
P_b(H(\wp, \varkappa, \varpi, \lambda), \wp_0) &= P_b(H(\wp, \varkappa, \varpi, \lambda), H(\wp_0, \varkappa_0, \varpi_0, \lambda_0)) \\
&\leq \kappa \left\{ \begin{array}{l} P_b(H(\wp, \varkappa, \varpi, \lambda), H(\wp, \varkappa, \varpi, \lambda_0)) \\[4pt] + P_b(H(\wp, \varkappa, \varpi, \lambda_0), H(\wp_0, \varkappa_0, \varpi_0, \lambda_0)) \\[4pt] - P_b(H(\wp, \varkappa, \varpi, \lambda_0), H(\wp, \varkappa, \varpi, \lambda_0)) \end{array} \right\} \\[4pt]
&\leq \kappa M |\lambda - \lambda_0| + \kappa P_b(H(\wp, \varkappa, \varpi, \lambda_0), H(\wp_0, \varkappa_0, \varpi_0, \lambda_0)) \\[4pt]
&\leq \kappa \frac{1}{M^{z-1}} + \kappa P_b(H(\wp, \varkappa, \varpi, \lambda_0), H(\wp_0, \varkappa_0, \varpi_0, \lambda_0)).
\end{aligned}
$$

Letting $z \to \infty$, we obtain

$$
\begin{aligned}
P_b(H(\wp, \varkappa, \varpi, \lambda), \wp_0) &\leq \kappa P_b(H(\wp, \varkappa, \varpi, \lambda_0), H(\wp_0, \varkappa_0, \varpi_0, \lambda_0)) \\
&\leq \varphi\left(\delta \max\left\{P_b(\wp, \wp_0), P_b(\varkappa, \varkappa_0), P_b(\varpi, \varpi_0)\right\}\right).
\end{aligned}
$$

Similarly

$$P_b(H(\varkappa, \varpi, \wp, \lambda), \varkappa_0) \leq \varphi\left(\delta \max\left\{P_b(\wp, \wp_0), P_b(\varkappa, \varkappa_0), P_b(\varpi, \varpi_0)\right\}\right).$$

and

$$P_b(H(\varpi, \wp, \varkappa, \lambda), \varpi_0) \leq \varphi\left(\delta \max\left\{P_b(\wp, \wp_0), P_b(\varkappa, \varkappa_0), P_b(\varpi, \varpi_0)\right\}\right).$$

Thus

$$\max\left\{\begin{array}{c} P_b(H(\wp, \varkappa, \varpi\lambda), \wp_0), \\ P_b(H(\varkappa, \varpi, \wp, \lambda), \varkappa_0), \\ P_b(H(\varpi, \wp, \varkappa, \lambda), \varpi_0) \end{array}\right\} \leq \varphi\left(\delta \max\left\{\begin{array}{c} P_b(\wp, \wp_0), \\ P_b(\varkappa, \varkappa_0), \\ P_b(\varpi, \varpi_0) \end{array}\right\}\right)$$

$$\leq \delta \max\left\{\begin{array}{c} r + P_b(\wp_0, \wp_0), \\ r + P_b(\varkappa_0, \varkappa_0), \\ r + P_b(\varpi_0, \varpi_0) \end{array}\right\}.$$

Thus for each fixed $\lambda \in (\lambda_0 - \epsilon, \lambda_0 + \epsilon)$, $H(., \lambda) : \overline{B_{P_b}(\wp_0, r)} \to \overline{B_{P_b}(\wp_0, r)}$, $H(., \lambda) : \overline{B_{P_b}(\varkappa_0, r)} \to \overline{B_{P_b}(\varkappa_0, r)}$ and $H(., \lambda) : \overline{B_{P_b}(\varpi_0, r)} \to \overline{B_{P_b}(\varpi_0, r)}$.

Since (i) also holds, Theorem 5.3.1 is satisfied in all of its conditions. Thus, we can conclude that $\overline{U}$ has a TFP for $H(., \lambda)$. Therefore, U must include this TFP because (i) holds. For any $\lambda \in (\lambda_0 - \epsilon, \lambda_0 + \epsilon)$, $\lambda \in A$. As a result, A is open in $[0, 1]$ since $(\lambda_0 - \epsilon, \lambda_0 + \epsilon) \subseteq A$.

We employ the identical method for the opposite inference.

$\square$

5.4 Conclusion

This study uses contractive mappings of the $(\alpha, \varphi) - K$ type contraction in the context of partial b-metric space to present some fixed point results and appropriate example that illustrate the main findings. Additionally, integral equation and homotopy applications are given.

BIBLIOGRAPHY

Bibliography

[1] Abbas, M., Ali Khan, M., Radenović, S., Common coupled fixed point theorems in cone metric spaces for ω-compatible mappings: *Appl. Math. Comput.*, 217(2010), 195 - 202.

[2] Abbas, M., Bashir, B., Suleiman, Y.I., Generalized coupled common fixed point results in partially ordered A-metric spaces: *Fixed point theory Appl.*, (2015), 2015:64.

[3] Afshari, H., Aydi, H., Karapinar, E., On generalized $\alpha - \psi$-Geraghty contractions on b-metric spaces: *Georgian Math. J.*, 27(1), (2020), 921.

[4] Aghajani, A., Abbas, M., Pourhadi Kallehbasti, E., Coupled fixed point theorems in partially ordered metric spaces and application: *Math. Commun.*, 17(2012), 497509.

[5] Alexendroff, P., Hopf, H., (1935) Topologie I: *Springer Berlin*.

[6] Ali Mutlu., Kübra Özkan., Utku Gürdal., Coupled fixed point theorems on bipolar metric spaces: *European journal of pure and applied mathematics*, 10(4),(2017), 655 - 667.

[7] Ali Mutlu., Utku Gürdal., Bipolar metric spaces and some fixed point theorems, *Journal of Nonlinear Sciences and Applications*, 9(9), (2016), 5362 - 5373.

[8] Alqahtani, B., Karapinar, E., Oztürk, A., On $(\alpha, \psi) - K$-Contractions in the Extended b-Metric Space: *Filomat*, 32:15(2018), 53375345. https://doi.org/10.2298/FIL1815337A.

[9] Alsulami. H. H., Agarwal, R.P., Karapinar, E., Khojasteh, F., A Short note on C^* -valued contraction mappings, *Journal of Inequalities and Applications*, 50(2016).

[10] Altun, I., Sola, F., Simsek, H., Generalized contractions on partial metric spaces: *Topology and its Applications*, 157(18), (2010), 2778 - 2785.

[11] Ansari, A.H., (2014) Note on $\varphi - \psi$-contractive type mappings and related fixed point: *The 2nd Regional Conf. Math.Appl.*, PNU, 377380. 1, 1, 1.11.

[12] Ansari, A.H., Kaewcharoen,A., C-class functions and fixed point theorems for generalized $\aleph - \eta - \psi - \varphi - F$-contraction type mappings in $\aleph - \eta$-complete metric spaces: *J. Nonlinear Sci. Appl.*, 9 (2016), 41774190.

[13] Ansari,A.H., Shatanawi, W., Kurdi,A., Maniu,G., Best proximity points in complete metric spaces with (P)-property via C-class functions: *J. Math. Anal.*, 7(2016), 5467.

[14] Aydi, H., Abbas,M., Sintunavarat, W., Kumam, p., Tripled fixed point of ω- compatible mappings in abstract metric spaces: *Fixed point Theory Appl.*, (2012), 20 pages.

[15] Aydi, H., Karapinar, E., Postolache, M., Tripled fixed point theorems for weak ϕ-contraction in partially ordered metric spaces: *Fixed Point Theory Appl.*, Vol.2012, ID: 2012:44, 12 pp.

[16] Banach, S., Sur les operations dans les ensembles abstraits etleur applications aux equations integrales: *Fundam. Math,* 3(1922), 133-181.

[17] Batul, S., kamran, T., C^* - valued contractive type mappings: *Fixed point Theory and Applications,* 2015(142), DOI10.1186/s13663-015-0393-3.

[18] Berinde, V., Borcut, M., Tripled fixed point theorems for contractive type mappings in partially ordered metric spaces: *Nonlinear Anal.*, 74(15), (2011), 4889-4897.

[19] Birkhoff, G.D., Kellogg, O.D., (1922) Invariant points in function spaces: *Amer. Math. Soc,* 23, 96-115.

[20] Borcut, M., Berinde, V., Tripled coincidence theorems for contractive type mappings in partially ordered metric spaces: *Appl. Math. Comput.*, 218(2012), 5929-5936.

[21] Borcut, M., Pacurar, M., Berinde, V., Tripled fixed point theorems for Mixed Monotone Kannan Type contractive mappings: *J. Appl. Math.*, 2014(2014), 8 pages.

[22] Brouwer, L.E.J., (1912) $\ddot{U}$ber die abbildung von mannig falting keiten: *Math. Ann.*, 71, 97-114.

[23] Cao, T., Some Coupled fixed point theorems in C^*-algebra valued metric spaces: *arXiv:1601.07168v1*, (2016).

[24] Caristi, J.V., Ph.D. Thesis: *University of Iowa*, (1975).

[25] Cesari, L., (1975) Alternative methods in nonlinear analysis: *International Conference on Differential equations, Ed. by H.A. Antosiewicz, Academic Press*, 95-149.

[26] Chuanzhi Bai., Coupled fixed point theorems in C^*-algebra valued b-metric spaces with application: *Fixed point theory and Applications*, 70(2016), DOI.10.1186/s13663-016-0560-1.

[27] Collatz, L., (1966) Functional Analysis and Numerical Analysis: *Academic Press, New York.*

[28] Cronin, J., (1964) Fixed points and topological degree in non-linear analysis: *Amer. Math. Soc,* (Mathematical Survey No. 11).

[29] Czerwik, S., Contraction mappings in b-metric spaces: *Acta Math. Inform. Univ. Osrav.*, 1(1993), 5-11.

[30] Czerwik, S., Nonlinear set-valued contraction mappings in *b*-metric spaces: *Atti Sem. Mat. Fis. Univ. Modena.*, 46(1998), 263-276.

[31] Dey, L.K., Mondal, S., Best proximity point of F-contraction in complete metric space: *Bull. Alahabad Math. Soc.*, 30(2), (2015), 173189.

[32] Dunford, N., Schwartz, J.T., (1957) Linear Operators, Part I, Interscience: *New York* .

[33] Dung, N.V., Hang, V. L., A fixed point theorem for generalized F-contractions on complete metric spaces: *Vietnam. J. Math.*, 43(4), (2015), 743753.

[34] Dur-e-Shehwar., Samina Batul., Tayyab Kamran., Adrian Ghiura., Caristi's fixed point theorem on C^*-algebra valued metric spaces: *Journal of Nonlinear Science and Applications*, 9(2),(2016), 584 - 588.

[35] Fréchet, M., La notion décart et le calcul fonctionnel: *C. R. Acad. Sci. Paris*, 140(1905), 772774.

[36] Gopal, D., Abbas, M., Patel, D.K., Vetro, C., Fixed points of α-type F-contractive mappings with an application to nonlinear fractional differential equation: *Acta Math. Scientia* , 36(3), (2016), 957970.

[37] Gnana Bhaskar, T., Lakshmikantham, V., Fixed point theorems in partially ordered metric spaces and applications: *Non-linear Anal.*, 65(7), (2006), 1379-1393.

[38] Guo, D.J., Lakshmikantham, V., Coupled fixed points of nonlinear operators with applications: *Nonlinear Anal.*, 11(5), (1987), 623-632.

[39] Guttia, V.R.B., Kumssa, L.B., Fixed points of (α, ψ, φ)-generalized weakly contractive maps and property (P) in S-metric spaces: *Filomat*, 31(14),(2017), 4469 4481.

[40] Hafid Massit., Mohamed Rossafi., Fixed point theorem for (ϕ, F)-contraction on C^*-algebra valued metric spaces: *Eur. J. Math. Appl.*, (2021), 1:14.

[41] Huaping Huang., Guantie Deng., Stojan Radenović., Fixed point theorems for C-class functions in b-metric spaces and applications: *J. Nonlinear Sci. Appl.*, 10(2017), 58535868.

[42] Husain, S.A., Sehgal, V.M., On common fixed points for a family of mappings: *Bull. Austral. Math. Soc,* 13(1975), 261-267.

[43] Istrátescu, V.I., Fixed point theory: *An introduction D. Reidel Publ. Comp.*, (1981).

[44] Jingren Zhou., Fixed point theorems in Partial b-metric spaces: *Applied Mathematical Sciences*, 12(13), (2018), 617-624.

[45] Jungck, G., Compatible mappings and common fixed points: *International Journal of Mathematics and Mathematical Sciences*, 9(4), (1986), 771-779.

[46] Jungck, G., Rhoades, B.E., Fixed point for set valued functions without continuity: *Indian Journal of pure and Applied Mathematics*, 29(3), (1998), 227-238.

[47] Kameswari, M.V.R., Sujatha, K., Kiran, D.M.K., Fixed Point Results in S_b-Metric Spaces via (α, ψ, ϕ)- Generalized Weakly Contractive Maps: *Global Journal of Pure and Applied Mathematics*, 15(4), (2019), pp 411428.

[48] Kamran, T., Postolache, M., Ghiura, A., Batul, S. and Ali, R., The Banach contraction principle in C^*-algebra-valued b-metric spaces with application: *Fixed Point Theory and Applications* , 10(2016), DOI10.1186/s13663-015-0486-z.

[49] Kannan, R., Some results on fixed points: *Bull Cal. Math.Soc,* 60(1968), 71-76.

[50] Kannan, R., Some results on fixed points II: *Amer. Math.,* Monthly, 76(1969), 405-408.

[51] Karapinar, E., Coupled Fixed Point on Cone Metric Spaces: *Gazi Univ. J. Sci.,* 1(2011), 5158.

[52] Karapinar, E., Czerwik, S., Aydi, H., (α, ψ)-Meir-Keeler contraction mappings in generalized b-metric spaces: *Journal of Function Spaces*, 2018, Article Id: 3264620.

[53] Karapinar,E., Kumam, P., Salimi, P., On $\alpha - \psi$-Meir-Keeler contractive mappings: *Fixed Point Theory Appl.*, 2013:9, 2013.

[54] Karapinar, E., Tripled fixed point theorems in partially ordered metric spaces: *Stud. Univ. Babes-Bolyai Math.*, 58(2013): 75-85.

[55] Karapinar, E., $\alpha - \psi$-Geraghty contraction type mappings and some related fixed point results: *Filomat* 28(1), (2014), 37 48.

[56] Khan, M.S., Swaleh, M., Sessa, S., Fixed point theorems by altering distances between the points: *Bull. Aust. Math. Soc.*, 30(1984), 19. 1.13.

[57] Khomdram, B., Bina Devi, M., Rohen, Y., Fixed point of theorems of generalised α-ratonal contractive mappings on rectangular b-metric spaces: *J. Math. Comput. Sci.*, 11 (2021), 991-1010.

[58] Kishore, G.N.V., Adilakshmi,G., Baghavan,V.S., Srinuvasa Rao, B., C^* -algebra valued fuzzy soft metric space and related fixed Point results by using triangular α-admissible maps with Application to nonlinear integral equations : *Jour of Adv Research in Dynamical & Control Systems*, 12(02), (2020).

[59] Kishore, GNV., Agarwal, R.P., Srinuvasa Rao, B., Srinivasa Rao, R.V.N., Caristi type cyclic contraction and common fixed point theorems in bipolar metric spaces with applications: *Fixed Point Theory and Applications*, 2018:21.

[60] Kishore, G.N.V., Rao, K.P.R., Panthi, D., Srinuvsa Rao, B., Satyanaraya, S., Some appli-

cations via fixed point results in partially ordered S_b-metric spaces: *Fixed point theory and applications*, (2017), 2017:10, doi: 10.1186/s13663-017-0603-2.

[61] Kishore, G.N.V., Srinuvasa Rao, B., Ram Prasad, D., Bhagavan, V.S., Some fixed point results of C^*-algebra valued fuzzy soft metric spaces with applications: *Journal of Critical Reviews*, 7(2), (2020).

[62] Kishore, GNV., Srinuvasa Rao, B., Subba Rao, R., Mixed monotone property and tripled fixed point theorems in partially ordered bipolar metric spaces: *Italian Journal of pure and Applied Mathematics*, 42(2019), 598-615.

[63] Kishore, GNV., Srinuvasa Rao, B., Radenović, S., Huang, H., Caristi Type Cyclic Contraction and Coupled Fixed Point Results in Bipolar Metric Spaces: *Sahand Communications in Mathematical Analysis (SCMA)*, 17(1), (2020), 1-22.

[64] Kolmogrov, A.M., Fomin, S.J., Functional Analysis: *Graylock Rochester*, Vol. I, (1957).

[65] Kreyszig, E., (1978) Introductory Functional Analysis with Applications: *John Wiley and Sons, New York*.

[66] Leggett, R.W., Williams, L.R., (1980) A fixed point theorem with applications to an infectious disease model: *J. Math. Anal.andAppl.*, 76, 91-97.

[67] Long, W., Rhoades, B.E., Rajović, M., Coupled coincidence points for two mappings in metric spaces and cone metric spaces: *Fixed Point Theory Appl.*, 66(2012), 9 pages.

[68] Maji, P.K., Biswas, R. and Roy, A.R., Fuzzy soft Sets: *Journal of Fuzzy Mathematics*, 9(3), (2001), 589 - 602.

[69] Mangapathi, N., Srinuvasa Rao, B., Rao, K.R.K., Pasha, M.I., On certain fixed point theorems in S_b-metric spaces with applications: *Int. J. Anal. Appl.*, (2023), 21:18.

[70] Manoj Kumar., Sushma Devi., Parul Singh., Fixed Point Theorems by Using Altering Distance Function in S-Metric Spaces: *Communications in Mathematics and Applications*, 13(2), (2022), 553573.

[71] Martin, R.H.Jr., (1976) Nonlinear operators and differential equations in Banach spaces: *John Wiley and Sons, New York.*

[72] Matthews, S.G., Partial metric topology: *in Proceedings of the 8th Summer Conference on General Topology and Applications, Annals of the New York Academy of Sciences*, 728(1994), 183-197.

[73] Matthews, S.G., Partial metric topology: *Research Report 212. Dept. of Computer Science. University of Warwick*, (1992).

[74] Mishra, V.N., Wadkar, B.R., Bhardwaj, R., Khan, I.A., Singh, B., Common Fixed Point Theorems in Metric Space by Altering Distance Function: *Advances in Pure Mathematics*, 7(2017), 335-344.

[75] Moore, R.E., (1985) Computational functional analysis: *Ellis Harwood Limited, New York.*

[76] Molodstov, D.A., Fuzzy soft Sets- First Result: *Computers & Mathematics with Application*, 37(4-5), (1999), 19-31.

[77] Murphy, G.J., C^{*}-algebras and Operator Theory: *Academic press, Boston*, Chapter2, (1990), 35-76.

[78] Mustafa, Z., Jaradata, M. M. M., Jaradat, H. M., Some common fixed point results of graphs on b - metric space: *Journal of Nonlinear Science and Applications*, 9(6), (2016), 4838-4851.

[79] Mustafa, Z., Roshan, J.R., Parvaneh, V., Kadelburg, Z., Some common fixed point result in ordered partial b-metric spaces: *Journal of Inequalities and Applications*, 2013:562.

[80] Naresh, P., Upender Reddy, G., Srinuvasa Rao, B., Existence Suzuki Type Fixed Point Results in A_b-Metric Spaces With Application: *Int. J. Anal. Appl.*, (2022), 20:67.

[81] Oltra, S., Valero, O., Banachs fixed point theorem for partial metric spaces: *Rendiconti dellIstituto di Matematica dellUniversit'a di Trieste* , 36(1-2), (2004), 17 - 26.

[82] Ozturk, V., Ansari, A.H., Common fixed point theorems for mappings satisfying (E.A)-property via C-class functions in b-metric spaces: *Appl. Gen. Topol.*, 18(1),(2017), 4552.

[83] Piri, H., Kumam, P., Some fixed point theorem concerning F-contractions in complete metric spaces: *Fixed Point Theory Appl.*, 2014:210, (2014).

[84] Piri, H., Rahrovi, S., Marasi, H., Kumam, P., F-contraction on asymmetric metric spaces: *J. Math. Computer Sci.*, 17(2017), 3240.

[85] Popa, V., Mocanu, M., Altering distance and common fixed points under implicit relations: *Hacettepe Journal of Mathematics and Statistics*, 39(3), (2009), 329 357.

[86] Ram Prasad, D., Kishore,G.N.V., Huseyin Isik., Srinuvasa Rao, B., Adi Lakshmi, G., C^*-algebra valued fuzzy soft metric spaces and results for hybrid pair of mappings: *Axioms* , 8(2019), 0099.

[87] Rao, K.P.R., Kishore, G.N.V., A unique common triple fixed point theorem in partially ordered cone metric spaces: *Bulletin of Mathematical Analysis and Applications*, 3(4), (2011), 213-222.

[88] Rao, K.P.R., Kishore, G.N.V., Sadik, Sk., A unique common coupled fixed point theorem for four maps in S_b-metric spaces: *Journal of linear and Toplogical Algebra,* 6(1), (2017), 29-43.

[89] Rao, K.P.R., Kishore, G.N.V., Sobhana Babu, P.R., Triple coincidence point theorems for multivalued maps in partially ordered metric spaces: *Universal Journal of computational Mathematics*, 1(2), (2013), 19-23.

[90] Rao, K.P.R., Kishore, G.N.V., Tas, K., A unique common tripled fixed point theorem for hybrid pair of mappings: *Abstract and Applied Analysis*, Volume 2012, Article ID 750403, 9 pages. doi:10.1155/2012/750403.

[91] Ravi, P.A., Kishore, G.N.V., Srinuvasa Rao, B., Convergence properties on C^*-algebra valued fuzzy soft metric spaces and related fixed point theorems: *Malaya Journal of Matematik,* 6(2),(2018), 310-320.

[92] Rhoades, B.E., A comparison of various definitions of contractive mappings: *Trans. Amer. Math. Soc,* 226(1977), 256-290.

[93] Rhoades, B.E., Contractive definitions revisted: *Contemporary Mathematics,* 21(1983), 189-205.

[94] Rhoades, B.E., Proving fixed point theorems using general principles: *Indian J. Pure Appl. Math.,* 27(8),(1996), 741-770.

[95] Roy, S., Samanta, T. K., A note on Fuzzy soft Topological Spaces: *Annals of Fuzzy Mathematics and Informatics,* 3(2), (2012), 305 - 311.

[96] Rus, I.A., Metrical fixed point theorems, *Clujnapoca,* (1979).

[97] Saluja, G.S., Common Fixed Point Theorems on S-Metric Spaces Via C-Class Functions: *International J.Math. Combin.,* 3(2022), 21-37.

[98] Samet, B., Vetro, C., Vetro, P., Fixed Point Theorems for $\alpha - \psi$–Contractive Type Mappings: *Nonlinear Analysis,* 75(2012), 2154-2165.

[99] Sanath Kumar, H.G., Ramakant Bhardwaj., Basant Kumar Singh., Fixed Point Theorems of Soft Metric Space Using Altering Distance Function: *International Journal of Recent Technology and Engineering (IJRTE),* 7(6), (2019).

[100] Satish,S., Partial b-metric spaces and fixed point theorems, *Mediter.J. Math.*, 11(2), (2014), 703-711.

[101] Schaiider, J., Der fixpunksatz funktional raumen: *Studio Math.*, 2(1930), 171-180.

[102] Schaiider, J., Zur theoric stetiger abbildungen in funcktional raumen: *Math. Z.*, 26(1927), 47-65, 417-431.

[103] Secelean, N.A., Iterated function systems consisting of F-contractions: *Fixed Point Theory Appl.*, 2013, 277(2013). doi:10.1186/1687-1812-2013-277.

[104] Sedghi, S., Gholidahneh., Dosenovic, T., Esfahani, J., Radenović, S., Common fixed point of four maps in S_b-metric spaces: *Journal of Linear and Topological Algebra*, 5(2),(2016), 93-104.

[105] Sedghi, S., Shobe, N., Aliouche, A., A generalization of fixed point theorem in S-metric spaces: *Mat. Vesnik*, 64(3), (2012), 258-266.

[106] Sessa, S., On a weak commutativity condition of mappings in fixed point considerations: *Publications de lInstitut Mathematique*, 32(1982), 149-153.

[107] Shukla, S., Partial b-metric spaces and fixed point theorems: *Mediterranean Journal of Mathematics*, (2013), doi:101007/s00009-013-0327-4.

[108] Smart, D.R., (1974) Fixed point theorems: *Cambridge University Press*.

[109] Souayah Nizar., A fixed point in partial S_b-metric spaces: *An. St. univ ovidius constante*, 24(3), (2017), 315-362.

[110] Souayah Nizar., Mlaiki., A fixed point theorems in S_b-metric spaces: *Journal of mathematics and computer science*, 16(2016), 131-139.

[111] Shatanawi, W., Postolache, M., Ansari, A.H., Kassab, W., Common fixed points of dominating and weak annihilators in ordered metric spaces via C-class functions: *J. Math. Anal.*, 8(2017), 5468.

[112] Stan, G., Popescu, O., Two fixed point theorems concerning F-contraction in complete metric spaces: *Symmetry*, (2020), 12, 58, doi:10.3390/sym12010058.

[113] Srinuvasa Rao, B., Kishore, G.N.V., Common fixed point theorems in bipolar metric spaces with applications to integral equations: *International Journal of Engineering & Technology*, 7 (4.10), (2018), 1022-1026.

[114] Srinuvasa Rao, B., Kishore,G.N.V., Muhammad Sarwar., Konda Reddy, N., Fixed point theorems in ordered S_b-metric spaces by using (α, β)-admissible Geraghty contraction and applications: *J. Applied Sci.*, 18 (1), (2018), 9-18.

[115] Srinuvasa Rao, B., Kishore,G.N.V., Vara Prasad,T., Fixed point theorems under Caristi's type map on C^*-algebra valued fuzzy soft metric space: *International Journal of Engineering & Technology*, 7 (3.31), (2017), 111-114.

[116] Taheri,A., Farajzadeh, A., A new generalization of α-type almost-F-contractions and α-type F-Suzuki contractions in metric spaces and their fixed point theorems: *Carpathian Math. Publ.*, 11(2019), 475-492.

[117] Taieb Hamaizia., Common Fixed Point Theorems Involving C-class Functions in Partial Metric Spaces: *Sohag J. Math.*, 8(1), (2021), 23-28.

[118] Thangaraj Beaula., Christinal Gunaseeli., On fuzzy soft metric spaces: *Malaya Journal of Matematik*, 2(3), (2014), 197 - 202.

[119] Thangaraj Beaula., Raja, R., Completeness in Fuzzy Soft Metric Space: *Malaya Journal of Matematik,* S(2),(2015), 438 - 442.

[120] Tridiv Joti Neog., Dusmanta Kumar Sut., Hazarika, G. C., Fuzzy Soft Topological Space: *International Journal of Latest Tends in Mathematics,* 2(1), (2012).

[121] Tychonoff, A., Ein fixpunksatz: *Math. Ann.,* 111(1935), 767-776.

[122] Wardowski, D., Dung, N.V., Fixed points of F-weak contractions on complete metric spaces: *Demonstr. Math.,* 47(1), (2014), 146155.

[123] Wardowski, D., Fixed points of new type of contractive mappings in complete metric spaces: *Fixed Point Theory Appl.,* (2012), 2012:94.

[124] Wardowski, D., Solving existence problems via F- contractions: *Proc. Amer. Math. Soc.,* 146(2018), 1585-1598.

[125] Zadeh, L. A., Fuzzy Soft: *Inform and Control,* 8(3), (1965), 338 - 353.